A GUIDE TO ORAL INTERPRETATION

A GUIDE TO ORAL INTERPRETATION

LOUISE M. SCRIVNER

THE ODYSSEY PRESS
THE BOBBS-MERRILL COMPANY, INC. PUBLISHERS
INDIANAPOLIS · NEW YORK

THE ODYSSEY PRESS

A Division of

THE BOBBS-MERRILL COMPANY, INC.

Library of Congress Card Number 67-20378

Printed in the United States of America

ISBN 0-672-63043-5 (pbk)

Fourth Printing

64054

PREFACE

This book grew from an effort to present the principles and skills of oral interpretation for practical use in a one-semester introductory course. The inspiration came from students whose encouragement and participation in the testing of exercises and methods in the classroom made much of the book a joint endeavor. Their questions, too, did much to direct the book's practical approach: "Do we need to read so much *about* oral interpretation?" "Can't this be said in fewer words?" "*How* do I find the tone of a particular selection?" "*How* can I learn to subordinate?" and so forth.

And so this text seeks to present course content as briefly and as concretely as possible. Its purpose is to show the student specific ways he may go about finding meaning in works of literary art and to suggest specific methods he may use to communicate this meaning effectively to an audience. But the "hows," as the title of the text implies, are not presented as mechanical processes but as "guides" which have been found useful.

The book, based on the philosophy that theory has more meaning when it is applied immediately, suggests a procedure or a mode of work that will enable the teacher to handle increasingly large classes, and, at the same time, to make provision for individual needs through laboratory assistance. The included exercises (class and laboratory) are, therefore, designed for these purposes.

Two approaches are presented: the technical and the psychological. The technical aspects draw upon the basic theories generally accepted in the field of oral interpretation. The credit for developing these principles belongs to many teachers and writers in this area. The psychological approach attempts to assimilate from the acting field the uses of concentration, imagination, and identification, and to apply them specifically to the art of interpretative reading. This approach draws upon the writings and teachings of followers of the Stanislavski method in acting. Credits are given to Michael Chekhov, Lee Strasberg, and others.

The text is organized into four parts. Part One deals with general principles. Chapter 1 is an introduction dealing with course content and goals. Chapter 2 is an overview which defines and discusses the general principles, methods, and processes used throughout the book.

Part Two is concerned with literary analysis. Chapter 3 discusses and attempts to clarify the elements and literary devices that go into the making of a work of literary art. Chapter 4 illustrates analysis procedures and relates them to the oral reading performance. The content of both chapters is further developed and related to the analysis of specific selections throughout the text.

Part Three is devoted to the technical and psychological approaches. Techniques for communicating meaning and for using the voice and body effectively are given specific treatment in Chapters 5, 6, and 7. Chapter 8 is concerned with the psychological approach, which deliberately undertakes to train the imagination.

In Part Four, "Literary Forms for Interpretation," Chapters 9, 10, and 11 illustrate specific problems and solutions in reading prose, poetry, and drama. Chapter 12 is unique in its treatment of two popular forms of group interpretation. Reader's Theatre is discussed more fully than is usual in oral-interpretation texts. The discussion of Chamber Theatre presents an actual project and furnishes a guide for those interested in experimenting with this relatively new form of narrative dramatization. The teaching and writing of Dr. Robert Breen of Northwestern University is gratefully acknowledged.

Four appendices include material of practical aid to both student and teacher. Included are annotated lists of material, suggestions for a workable speech laboratory and suggestions for its use in oral interpretation, a plan applicable to this text, and detailed explanations of suggested oral projects. Evaluation forms that may serve as a cumulative record of the student's class progress are also included.

By considering prose, poetry, and drama, as well as special forms for group interpretation, it is hoped that the book may serve teachers and students in various situations. In speech departments where an advanced course in oral interpretation is offered, the content of an introductory course is often confined to the interpretation of the shorter literary forms—the essay, the short story, and lyric and narrative poetry; the longer and more dramatic forms are reserved for the advanced course. But in departments of English where only one course in interpretation is offered, the teacher may wish to include various forms (depending, of course, upon the general class level and interests). It is the intention of this text to offer such a choice. The forms included here focus on the more imaginative types of writing. The essay is given only a brief consideration in order to concentrate on the more dramatic forms of narrative fiction, poetry, and drama.

Initially in this text, prose, poetry, and drama are considered together. This approach implies that technically and psychologically the analysis and oral communication of all literary forms have much in common and that at first they may conveniently be considered together. In later chapters the more subtle problems related to each genre are discussed. An effort is made to integrate the discussion of the literary elements through full analyses of the various genres and through the use of one example to point out various elements and relationships. Throughout, the text emphasizes the fact that there can be no exact process for analyzing literary works, just as there can be no exact formula for conveying logical and emotional meaning to an audience. Both literature and oral communication are recognized as intangibles, and each literary work and each oral presentation is recognized as a unique creative experience.

My thanks go to many friends and colleagues for specific help and general support. I owe a special debt to Edward de Rosset, my student secretary, who stayed with me through the revisions and helped me keep in mind the student view.

LOUISE M. SCRIVNER

CONTENTS

ix

Part One

GENERAL PRINCIPLES

1 INTRODUCTION

ORAL READING

The term *oral reading* covers a wide area. It extends from the most practical purpose (a secretary reading a club report) to professional entertainment (John Gielgud interpreting a Shakespearean soliloquy for the aesthetic pleasure of an audience). Good oral-reading techniques are of concern to the layman taking part in the ordinary social, professional, and cultural activities of contemporary life as well as to the person more actively engaged in public speaking, acting, or interpretative reading. Alike, they are interested in acquiring the ability to convey effectively previously worded material to enlighten, to influence, or to entertain their listeners. The techniques involved in reading a club report and interpreting a Shakespearean soliloquy do overlap, but, obviously, the latter makes greater demands on the reader.

Our particular concern is the oral reader who interprets literature for the pleasure of an audience. Anyone who can accomplish this successfully will have no difficulty reading aloud when his purpose is less demanding.

ORAL INTERPRETATION OF LITERATURE

Oral interpretation of literature may be defined as *the art of re-creating an author's recorded experience in a work of literary art and of communicating this to an audience so as to arouse a meaningful response.*

But a general definition does not begin to clarify or suggest the subtleties of the art. In Chapter 2 we will discuss this in detail. For the present, let us consider oral interpretation as a course of study—its subject matter, goals, and values, and its relationship to other speech activities.

3

Course Content, Goals, and Values

Oral Interpretation of Literature is a course offered in the interpretative area of speech arts, on the college level, which concerns the twin arts of literature and oral communication. Course content, then, is geared to aid the student in his pursuit of two goals: understanding specific literary works and effective communication. He must be given a means to understand an author's intellectual and emotional meanings and to "interpret" these in relation to his own experience; and he must be given a means to communicate effectively his interpretation so as to arouse a meaningful response from an audience.

The history of instruction in this area of the performing arts is an interesting one.[1] At one time oral interpretation centered more on a student's oral performance than on his comprehension and interpretation of the "matter" on which his oral skills were directed. Today, major emphasis is placed on the subject matter: the interpretation of the literary text. The techniques of oral communication (voice, body, and so forth) are considered not as an end in themselves, but as a means of communicating the thought and feeling within a literary work. Though some students may take a beginning course in interpretation for additional training in speech, few expect to be actively engaged as professional "readers." All students, however, expect to be actively engaged in living and in extending their awareness of life experience through the reading and understanding of literature.

Oral Interpretation, as any course study of literature, is an important academic discipline. Because effective communication of the author's meanings is expected by the listeners, the student of interpretation is not likely to settle for a superficial understanding. When he studies literature with the intent of giving physical expression to the literary material, his responses must be *active*; he must "experience" more fully than the silent reader. Also, as he seeks aids that bear directly on understanding literary art, his acquaintance with important critical and theoretical studies is extended. Biographical and historical studies may also extend his general background knowledge.

Oral interpretation as a speech art takes a middle position between public speaking and acting. The disciplines learned for effectively communicating a selection of literature may serve to improve the student's speech skills in related speech activities or in social situations.

From a course combining the twin arts of literature and speech the student should expect to extend his acquaintance with literature and to gain

[1] For a discussion of the history and theories of interpretation see Charlotte I. Lee, *Oral Interpretation*, 3rd ed. (Boston, 1965), pp. 449–456.

competence in both silent and oral reading. The oral skills serve to make him a more effective person in any life situation; the ability to experience literature more fully, either silently or orally, serves to make life more interesting and enjoyable. Dr. Robert Breen speaks of "experiencing literature" as

> ... one of the most profoundly civilizing processes—the education of the senses and the pleasurable acquisition of that knowledge which is necessary for our understanding of human experience.[2]

Relationship to Related Speech Activities

Oral Interpretation is not public speaking, and it is not acting; and yet at times it is very close to both. The interpreter's reading performance may take on the characteristics of the public speaker's. This occurs when the reader addresses the audience directly with introductory or transitional remarks. His manner, at such times, is like that of the public speaker when he "reaches out" to his audience to clarify. His speech behavior at such times usually appears relaxed and conversationally direct.

When an address or an essay is interpreted, the oral reader approaches the role of the public speaker, but there is a difference. The public speaker's words are his own, and he is intent on influencing the audience with his own ideas in some way. The reader, when he interprets an address or essay orally, is trying to stimulate his audience to an appreciative response of someone else's ideas. Though the audience is addressed directly (as in public speaking), his attitude suggests that he is joining his audience in appreciating the ideas and attitudes of the author rather than in influencing them directly with his own. The difference, then, is a matter of attitude which is brought about by the contrast in purposes.

When an oral interpreter reads certain material, he approaches the role of the actor. How far may he go into the acting area in his character interpretations? How closely may he "identify" with a character? Just what is the difference between the role of the actor and the role of the interpreter? These are some of the questions he wants answered.

We can say that the chief difference between oral interpretation and acting arises from a very natural cause: the difference in the performing situations. The actor, on a stage set, with freedom to move about, speaking the lines of one character and reacting to other live "characters," has a different environment from that of the oral interpreter. In the usual reading situation the interpreter uses a script placed on a lectern. His position is confined; he has no costume, no set, no lighting effects, and no other live "character" about.

---

2 From *Literature as Experience* by Wallace A. Bacon and Robert S. Breen. Copyright © 1959 by McGraw-Hill Book Company. Used by permission.

The actor has the physical environment and the motivations to identify with his character completely, to *be* the character. The interpreter's situation discourages identification with the character or characters he is interpreting. He would look and feel silly trying to "be" many people all at the same time, and he should find it literally impossible to perform his character's actions in his confined position. So what does he do when he has the responsibility of reading the parts of many characters in a play or story?

The interpreter takes a re-creative role. Retaining his own identity, he *suggests* a character or characters. The actor, on the other hand, takes a creative role, attempting to identify with his character completely and to represent him—literally.

The interpreter, then, must learn the art of suggestion. Happily, audiences respond to suggestion; modern experimental theatre is proof of this. More and more plays are staged with suggestive set pieces and suggestive props and costumes. Audiences like this. They like being given the chance to use their imaginations.

The line between the suggestive role of the interpreter and the more literal role of the actor must remain a vague one. But is it so bad if, when reading a dramatic part, the interpreter slips over into the actor's realm and "identifies"? We think not, so long as he does not call attention to *himself.* There must be a degree of flexibility between suggestion and representation of character. Ralph Dennis, former head of the speech department at Northwestern University, stated a sensible philosophy in regard to the interpreter's role:

> How can we measure platform art? . . . By this: does it appeal, does it get over *to the judicious few as well as to the many?* That's a high standard, a practical standard. . . . If we accept such measurements what care we about personation or impersonation, characterization, or acting, except as they be good or bad mediums for the individual under discussion. . . .
>
> If a reader . . . shows me life through his personal slant, his concept, his vision; if he is sincere, true, honest, does not offend, if he moves me, makes me think, I am for him. . . . Let's not quibble over terms, over methods. . . . Let's learn how to retranslate, into living words and actions that will be understood by all, the thoughts, the life values, the life interpretations which men have put into books.[3]

[3] Ralph Dennis, "One Imperative Plus," *Quarterly Journal of Speech,* Vol. 8 (June, 1922), pp. 218–23. Reprinted by permission.

2 OVERVIEW OF THEORY AND METHODS

ORAL INTERPRETATION DEFINED

We defined oral interpretation as the art of re-creating an author's recorded experience in a work of literary art and of communicating this to an audience so as to arouse a meaningful response.

Let us begin our discussion of this definition with *an author's recorded experience in literature,* the subject matter of oral interpretation.

"Experience" is the key word. We are saying that what the author transforms, molds, and shapes into a form of literature (be it prose, poetry, or drama) is his own experience: what he has actually experienced and what he has experienced vicariously.

Here is an explanation of how Robert Frost "just came" to write "Stopping by Woods on a Snowy Evening."

> Once at Bread Loaf, however, I heard him add one very essential piece to the discussion of how it "just came." One night, he said he had sat down after supper to work at a long piece of blank verse. The piece never worked out, but Mr. Frost found himself so absorbed in it that, when next he looked up, dawn was at his window. He rose, crossed to the window, stood looking out for a few seconds, and *then* it was that "Stopping by Woods" suddenly "just came," so that all he had to do was cross the room and write it down.[1]

That the poem "just came" was, in part, due to the fact that the poet had memories, both real and imagined, on which to draw. As a creative artist Frost was able to see in a simple experience something of general signifi-

[1] From "Robert Frost: The Way to the Poem" by John Ciardi. *Saturday Review,* April 12, 1958. Reprinted by permission.

cance. And as a creative artist he was able to find the right words, just the right words, to record this in a form which is now recognized as one of the classics in lyric poetry.

The author, then, with his sensitivity to language and form and with his special talent for perceiving the relationships of human experience, "modifies" or "extends" his experiences into a form of literary art.

And, after the writer, there is the reader who must use his thought and imagination to understand. The interpretation of the text for meaning we call *the art of re-creating*. The words *art* and *re-creating* suggest that the reader's interpretation is a creative process, and, in part, it is. What does the reader have that can help him understand an author's sometimes complex modification and extension of human experience? He has his own background of experiences, both real and vicarious. The author's world may differ greatly from his own; but if the author has successfully communicated, the reader finds "public" meanings within the selection. These can be related to the experiences of all men. When the interpreter relates his own life experiences to an author's recorded experience something new is created. His experiences fuse with the author's to illuminate the text in a particular way. Each interpretation is to a degree original. All art implies originality. This is why actors may give slightly different interpretations of the same character role and all receive high praise. However, an interpreter's creativity should be based on, and guided by, a thorough understanding of the author's meaning; he should not base his reactions on "private impressions."

The creative element is only one part of the art of re-creating. Art also implies discipline. It is necessary for the interpreter to know how literature works, what its elements are, and how to apply this knowledge in a careful analysis of a given piece of writing.

"A work of literary art," from our definition, suggests that the interpreter is concerned with developing standards for judging the literary worth of a selection. He must know what constitutes a work of literary art and be able to apply this criterion to his own choices. He should also give attention to studies in literary criticism or to biographical or historical studies that bear directly on understanding a particular piece of literary art.

Finally, consider ". . . communicating this to an audience so as to arouse a meaningful response." "Communication," of course, implies the effective use of vocal, facial, and body expression. But this also embraces the whole aesthetic effect of a reading performance. It means the interpreter's control of his material, himself, and the audience. These are very subtle matters that apply to every aspect of an interpreter's performance and to the total effect. These will be discussed at appropriate points throughout the text.

This discussion of the definition of oral interpretation has touched on some of the basic theories that will be enlarged upon and applied as we proceed. We will continue this overview with a general look at the processes and methods used throughout the text.

The divisions, it should be noted, are intended to facilitate matters; we cannot study everything at once. Actually, content (interpretation) and delivery (projection) cannot be separated. All of these aspects merge, and something more is added in the final creative performance. The reader is more than the sum of his attributes as the reading is more than the sum of its parts.

We begin with the process of interpreting material.

INTERPRETING

The interpreter should, first of all, be concerned with ways and means to understand the author's ideas and emotions. He has an obligation to understand the author's experience if he is to be an honest spokesman.

We must possess something before we can share it. But is it possible to "possess" another's experience? Even when two people have the same sensory experience, the interpretations of the experience differ because of individual differences. As we have just pointed out in our discussion of the definition, each interpretation is colored by the reader's personal response because he is influenced by his own background and knowledge. Each response is also influenced by time and mood. A good piece of literature can be read again and again and still hold something to be found in the next reading. With every reading the interpreter has changed, and he will never be twice in exactly the same mood. So it is that the meanings of literature are always "on the wing," and no one can expect to capture the exact experience. It follows that the interpreter can never "possess" the experience, in the usual sense of the word; but he can, at a given time, be made alive to, be "possessed of," the author's experience. How does the student pursue such an understanding? As we have said, the pursuit should be both a discipline and a creative process.

With the hope of making the intangible aspects of interpretation more tangible, we will suggest four steps that may lead the student to an understanding and appreciation of a work of literary art:

Responding to the total experience
Analyzing the author's experience
Relating the author's experience to one's own
Assimilating the total experience

Responding to the Total Experience

What is the total experience in a piece of literature? In regard to the short story, Eudora Welty says:

> The first thing we see about a story is its mystery. And in the best stories, we return at the last to see mystery again. Every good story has mystery—not the puzzle kind, but the mystery of allurement. As we understand the story better, it is likely that the mystery does not necessarily decrease; rather it simply grows more beautiful.[2]

When an interpreter looks at the total effect of a selection of literature, he should be sensitive to this "mystery." We may define this as an "imperative extra" that comes across to the sensitive reader as a result of the fusion of all the properties of the writing (content, form) to give aesthetic pleasure. It is the special quality of the whole creation, rather than any one element or technique of form.

A student may find that he is more sensitive to this quality of the whole when he is familiar with the author's writing. Someone who is familiar with Hemingway's writing, for instance, may be aware that over and over he is telling us that the only way to live in this world of pain and violence is to be brave, courageous, and tough. This essence of content he makes clear with such gusto and terseness that the effect is magic. In contrast, Eudora Welty's stories are completely lacking in violence, and she never points a moral. She takes us with her into a simple situation and shows us life in a setting. Her magic lies in how "finely" she catches the atmosphere —the sound, the smell, the feel of a place—and in how rightly she catches the tone and rhythm of the people she places in the setting.

A student, reading a selection for the first time, may not be able to respond on this level; but usually, he has some immediate awareness of why the material holds his attention and why it has appeal for him. He should begin *where he is,* expressing his initial response as best he can. Sensitivity to literature grows with use.

But why should the interpreter start with a response to the whole? He should start here because the whole must always be kept in mind as he analyzes the parts; each part should be considered, not as an end in itself, but as a means of understanding the end result—the total experience.

Analyzing the Author's Experience

The process of analysis recommended in Chapters 3 and 4 is based on the philosophy of leading literary critics. We consider a work of literary art

[2] From "The Reading and Writing of Short Stories." Copyright © 1949, by Eudora Welty. Reprinted by permission.

as an action. In seeking to understand the situation (what happens—to whom, where, when, and why?) and the attitudes of the author or characters toward the situation, we arrive at an understanding of what the author is saying (theme). Such an investigation should reveal surface meaning which, in many cases, can be considered sufficient for oral interpretation. For a fuller understanding an extended investigation of symbolic meanings is suggested.

Chapter 3 discusses the technical elements found within a literary selection (plot, character, setting, theme) and literary devices used by authors (such as point of view, uses of language) to reveal attitudes and style. In Chapter 4 actual procedures for analyzing are suggested.

Relating the Author's Experience to One's Own

It is a very natural thing to relate our own personal experiences to fictional experiences. An author's imagery will suddenly remind the reader of a scene he has witnessed, a sound he has heard, or an emotion he has felt. While walking across campus, a student may reflect on the relationship of certain characters in the material he is preparing and recall an occasion when he experienced a similar relationship. When or where this relating process takes place is not important—so long as it does occur.

Through the imagery of words, an author hopes to stimulate the reader to share his experience. In life, we experience the sensory responses of sight, sound, taste, smell, and touch directly; in reading, we experience them indirectly. If a reader lets the author's words stimulate him to imagine or to recall sensory responses from his own life as he reads, he becomes immediately involved in the recorded experience.

Though a person has never seen the inside of a fish, he could imagine the sight from this description:

> I thought of the coarse white flesh
> packed in like feathers,
> the big bones and the little bones,
> the dramatic reds and blacks
> of his shiny entrails,[3]

But if the reader could recall an experience—a time when he actually cut into the soft belly of a fish, observed, and reacted to the sight—he would respond more fully to the poet's imagery. We are more likely to respond to any recorded sensory experience when we have been emotionally involved in a comparable one. Here is a passage in which a mother grieves for a lost son:

[3] From "The Fish" from *Poems—North and South—A Cold Spring* by Elizabeth Bishop, published by Houghton Mifflin Company.

I am not mad; this hair I tear is mine;
My name is Constance; I was Geffrey's wife;
Young Arthur is my son, and he is lost.
I am not mad; I would to heaven I were!
For then 'tis like I should forget myself.
O, if I could, what grief should I forget! . . .
For, being not mad, but sensible of grief,
My reasonable part produces reason
How I may be delivered of these woes,
And teaches me to kill or hang myself.
If I were mad, I should forget my son;
Or madly think a babe of clouts were he.
I am not mad; too well, too well I feel
The different plague of each calamity.
    . . . my poor child is a prisoner.—
And, father cardinal, I have heard you say,
That we shall see and know our friends in heaven.
If that be true, I shall see my boy again; . . .
But now will canker sorrow eat my bud,
And chase the native beauty from his cheek,
And he will look as hollow as a ghost;
As dim and meagre as an ague's fit;
And so he'll die; and, rising so again,
When I shall meet him in the court of heaven
I shall not know him. Therefore never, never
Must I behold my pretty Arthur more. . . .
Grief fills the room up of my absent child,
Lies in his bed, walks up and down with me;
Puts on his pretty looks, repeats his words,
Remembers me of all his gracious parts,
Stuffs out his vacant garments with his form;
Then, have I reason to be fond of grief.
Fare you well; had you such a loss as I,
I could give better comfort than you do.—
I will not keep this form upon my head,
When there is such disorder in my wit.
O Lord, my boy, my Arthur, my fair son!
My life, my joy, my food, my all the world!
                    (Shakespeare, *King John,* Act III, sc. 4)

Listening to this passage interpreted by Helen Hayes, an actress with the technical skill to give subtle nuances and shadings to the words, we can appreciate the depth of this Queen Mother's grief over the loss of her child. Listening to it with the knowledge that Helen Hayes has in her own life suffered the death of a beloved child, we are even more moved by her performance. We cannot say that Miss Hayes is thinking of her own personal grief while reading, but we can be sure that at some point she has related this grief to her own. Her experience has given her great understanding so that she can sincerely experience this mother's grief as she reads the lines.

In relating his own experience, the interpreter becomes more personally involved. What Charles McGaw says in regard to the actor's inner resources can apply as well to the reader: "What the actor has 'in him' is his own experiences. His *inner* resources are everything that he has ever seen and felt and thought."[4]

Assimilating the Total Experience

Once again, the interpreter should return to the selection as a whole as his final step in the interpretative process. As a result of his analyzing and "relating," the meaning is clear and he is more personally involved in the material. But at this point, he may find he cannot respond to the thought and feeling because he is too concerned with details. He must forget the parts and focus on the whole. If he is able to leave the material for a few days, he may find when he goes back to it that the meanings have been assimilated. Another person may assimilate the new meanings and associations by reading the selection over and over many times.

PROJECTING

Now we are concerned with the student reader's ability to get an audience to respond to his interpretation. There is no formula for conveying logical and emotional meaning to an audience. We can only offer guidelines. The interpreter's success is dependent upon the use he makes of his voice and body and his ability to respond at the moment to an author's ideas and emotions.

A *possible* way to aid communication is offered here. The process includes two approaches, technical and psychological. In this chapter we will only clarify the two approaches. Chapters 5, 6, and 7 will be devoted to theory and practice material for the techniques. Chapter 8 will further amplify the psychological approach.

Technical Approach

Techniques are the "hows" of learning something—anything: playing the piano or playing football, playing tennis or painting a portrait, making a

---

4 Charles McGaw, *Acting Is Believing* (New York: Holt, Rinehart and Winston, Inc., 1955), p. 4, Copyright ©,1966 by Holt, Rinehart and Winston, Inc. By permission of the publishers.

cake or writing a story. Art forms and simple activities require skills. In this case, the techniques are tools for learning how to use the voice and body effectively and how to employ controls to aid in the projection of logical and emotional meanings in literature.

The hows for voice and body should never be considered as rules that must be followed by every student, every time. They are, rather, possible means to reach a good result, but the extent of their use should be measured in terms of where the student is and where he wants to go. In an oral interpretation class there are usually found different levels of native talent and variations of purpose. One student who plans to teach may have a pleasing voice which he uses naturally and effectively. Both he and the teacher are likely to think his present vocal control adequate for his work in the course and for his future profession. It makes better sense for him to devote his time to the reading and analysis of literature which will be of more personal profit than working with voice exercises. Another student, whose voice and speech control are good, wants to become an actor; since his future profession makes rigid demands on the perfecting of voice and diction, he had best continue work on techniques. But these are exceptions. In an average class, the majority of students have voice and body problems that interfere in varying degrees with oral communication. In each case the student should learn, with the teacher's guidance, where he has the greatest need for acquired techniques and plan his practice exercises accordingly. Concentrated effort on a few significant points is usually the best way to get results.

There are certain principles that the student should keep in mind while working on voice and body techniques. As we said earlier, the interpreter's techniques should never intrude, offend, or interfere with his communication of meaning and feeling. In other words, they should never "show" or draw attention as techniques; and they should never be used to display ability. The author's experience in the material is what the listener should remember—not the interpreter. Sometimes the listener is made aware of techniques, not because they have been exhibited as effects, but simply because the reader seems to be *aware* of using them. Communication becomes an art form when there is sufficient refinement of techniques and when they are used easily without apparent effort.

But at what point can the student be expected to use good techniques without effort? As he begins to work on exercises, he may feel as if he is progressing backward instead of forward. At this point he becomes overly conscious of the "hows." To avoid this awareness of mechanics in performance, he should work on techniques *only* in practice session. In these practice periods the student should use prescribed exercises with short reading passages, concentrating on one problem at a time. In performance, he should forget techniques, put his problems aside and concentrate only on the author's ideas and feelings. Improvement in techniques, as a result of his practice sessions, may be slight at first; the carry-over from practice to performance is slow, for it takes time to break a bad voice or diction habit and to replace it with a good one. The mastery of oral communication is forever ahead. No one attains "perfection," but improvement is always possible.

A student's attitude toward technique plays an important part in his degree of success. Because changing a habit is slow and hard to measure, he may become discouraged or discredit the whole process. This can be avoided if he realizes, at the beginning, that any degree of mastery of a technique takes discipline, patience, and effort. What Stanislavski, the well-known director of the Moscow Art Theatre, had to say about the actor's "work" applies as well to students in any of the speech arts:

> Let some one explain to me why the violinist who plays in an orchestra on the tenth violin must daily perform hour-long exercises or lose his power to play? Why does the dancer work daily over every muscle of his body? Why do the painter, the sculptor, the writer practice their art each day and count that day lost when they do not work? And why may the dramatic artist do nothing, spend his day in coffee houses and hope for the gift of Apollo in the evening? . . . There is no art that does not demand virtuosity.[5]

Making any noticeable improvement in the use of voice and speech depends upon knowledge and artistic application of technique. This demands work.

Psychological Approach

The psychological approach is based on the simple theory that if you think about the meaning as you read aloud, your expression of the thoughts will be good. The validity of the theory has long been recognized in the interpretation field. Though the general theory is reasonable, it is usually recommended with reservation, and the "hows" of such an approach remain rather "mystic" and undefined. To argue which is better—the technical or the psychological approach—is useless. Both methods can be useful. It is a matter of individual needs and talents.

The psychological method, however, is not as simple as it might appear. There is more to it than "just think the thought and feel the emotion at the moment, and the voice and body will respond—naturally." In the first place, the voice and body response must be naturally good. It is true that concentration on the thoughts and feelings may bring about a marked improvement in control of voice and body, but the method cannot correct a lisp or a

---

5 *My Life in Art.* Copyright 1948 by Elizabeth Reynolds Hapgood. Reprinted by permission of the publisher, Theatre Arts Books, New York.

flat vowel sound. And, how does one discipline himself to concentrate, to use his imagination, and to relate his own experience when reading aloud? In Chapter 5 we will include exercises which are sometimes helpful in that they may assist the student in gaining enough freedom to respond to emotional meanings—a necessity if the psychological approach is to work. In Chapter 8 we will draw upon some aspects of the Stanislavski method in acting to aid in the application of concentration, imagination, and identification. An attempt is made to adapt these acting techniques to the practical needs of the interpreter.

APPLYING AESTHETIC PRINCIPLES

The final test for an interpretative performance is that it be aesthetically pleasing. Aspects of good taste in relation to choice of material, emotional control, and use of voice and body are discussed throughout this text. There are three general principles regarding aesthetic criteria that seem appropriate to include here in this overall discussion: appropriateness of speech level, empathy, and aesthetic distance.

Appropriateness of Speech Level

Our material makes different demands on the degree of "naturalness" we can use and still stay within the bonds of appropriateness. The poetic and elegant language of the Bible, of Shakespeare, or of the Greek classics must be lifted above "natural" speech and given appropriate dignity and beauty. Our aesthetic sense of beauty might well be offended if we heard Medea's passionate lines read with the "natural" flavor of colloquial speech.

In lifting such language to an appropriate level of utterance, we find there is always the fear of overdoing, and rightly so. Nothing is more offensive than affected, artificial speech. Somehow the interpreter must "sense" a rightness. Listening to others in class, he becomes aware of the underplay or overplay of precision and beauty of speech in relation to the demands of the material. Remembering Hamlet's advice to the players,

> Suit the action to the word, the word to the action; with special observance that you o'er step not the modesty of nature . . .   (Act III, sc. 2)

and listening to professional readers, the student becomes sensitive to the artistic demands of literary art.

Empathy

The dictionary defines empathy as "the imaginative projection of one's own consciousness into another being." Like most dictionary definitions this is accurate so far as it goes. But empathy includes a kind of "physical sympathy" with another person or situation in which we are not actually participating. We have all experienced that unconscious human tendency to "feel into" a situation: to laugh or cry at the movies, to pucker our lips when we see someone eating a lemon, to move our bodies to follow the ball down the basketball court. We respond in this way because, in each case, we are feeling into the experience we are observing, and, as a result, the body tends to imitate the observed action.

As he reads aloud for an audience the interpreter becomes involved in the material he is reading to the extent that he feels into the author's experience and his body responds to the inherent action in the ideas and feelings expressed by the author's words. If successful, he arouses a reponse from his listeners that causes them to feel into the experience in the literature. Whether the listener's response is physical in such a form as leaning forward, or spiritual, in the *feel* of mind meeting mind, the interpreter senses the response. When this happens a kind of magic circle is completed, and communication is at its best. But the circle can be broken at any point by various distractions caused by the situation, the listener, or the reader. For example, if the reader fails to empathize with his material, his listeners do not respond; if he empathizes with his material too much, he calls attention to himself and the audience response is one of disapproval or embarrassment.

How to arouse empathy is the concern of all artists. Aesthetic distance is a means of arousing the right kind of empathic response.

Aesthetic Distance

Aesthetic distance may be defined as a physical distance, detachment, or a degree of "disinterest" that permits interest in the immediate activity.

People caught in New York's stalled elevators or black subway tunnels on the night of November 9, 1965, were too emotionally involved in surviving the ordeal to feel any detachment from the matters at hand. They were interested only in the culmination of the experience. But those viewing the black-out on television the next morning were able to see the experience with detachment, to look at the event with a degree of "disinterest." A physical distance or removal allowed them to see the whole event in perspective.

The principle of aesthetic distance is the artist's tool in arousing the audience to appreciate the significance of a situation or the beauty of an object. When an object is too physically near, aesthetic pleasure may be destroyed: a painting may fail to give aesthetic pleasure when you stand too close; loud music in a small room may offend a person's aesthetic taste; the nearness of the actors in a play-in-the-round may destroy the illusion;

a dramatic reading given in a small room may embarrass the listeners. The response in this last example may, of course, be due to lack of restraint on the part of the reader in addition to the fact that his vocal and physical "effects" are too close for comfort.

The student, reading various types of material in the classroom, senses that highly emotional material needs to be somewhat removed from the audience; but, in a small room what can one do? An arrangement of the chairs to increase the actual distance between reader and listeners can help. The use of the reading stand also serves to increase the distance. But in addition, the student interpreter can control the distance by using a level of restraint required for this physical nearness. He must learn to sense what the audience can take.

To determine the right degree of physical detachment, the interpreter should consider the audience's role. When the audience is to be directly involved, as in public speaking, the interpreter tries to reduce aesthetic distance in order to draw the listeners in. In reading expository material, then, the reader's contact with his listeners would be direct as in the public speaking situation. But when the listener's role is to overhear, to look in on a scene unobserved (as in drama), the interpreter withdraws, increasing the aesthetic distance. To determine the appropriate degree of aesthetic distance, the interpreter must study the particular selection to learn the author's intent—that is, the role he has given to the audience. For the interpreter, aesthetic distance is often a means of maintaining an illusion.

What well might be a student's first consideration as he begins his work in an interpretation class is our last one in this overview: *what* to choose to read aloud.

CHOICE OF MATERIAL

Within each literary form (prose, poetry, and drama) the interpreter has an unlimited amount of material from which to choose. He can to some extent be guided by his own tastes, but he must also consider the literary worth of his choice and its appropriateness for a particular audience.

Audience response is a good proving ground for standards. When selecting material to share with a particular audience, it is wise to consider details regarding the group, the place, the time, and so forth. Age, sex, level of intelligence, interests, and mood of the occasion are some of the things that influence the tastes of an audience. Just as no song is beautiful in a place where persons desire quiet, so, no serious poem, however beautiful, will be appropriate for a group which, at that moment, desires only light entertainment. Then, too, if the material is beyond or below the comprehension level of the listeners, they will be bored or offended by the choice. Each selection must be made in relation to each particular audience at each particular time. The interpreter should ask, "Will this selection be interesting, understandable, suitable, worth the listening time of this group—at this time?"

In the classroom the student is influenced by what his classmates select to read aloud. A student with a weak background in literature makes discoveries as he listens, and he is challenged by the highest level of intelligence and sensitivity in the class. If he accepts this challenge, his own values and tastes in literature will grow, and his choices, as a result, will contribute to the growth and interest of the entire group.

It is difficult to set up standards for judging the literary worth of a piece of literature; each must be read as a unique literary experience. Yet, if we are to make critical judgments of what is good and bad writing, we need guides. Factors concerning literary evaluation will be dealt with more specifically in the chapters on prose, poetry, and drama. For the present, let us consider general criteria applicable to any type of literature. These questions may guide the student in his consideration of the literary value and attention factors of materials:

Does this material reveal truths about life experience?

Does this material touch my own life experience, and is it likely to touch the experience of my listeners?

Will this material give pleasure, intellectual and sensory, or in combination?

Does this material have individuality of style?

Do the author's structure, imagery, and power of suggestion have special appeal?

Will this material read aloud well and hold the attention of my listening audience?

In regard to this last point, it is important to remember that the listener must "get" each idea and each nuance—at the moment; he cannot look back a few pages to pick up a cue as the silent reader may do. The interpreter is wise to select material that can be most easily followed by the listening ear. These points should be kept in mind:

Vivid and emotionally toned action material will hold attention; abstract philosophical thought will not.

The ear prefers simplicity to complexity, concreteness to generality, and vivid imagery to vague abstraction.

Some authors seem to have an ear attuned to the sound of words and their combinations; their writing seems to flow with the natural cadence of human speech in a way that calls for oral communication.

Part Two

LITERARY INTERPRETATION

3 LITERARY ANALYSIS

This chapter and the next will be closely related; both will concern interpretation of literary material. In this chapter the emphasis will be on clarifying the elements and literary devices that go into the making of a work of literary art. The purpose of this is to furnish the student with an adequate background in these matters that he can use in his analyses of particular selections of prose, poetry, or drama. The manner in which the student may utilize such an analysis in his oral-reading performance will be referred to only generally in Chapter 3, but Chapter 4 will be devoted to more specific application. There, actual analysis procedures will be illustrated and related to the oral-reading event. The content of both chapters will be further utilized and related to the analysis of specific selections throughout the text.

In discussing the elements found within literature, we shall use the following analysis guide:

The Situation and Its Movement

Who is speaking?
To whom is he speaking?
What happens?
Where and when does the action take place?

Tone

What is the author's attitude toward his subject?
What is the author's attitude toward his audience?

Theme

What is the author saying?

THE SITUATION AND ITS MOVEMENT

The situation (circumstances that exist at the beginning of an action) and its movement (what happens) are important aspects of any form of literary art. These matters comprise the content, the substance of a selection. In a literary work a situation exists even though it may be only implied, and something is happening, or has happened, that comprises or implies a dramatic action.

The first two aspects of the situation to be investigated have to do with an author's point of view.

POINT OF VIEW

Answers to the two questions "Who is speaking?" and "To whom is he speaking?" are important for the oral interpreter because he must understand the manner in which the author uses a narrator in order to adjust his oral style to the author's written style. He must know the nature of the storyteller so that he may project attitudes and an appropriate degree of characterization; he must recognize the listener so that he may establish proper speaker–audience relationships.

An author may choose one of three points of view: exterior omniscient, exterior third-person observer, or interior first person. Having chosen the view, the author creates a narrator, one who tells the story to us, the audience.

Omniscient Point of View

If the author has chosen the omniscient point of view, he may create a third-person narrator who possesses the power of omniscience. With his omniscience, the narrator may enter the consciousness of any of the characters; he knows and may express the thoughts and feelings of the characters. Here is an example where the narrator uses his omniscient power to see into the consciousness of all the characters. He uses his freedom to comment and judge as well:

> "Come, come, sir, walk downstairs with Miss Sharp, and I will follow with these two young women," said the father, and he took an arm of wife and daughter and walked merrily off.
>
> If Miss Rebecca Sharp had determined in her heart upon making the conquest of this big beau, I don't think, ladies, we have any right to blame her; for though the task of husband-hunting is generally, and with becoming modesty, entrusted by young persons to their mammas, recollect that Miss Sharp had no

kind parent to arrange these delicate matters for her, and that if she did not get a husband for herself, there was no one else in the wide world who would take the trouble off her hands.[1]

This *subjective*[2] use of omniscient power tends to direct the reader's attention to the narrator (in this case the author) rather than to the situation. The constant interruptions of the narrator to make personal comments tend to disrupt the reader's imaginative participation in the story's action. In the following passage from Thomas Hardy's story "The Three Strangers," we recognize again the subjective use of omniscient power, but it is, perhaps, less obtrusive because the author's personality is less evident.

> Oliver Giles, John Pitcher the dairyman, the parish-clerk, the engaged man of fifty, the row of young women against the wall, seemed lost in thought not of the gayest kind. The shepherd looked meditatively on the ground, the shepherdess gazed keenly at the singer, and with some suspicion; she was doubting whether this stranger were merely singing an old song from recollection, or was composing one there and then for the occasion. All were as perplexed at the obscure revelation as the guests at Belshazzar's Feast, except the man in the chimney corner, who quietly said, "Second verse, stranger," and smoked on.[3]

A variant of the omniscient is a limited view where the the narrator enters into the thoughts of only one of the characters, and what he reports is from that character's, or his own, view. In "The Marriages" by Henry James the narrator's omniscient power extends only into the character of Adela.

> "Won't you stay a little longer?" the hostess said, holding the girl's hand and smiling. "It's too early for everyone to go; it's too absurd." Mrs. Churchley inclined her head to one side and looked gracious; she held up to her face, in a vague, protecting, sheltering way, an enormous fan of red feathers. Everything about her, to Adela Chart, was enormous. She had big eyes, big teeth, big shoulders, big hands, big rings and bracelets, big jewels of every sort and many of them. The train of her crimson dress was longer than any other; her house was huge; her drawing room, especially now that the company had left it, looked vast, and it offered to the girl's eyes a collection of the largest sofas and chairs, pictures, mirrors, and clocks that she had ever beheld. Was Mrs. Churchley's fortune also large, to account for so many immensities? Of this Adela could know nothing, but she reflected, while she smiled sweetly back at their entertainer, that she had better try to find out. Mrs. Churchley had at least a high-hung carriage drawn by the tallest horses, and in the Row she was to be seen perched on a mighty hunter. She was high and expansive herself, though not exactly fat; her bones were big, her limbs were long, and she had a loud, hurry-

---

1 From *Vanity Fair* by William Makepeace Thackeray.

2 *Subjective* may be used in another sense. It may refer to the relating of an emotional response by a character who is feeling emotion peculiar to the dramatic situation and not necessarily those of the author. This kind of subjectivity is considered admirable; the kind in this story is no longer popular.

3 From *Wessex Tales* by Thomas Hardy.

ing voice, like the bell of a steamboat. While she spoke to his daughter she had the air of hiding from Colonel Chart, a little shyly, behind the wide ostrich fan. But Colonel was not a man to be either ignored or eluded.

"Of course everyone is going on to something else," he said. "I believe there are a lot of things tonight."

"And where are *you* going?" Mrs. Churchley asked, dropping her fan and turning her bright, hard eyes on the Colonel.

"Oh, I don't do that sort of thing!" he replied, in a tone of resentment just perceptible to his daughter. She saw in it that he thought Mrs. Churchley might have done him a little more justice. But what made the honest soul think that she was a person to look to for a perception of fine shades?

Third-Person Observer Point of View

The third-person narrator who merely observes and reports does not enter the thoughts and feelings of a character; he simply relates what he has seen or heard. Usually the narrator's descriptions and summaries (narrative elements) alternate with brief character scenes (dramatic episodes). In some cases the narrator's presence almost drops from view. He becomes a mere reporter of scenes, and the reader is shown rather than told the story through the dramatic interplay between the characters or through the thoughts in a character's mind (interior monologue). This is the *objective* use of the third-person view which allows the situation to unfold dramatically as in a play. Erskine Caldwell's story "Daughter" is an example. In "Daughter" the sense of the situation, of what is happening, is sharply focused through the dialogue of Jim (a share cropper who has shot his daughter because he could not bear to see her starve), the sheriff, and unidentified persons in the crowd. Though the third-person narrator briefly addresses the reader, the story is told dramatically; an illusion of an actual happening is created.

"You ought to have sent her over to my house, Jim. Me and my wife could have fed her something, somehow. It don't look right to kill a little girl like her."

"I'd made enough for all of us," Jim said. "I just couldn't stand it no longer. Daughter'd been hungry all the past month."

"Take it easy, Jim boy," the sheriff said, trying to push forward.

The crowd swayed from side to side.

"And so you just picked up the gun this morning and shot her?" somebody asked.

"When she woke up this morning saying she was hungry, I just couldn't stand it."[4]

4 From *Jackpot,* copyright, 1940, by Erskine Caldwell; by permission of Duell, Sloan and Pearce, Inc.

Obviously there is a difference in the degree of personality which authors allow third-person narrators to develop, and this would concern the oral interpreter. How would these narrators be characterized orally? By studying the style and tone of the story "The Three Strangers," the reader would discover that the narrator is in sympathy with the folk customs and the healthy attitudes of the simple folk he is describing; he enjoys their crude but effective management of the more sophisticated forces of the law. So the oral interpreter might suggest the physical characteristics of a well-educated but "earthy" middle-aged man. His mental attitude would reflect the sympathies and sense of humor evident in the narration. The characterization would not be full, but the audience would be able to recognize the narrator as a personality who is a product of the same place and time as the characters in the story. The direct speeches of the other characters would be given through the narrator; his voice would color the character interpretations, and these as well as his own comments would be addressed directly to the listening audience.

In the story "Daughter" the objective view lessens the importance of the narrator. In an oral reading, the interpreter would present this narrator as an unidentified observer, without personality. He would address the narrator's brief interruptions to the outside audience (or cut them; see Chapter 9), and he would characterize the other speakers as they address each other placing them out front in the realm of the audience.

Interior First-Person Point of View

If an author uses the interior, first-person point of view, the reader must determine whether the "I" of the narrative is a character telling his own story, a minor character involved in the action telling the story of a leading character, or a narrator who is reporting what he has observed or heard. In Mark Twain's *The Adventures of Huckleberry Finn,* Huck tells his own story and reveals, in the telling, himself and adults seen through his eyes. In the following passage we enter the story where Huck, to relieve his troubled mind, has just written a letter to Miss Watson to report the whereabouts of Jim, her runaway slave. He says:

> I felt good and all washed clean of sin for the first time I had ever felt so in my life, and I knowed I could pray now. But I didn't do it straight off, but laid the paper down and set there thinking—thinking how good it was all this happened so, and how near I come to being lost and going to hell. And went on thinking. And got to thinking over our trip down the river; and I see Jim before me all the time: in the day and in the nighttime, sometimes moonlight, sometimes storms, and we a-floating along, talking and singing and laughing. But somehow I couldn't seem to strike no place to harden me against him, but only the other kind. I'd see him standing my watch on top of his'n 'stead of calling me, so I could go on sleeping; and see him how glad he was when I came back

out of the fog; and when I come to him again in the swamp, up there where
the feud was; and such-like times; and would always call me honey, and pet me,
and do everything he could think of for me, and how good he always was; and
at last I struck the time I saved him by telling the men we had smallpox aboard,
and he was so grateful, and said I was the best friend old Jim ever had in the
world, and the *only* one he's got now; and then I happened to look around
and see that paper.

It was a close place. I took it up, and held it in my hand. I was a-trembling,
because I'd got to decide, forever, betwixt two things, and I knowed it. I studied
a minute, sort of holding my breath, and then says to myself:

"All right, then, I'll *go* to hell"—and tore it up. . . .

A contemporary "blood-brother" of Huck Finn is Holden Caulfield in
J. D. Salinger's *Catcher in the Rye.* He too tells his own story, and from his
view we get an amazingly realistic vision of an adolescent boy in our own
time. Both authors demonstrate unusual skill in presenting the first-person
interior view.

But the first-person narrator does not always tell his own story. In the
novel *The Great Gatsby* F. Scott Fitzgerald has a character who is closely
involved in the action tell the story of the leading character. We see Gatsby
through the eyes of Nick Carraway. Nick gives us a close-up view of Gatsby,
and his view is credible because the author places him in a position to observe closely, to receive reports from others and to participate in Gatsby's
experience.

... my eyes fell on Gatsby, standing alone on the marble steps and looking from
one group to another with approving eyes. His tanned skin was drawn attract-
ively tight on his face and his short hair looked as though it were trimmed every
day. I could see nothing sinister about him. I wondered if the fact that he was not
drinking helped to set him off from his guests, for it seemed to me that he grew
more correct as the fraternal hilarity increased. When the "Jazz History of the
World" was over, girls were putting their heads on men's shoulders in a puppy-
ish, convivial way, girls were swooning backward playfully into men's arms,
even into groups, knowing that some one would arrest their fall—but no one
swooned backward on Gatsby, and no French bob touched Gatsby's shoulder. . . .

Rather ashamed that on my first appearance I had stayed so late, I joined the
last of Gatsby's guests, who were clustered around him. I wanted to explain that
I'd hunted for him early in the evening and to apologize for not having known
him in the garden.

"Don't mention it," he enjoined me eagerly. "Don't give it another thought,
old sport." The familiar expression held no more familiarity than the hand
which reassuringly brushed my shoulder.

"And don't forget we're going up in the hydroplane tomorrow morning, at
nine o'clock."

Then the butler, behind his shoulder:

"Philadelphia wants you on the phone, sir."

"All right, in a minute. Tell them I'll be right there. . . . Good night."
"Good night."
"Good night." He smiled—and suddenly there seemed to be a pleasant signifi-
cance in having been among the last to go, as if he had desired it all the time.
"Good night, old sport. . . . Good night."[5]

The first-person view gives the oral reader the opportunity to characterize the narrator fully. He can suggest the character through voice and
body tones and through speech and body rhythms. Mark Twain makes it
easy for a reader to capture the movement and rhythm of Huck Finn's
speech. In *The Great Gatsby* the narrator's story is almost as important
as Gatsby's. Nick Carraway is a personality in his own right, and so he is
fully characterized. Usually the minor character telling another's story is
not so near center as Nick, but in any case, this narrator's personality and
his relationship with other characters should be discovered and projected
orally. When the narrator's direct speech is broken by dialogue, the oral
reader's direct contact with the audience (as narrator) would change. His
eye focus and characterization of the speakers would suggest who is speaking to whom (see "Differentiation," pp. 144–45).

The point of view in a poem may be recognized as it is in a fictional
story: a narrator tells a story from an external third-person view (omniscient or observer) or from an interior first-person view. In both narrative
fiction and poetry a narrator's presence may be clearly established and
maintained, or it may be only vaguely evident. But there are a few distinctions in the way a short-story writer and a poet may handle point of
view. In fictional prose a narrator is created by the author; the narrator
should not be considered as the author's voice. But in poetry the speaker
may or may not be the poet's voice. Furthermore, in narrative poetry a
story may be told through face-to-face dialogue between characters without
the use of a narrator. Let us cite these distinctions as evidenced in particular poems.

The unknown author of the ballad "Lord Randal" uses the dialogue of
the mother and son to tell the story; a narrator is not present.

LORD RANDAL

Anonymous

"O where hae ye been, Lord Randal, my son?
O where hae ye been, my handsome young man?"
"I hae been to the wild wood; mother, make my bed soon,
For I'm weary wi hunting, and fain wald lie down."

[5] Reprinted with the permission of Charles Scribner's Sons from *The Great Gatsby*,
pages 60–65, by F. Scott Fitzgerald. Copyright 1925 Charles Scribner's Sons; renewal copyright 1953 Frances Scott Fitzgerald Lanahan.

"Where gat ye your dinner, Lord Randal, my son?
Where gat ye your dinner, my handsome young man?"
"I din'd wi my true-love; mother, make my bed soon,
For I'm weary wi hunting, and fain wald lie down."

"What gat ye to your dinner, Lord Randal, my son?
What gat ye to your dinner, my handsome young man?"
"I gat eels boiled in broo; mother, make my bed soon,
For I'm weary wi hunting, and fain wald lie down."

"What became of your bloodhounds, Lord Randal, my son?
What became of your bloodhounds, my handsome young man?"
"O they swelld and they died; mother, make my bed soon,
For I'm weary wi hunting, and fain wald lie down."

"O I fear ye are poisond, Lord Randal, my son!
O I fear ye are poisond, my handsome young man!"
"O yes! I am poisond; mother, make my bed soon,
For I'm sick at the heart, and I fain wald lie down."

This little drama in one scene takes place after the real action, and we learn of the happenings through the dialogue. We are *told* nothing; we are allowed to overhear and to infer the meaning from the terse little scene. The realization of what has happened comes to us through simple questions that build in intensity, creating suspense. The poem has more to say than it states; the bare details given may suggest a complicated relationship among the three people: the mother, the son and his true-love, and suggestion is more effective in arousing an emotional response than facts given by a narrator. Presenting a story through dialogue is often used in the old ballads, and Robert Frost and other modern poets have used this method effectively.

In the ballad "Two Corbies" the narrator merely introduces the speakers: "As I was walking I heard two corbies making a mane," and from there the story is told through the dialogue of the two ravens without further directives from the narrator. This same dramatic technique is used by Robert Frost in "The Witch of Coos." A narrator's voice is evident only at the beginning and end of the poem for the purpose of setting and concluding the scene; the story itself comes to us through the talk we overhear between the mother and son. Many of Frost's poems could be cited as examples of dramatic dialogue (narrators used sparingly), among them "The Death of the Hired Man" and "West Running Brook."

The dramatic monologue and the soliloquy are two forms of poetry in which a story is told or implied without the assistance of a narrator. In the dramatic monologue the speaker is always a character, clearly identified, who speaks in the first person and reveals the situation (past and *present*) through words directed to a silent character (see "The Laboratory" by

Robert Browning, p. 55). The soliloquy differs from the dramatic monologue only in the fact that the speaker is not talking with or to anyone.
In both forms the narrator is a fictional character outside the personality of
the author.

In reading these dramatic forms aloud, the oral interpreter would characterize the speaker, and he would indicate through eye focus and other
subtle means that the character is speaking either to another character, to
a silent character, or to himself. In each case he is unaware of anyone over-
hearing.

A lyric poem may be close to the soliloquy in that a speaker expresses his
inner thoughts (implying a dramatic action). But the speaker in the lyric
may be the poet; he is not a fictional character created outside the personality of the poet as the speaker in the soliloquy is. In the lyric it is not always
possible to be sure who is speaking (the author or his narrator), and, on first
reading, the listener may not be easily identified. Notice the following:

A DEEP-SWORN VOW[6]
William Butler Yeats

Others because you did not keep
That deep-sworn vow have been friends of mine;
Yet always when I look death in the face,
When I clamber to the heights of sleep,
Or when I grow excited with wine,
Suddenly I meet your face.

Here we have no sure way of knowing whether Yeats or his narrator is
speaking. The situation—what has happened between two people—might
lead one to believe that either the man or the woman is speaking; but,
since the author is a man, we are inclined to agree that the narrator is a
man. The speaker appears to be addressing his words to a specific listener,
but on second reading we sense that the "you" of the poem is not present.
The narrator is reflecting on a past experience and the "you" of the poem
is present only in his memory. The oral reader would suggest that the
speaker (vaguely identified) is addressing himself in an internal reminis-
cence.

The reader may find narrative writers and poets who complicate matters
by using combinations or shifts in point of view; but even from this discussion of the most obvious problems, it should be evident that point of
view affects oral reading considerably and that in some cases it is no easy
matter to discover or project the qualities of the narrator found in a story
or poem.

[6] Reprinted with permission of The Macmillan Company from *Collected Poems* by
William Butler Yeats. Copyright Margaret C. Anderson 1917, 1918; renewed 1946 by
Bertha Georgia Yeats.

To chart the movement of the situation and to answer the question "What happens?" we need to examine another of the author's "hows": the way he has put his material together, the structuring. By studying this we discover what happens, and we get a sense of how the author gets the situation to move where he wants it to move and why.

FORM AND STRUCTURE

Some authors of narrative fiction stay close to such traditional plot forms as the beginning–middle–end pattern. They insist on satisfying resolutions, on answering for the reader all the questions aroused by the conflict. Other writers direct the reader's interest through conflict and actions, but they force the reader to use his imagination and to find his own answers. Modern writers tend to deviate from the traditional patterns and to find new shapes for narrative fiction. But even the most nonconventional form may be said to have a pattern of a kind which controls the author's purpose.

Plot

E. M. Forster in his *Aspects of the Novel* points the distinction between story and plot:

> Let us define a plot. We have defined a story as a narrative of events arranged in their time-sequence. A plot is also a narrative of events, the emphasis falling on causality. "The king died and then the queen died," is a story. "The king died, and then the queen died of grief" is a plot. The time-sequence is preserved, but the sense of causality overshadows it. . . . If it is in a story we say "and then?" If it is in a plot we ask "why?"[7]

A plot line can be evident in narrative or dramatic poetry; and lyric poetry, too, can be seen as an action with narrative elements (story) and dramatic conflict (plot) implied. But—and this need hardly be said—it is in the novel, short story, and drama that the plot is of prime importance.

The plot structure can be charted simply by asking, "What happens next?" and "Why?" We can see these divisions (something happens and then something else happens) as motivational units or "acts." This divisioning by units can be compared to the analyzing method used by many theatre directors. Analyzing a play, a director divides an act into scenes determined by entrances and exits. In either case, the interpreter or the director studies each unit or scene as to purpose and as to what each scene or unit accomplishes in relation to the whole. This will be illustrated in Chapter 4.

---

[7] E. M. Forster, *Aspects of the Novel* (New York: Harvest Books, Harcourt, Brace & World, Inc., 1927), p. 86. By permission of the publishers.

Rhythm of Content

The accents and descents of tension throughout a selection make up the rhythm of content. High points of excitement are usually followed by descents in excitement. A reader or an audience cannot be held in a state of tension too long; some relief must follow. It is helpful to think in terms of planes in tracing the rise and fall of tension: one high point reaches one plane and then the tension descends slightly before another build which ends on a higher plane than the one before.

Within each major structural division or unit a high point (or minor climax) can be detected. The highest point in the selection as a whole is the structural climax. This is the highest peak of interest, or the turning point in the situation. The minor climaxes may build in intensity to the climax of the whole and then descend quickly, or the climax may come early with a slow descent; there are countless ways. When the emotional peak comes at a different point than the structural climax, it is helpful for the oral interpreter to consider two climaxes: structural (or logical) and emotional. Charlotte Lee says in her text *Oral Interpretation:*

> Often the highest emotional intensity will come at the logical climax. Occasionally, however, this is not the case. The logical climax may precede the emotional high point and prepare for it. This will be true, for instance, when the emotional climax depends upon a character's or a writer's response to a completed cycle of events. On the other hand, if the outcome of events depends upon a character's emotional reaction, the emotional climax will precede the logical one. . . .[8]

In the poem "Bredon Hill," by A. E. Housman, the rhythm changes abruptly in the middle of the poem and the structural climax follows almost immediately:

> My love rose up so early
> And stole out unbeknown
> And went to church alone.

The highest emotional peak, however, comes in the last lines:

> Oh, noisy bells, be dumb;
> I hear you, I will come.

In the episode from *My Little Boy* by Carl Ewald, the structural climax comes near the beginning:

> I hear them shouting "Jew!" and I go to the window and see my little boy in the front rank of the bandits, screaming, fighting with clenched fists. . . .

The emotional climax, dependent upon this climactic action and the events that follow, is expressed at the end:

8 (Boston: Houghton Mifflin Company, 1965), p. 20. Reprinted by permission of the publishers.

... Today I have vaccinated him against the meanest of all mean and vulgar diseases.

The interpreter must use his vocal techniques for building in accordance with the material, so it is important that he be able to identify the climax (or climaxes) and the way the author builds and descends to and from the peaks of structural and emotional intensity.

There is not enough time for any noticeable change in rhythm of content in Yeat's short poem, but even here we can see three divisions with high points or key words in each unit:

UNIT 1   Others because you did not keep
         That *deep-sworn vow* have been friends of mine;

UNIT 2   Yet *always* when I look death in the face,
         When I clamber to the heights of sleep,
         Or when I grow excited with wine,

UNIT 3   *Suddenly* I MEET YOUR FACE.

Structural divisioning of other types of literature may be found in later chapters: short story (p. 151), play cutting (p. 190).

PLACE AND TIME (WHERE AND WHEN?)

No story would be the same if it were transferred to another place and time. Huck Finn would not be Huck Finn in a modern setting. Believable fictional characters seem to belong to a certain place and time, which act upon them. So these two elements are keys to understanding characters. In Thomas Hardy's stories his settings act upon the characters and influence their actions. It seems that the characters do what they do and are what they are because of where they are in place and time. In Joseph Conrad's "Heart of Darkness," setting is the source of a character's destruction: the character, Kurtz, identifies with the African jungle, and in the end, this destroys him. William Faulkner's characters are believable because they spring from their place—Yoknapatawpha County, Mississippi. Though the Snopeses are found everywhere, they belong to this particular place. Hemingway's places sometimes take on symbolic meanings: in the story "A Clean Well Lighted Place," the place, a cafe in Paris, *well lighted* and *clean*, is a symbol of what one character is searching for in his fellow man and, perhaps, what all men are searching for in life.

Location and time are closely bound to feeling. An author's selection of details and imagery evokes an atmosphere, a mood, that surrounds the physical scene and the characters—decadence and terror in Conrad's "Heart of Darkness," cynicism, loneliness, and despair in Hemingway's "A Clean

Well Lighted Place." There is often a close relationship between place and time and the pervading tone of a literary work.

TONE

The word *tone* can have many meanings: it can refer to vocal sound, the intonation of voice that expresses a particular attitude; it can refer to the feeling or attitude created by a word or word arrangement in a certain context; or it can be used in a larger sense to refer to the pervading attitude or predominant spirit of a piece of writing, an effect produced by the author's handling of language and his expression of mood. In this text, it will be used in all of these ways.

We may recognize the pervading tone or atmosphere of a piece of literature as being dark, light, serious, playful, intimate, approving, disapproving, or any of the many other possible attitudes. The author creates an atmosphere, a tonal effect which is a synthesis of a selection's subject and style. The oral reader must be prepared to project this overall tone or atmosphere as well as the subtleties of tone that contribute to it.

To determine the pervading tone, the interpreter may need to give first consideration to a literary work's place in time. A reader's recognition of attitudes may be blocked because he does not understand the language used, the attitudes and values of a past era. Usually, however, tonal effect is due to an author's attitude toward his subject or toward his readers, or to the way he combines these. So, as a guide to discovering overall tone, we can seek answers to two questions: What is the author's attitude toward his subject? and What is the author's attitude toward his audience?

The Author's Attitude Toward His Subject

As an author records his own or another's experience, he reveals his emotional response toward that experience (his subject). This emotional response may be referred to as the mood. An author seldom tells us how he feels, but he shows us how he feels through his description of the setting, through the movement of the situation, and through his choice and arrangement of words. Responding to these, we are made to feel the author's response: sadness, joy, anger, happiness, bitterness, indignation, acceptance— or any one of the whole range of emotions. Within a selection, an author's moods may vary from light to dark, from comic to tragic; but in the material as a whole we can find a dominant mood. A study of mood change within a selection helps the oral interpreter put these changes in proper relation to the dominant mood and to prepare for smooth transitions. No part of the oral interpreter's analysis is more important, for he must be prepared to project every gradation of feeling within a selection.

Even in a short poem changes in attitude may be evident. In "Deep-Sworn Vow" the speaker seems at the beginning to have a casual attitude toward his subject ("others" has an impersonal connotation), but in five short lines the simple words build a deeply personal tone. The general mood evoked is reflective; the speaker is not bitter, but he is deeply concerned in his realization. In reading the poem aloud the interpreter would, through his awareness of the emotional meaning of the simple words, project changes in attitude, but at the same time he would maintain the dominant reflective mood.

The Author's Attitude Toward His Audience

An author's attitude toward his audience may be the same as his attitude toward his subject, and, in such a case, his attitude simply invites the reader to share his mood. But the author's attitude toward his subject and toward his audience can be quite distinct. An author may express an attitude of sympathy for his subject at the same time he reveals a tone of warning or condemnation for his readers. John Steinbeck in his novel *The Grapes of Wrath,* for example, expresses an attitude of sympathy for a dislocated group of Americans. At the same time, he is pointing an accusing finger at the American reader who, he is saying through his tone, is responsible for the plight of the group.

In narrative fiction, dramatic poetry, and in the drama, the author's imaginary characters are often the chief means through which his attitudes are disclosed. In the brief passage from Caldwell's "Daughter" (p. 26), we can detect a note of sympathy for the prisoner Jim. Fellow sharecroppers, addressing Jim, express attitudes of regret for this terrible act, but they are in sympathy with Jim because they understand what has led him to this state. The characters are revealing Caldwell's attitudes toward injustice. Toward his subject Caldwell's attitude is one of sympathy; toward his readers his attitude is one of accusation. Together these attitudes say what the author wishes to say and establish a pervading tone of disapproval for the existing condition in the South at that time.

In life we reveal our attitudes toward individuals and situations by our tonal inflections and our bodily reactions. As an author writes, he reveals his attitudes through his choice and arrangement of words. He must attempt to convey by words alone all the subtleties that vocal tone and bodily gestures may express in direct communication. So if the interpreter is to discover subtle attitudes, he must become aware of the tonal quality or the tonal gestures suggested by words—words alone and words in combination —in their emotional environment. The scientist attempts to hold words to their denotative, literal meanings; he abstracts meaning. The literary artist, on the other hand, selects his words to connote, to imply emotional meanings. His words have the power to awaken in the reader an intimate *sense* of things and relationships. So now we will consider the author's most important means of projecting attitudes—his language.

LANGUAGE

Connotation and Imagery

To read poetry and descriptive prose aloud effectively the reader must be aware of the emotional association that words take on in a particular context (connotative meaning), and he must be sensitive to the sensory appeals an author makes through imagery.

In "A Deep-Sworn Vow" (p. 31) the simple words imply meanings that can be shared by all: our common knowledge of the marriage vows leads us to believe that "deep-sworn vow" implies a spiritual bond (outside the bonds of law) between a man and a woman; "friends," as it is used with "others" in this context, seems to suggest a casual relationship; "clamber to the heights of sleep" suggests a dream state between consciousness and unconsciousness, and "suddenly I meet your face" suggests an impact of realization with deep emotional connotations.

Images can be created to call to memory all the senses: sight, hearing, taste, smell, and touch. An author's words stimulate the reader to mentally reproduce something not actually present; his imagination is aroused to recall sensory impressions from his own experience. Here is a sentence from Thoreau's *Walden* that may awaken a reader's sense of sound:

> Late in the evening I heard the distant rumbling of wagons over bridges,—a sound heard farther than almost any other at night,—the baying of dogs, and sometimes again the lowing of some disconsolate cow in a distant barn-yard.

In these lines from Matthew Arnold's "Dover Beach," notice how vividly the poet suggests the sounds of the sea:

> Listen! you hear the grating roar
> Of pebbles which the waves draw back, and fling,
> At their return, up the high strand,
> Begin, and cease, and then again begin,
> With tremulous cadence slow, and bring
> The eternal note of sadness in.

And notice in these lines from Hans Zinsser's "Young Love" how the concrete details make us see, sense movement, and taste!

> Mamie and I sat close together, for we were damp and a little chilly. She stuck up her wet face to be kissed, and I gazed down at her with the warm intention

of kissing her. But when I looked into her face, I saw two little rivulets running from Mamie's nose to her pouted upper lip. I had never noticed them before, although I had often observed her sticking her tongue out and upward, whenever she sniffed. For ours was a catarrhal climate. Now I looked and saw. But I have always been proud in later days that, even at this early age, I mastered my repulsion and kissed Mamie on her salty lips.[9]

When an oral reader recognizes and reacts to an author's sensuous imagery, he tends to "make real" what he reads aloud, and his word pictures and other sensory projections affect the audience so that they may "feel into" the recreated experience.

Figurative Language

There are many classifications of figures of speech, but it is less important to classify them than to see them at work as an author's means for evoking intellectual and sensual response. We shall briefly consider those figures which have the most significant bearing on the oral interpretation of literature.

Irony

The presence of irony is marked by a sort of grim humor. It is lighter and more indirect than sarcasm, but it is often more biting because it is indirect. An ironic statement contains an element of contrast; it has a double significance. Its intent is to imply that the opposite of what is said is meant. There are many devices through which irony may be achieved, among them overstatement, understatement, and paradox.

Overstatement is an exaggeration. Mark Anthony's funeral oration is the classic example: "Brutus is an honourable man." The speaker intends to have his audience believe, not what he says but the direct opposite of it.

Understatement is an ironical statement that appears to be less important than it actually is; what is left unsaid becomes important. Underplay has the effect of emphasizing and making a reader more aware of the reality. Notice in these lines from Marvell's "To His Coy Mistress" the effect obtained because the poet says less than could be said:

> The grave's a fine and private place,
> But none, I think, do there embrace.

In the poem "Does It Matter?" by Siegfried Sassoon understatement is deeply satirical:

9 From As *I Remember Him* by Hans Zinsser, copyright 1940, by Hans Zinsser, with permission of Atlantic–Little, Brown and Company.

Does it matter?—losing your sight? . . .
There's such splendid work for the blind . . .[10]

Paradox may be considered as a form of irony. It is a statement which though it seems contradictory may reveal a truth. It often suggests a mixture of attitude, as Juliet's line, "Parting is such sweet sorrow."

Irony may extend to situation or to character: we expect a certain thing to happen, but the opposite occurs. James Thurber's fables are examples of light irony applied to situation. In drama and in dramatic poetry irony is found in the situation when a character is revealed as opposite from what he seems to be or when words or acts of a character carry a meaning unperceived by himself but understood by the audience.

Metaphor and Simile

Metaphor and simile are, perhaps, the most widely used types of figurative language. A *simile* is a figure of speech in which a similarity between two objects is pointed out with the use of *as* or *like*. "March came in like a lion" is a common simile: the primary term of the comparison, March, acquires from the secondary term, lion, the qualities of "the king of beasts." In the *metaphor* the likeness between two objects is not pointed out. It is a figure which imaginatively identifies one object with another, and the reader must figure out how two things, seemingly unrelated, relate. When Shakespeare compares the world to a stage—"And the world's a stage . . ."—the relationship is clear. But when he compares old age to the season of late fall or early winter:

That time of year thou mayst in me behold
When yellow leaves, or none, or few, do hang
Upon those boughs which shake against the cold,
Bare ruined choirs, where late the sweet birds sang,

the meaning is not so evident because the comparison is conveyed through a group of complex images. In the modern poem "Auto Wreck" by Karl Shapiro (p. 60), we see metaphors and similes at work in conveying a powerful emotional impact: the ambulance is "the little hospital" (metaphor); its warning light is a "ruby flare pulsing out red light like an artery" (simile), and the wrecks are "empty husks of locusts" (metaphor).

Personification is a metaphor which gives human qualities to lifeless objects, animals, or abstractions: Keats refers to the Grecian urn as an "unravished bride of quietness," and an urn takes on the human qualities of purity; Donne refers to the sun as "Busy old fool, unruly Sun . . ." and the sun takes on the human qualities of a meddlesome old man.

[10] *Does It Matter* by Siegfried Sassoon. From *Counter Attack*. Pub. E. P. Dutton & Co., Inc. Copyright, 1940 by Siegfried Sassoon. Reprinted by permission of Brandt & Brandt.

Symbolism

On a literal level a symbol is something which stands for or suggests something else. It is a tangible thing (object, person, or action) that stands for something intangible: a lion is an animal which stands for courage; a flag is a piece of cloth which stands for a nation. The tangible object (lion or flag) has within itself the suggestion of a universal meaning. Such symbols are inherent in the language; they come into our daily conversation with perfect naturalness.

Another type of symbol suggests another meaning only because of the way it is used in a given text. For example, in Carl Sandburg's poem "Prayers of Steel,"

> Let me pry loose old walls;
> Let me lift and loosen old foundations.[11]

"old walls" and "old foundations" might be thought to stand for an outdated convention (segregation, nationalism . . .) or conformity in general. Usually many associations are attached to a symbol. Objects, people, and happenings may take on symbolic meanings because of the way they are handled in a piece of literature: rain becomes a symbol of death in a novel by Hemingway; snow becomes a symbol of death in a poem by Emily Dickinson; the apple tree is a symbol of death in Arthur Miller's *All My Sons*.

To understand an author's symbolism the reader must first of all recognize certain details as symbols, and then he must discover what meaning the author intends to have the reader attach to them. As the situation unfolds in Tennessee Williams' play *The Glass Menagerie*, we begin to associate the glass objects with a certain character, and then the objects take on symbolic meaning. We realize that it was the author's intent to have the objects represent the character's means of escape from her personal inadequacies and fears of life. Any element in a work of literary art (characterization, place, time, structure, and so forth) can take on symbolic meaning, but the reader must always be able to see the associations as related to the author's purpose.

Sound Symbolism

Recognizing the way the author has used sound to reinforce meaning is a means of understanding and projecting his more subtle emotional connotations. An author may select words with pleasant sounds to suggest beauty (*l, au,* and so forth), or he may choose words with unpleasant sounds to sug-

---

[11] From "Prayers of Steel" from *Cornhuskers* by Carl Sandburg. Copyright 1918 by Holt, Rinehart and Winston, Inc. Copyright 1946 by Carl Sandburg. Reprinted by permission of Holt, Rinehart and Winston, Inc.

gest harshness or abruptness (*p, b, t, k, g,* and so forth). *Onomatopoeia* is the imitation of actual sounds; the sound suggests the sense, as in the words "hiss" and "bubble." *Alliteration* is the repetition of identical consonant sounds: "what a tale their terror tells . . . ," and *assonance* is the repetition of vowel sounds: "To the moaning and the groaning of the bells!" (Poe's "The Bells"). In the prose selection "The Bombardment" by Amy Lowell (p. 58), sound symbolism is strikingly evident, and in most poerty it is used as a way of intensifying emotional response.

Rhythm

Rhythm is an element that is especially important in poetry, but in both prose and poetry the rhythmic patterns of recurrent beat or stress lend both pleasure and heightened emotional response to the listener or reader. This element will be discussed in some detail in Chapter 10.

THEME

The theme of a selection is not the subject, but what the author is saying about his subject. It is both the point of the whole writing and the reason why the author wrote it.

General themes concern conflicts: a character's search for identity, love, real-life values, and the like may be blocked by personal frustrations, man's inhumanity to man, fate, and so forth. The theme may be seen as the result of such a conflict. But sometimes a conflict is only implied. In a poem or in a modern short story an author's theme may be nothing more than a comment on life. In modern literature the theme more often points some aspect of truth rather than a "moral." In the (now familiar) poem "Deep-Sworn Vow," Yeats is simply giving an interpretation of a life experience and saying that it is possible for a past love affair to make a lasting impression on the unconscious mind. What the author is saying is highly colored by emotional connotations. This reminds us that thought and feeling can never be divorced in considering the theme of a piece of literature.

Study of a selection itself is the best way to find the underlying central meaning. Everything in the selection helps to point the theme, but the conflict, the emphasis given to certain words or phrases, and the title are all important clues. Means of discovering theme will be illustrated in the next chapter.

In this chapter we have examined the elements found within all forms of literary art for the purpose of understanding and appreciation. The next step in the student's preparation is to apply his understanding of literary form in an analysis of a selected piece of literature so that he may share more effectively the author's experience with a listening audience.

4 ANALYSIS PROCEDURES AND APPLICATIONS

Though a piece of literature exists in a form (narrative fiction, poetry, drama), we can see these forms as variants of the same art. All literary forms seek to reveal some truth about human experience through a dramatic situation, and all employ elements of language, character, structure, and tone to express or imply a comment on experience. It follows that the interpretation of the various forms would present similar problems and that general analysis procedures would be applicable to all the forms. Initially, then, we will consider the procedures suggested here as applicable to prose, poetry, or drama, leaving the subtle differences to be pointed out in later chapters.

The method for analyzing offered here is *one* way to go about a study of the parts in relation to the whole. The procedures are set down in a systematic order, but this does not mean that they cannot be modified; they are guidelines, and, as such, the complexity of the literary work under consideration and the individual interpreter's comprehension level should determine the extent of their use.

ANALYSIS PROCEDURES

Reading for a General Impression

Read the selection for a general impression of the total effect.

Clarifying Details

Clarify details that block comprehension. Comprehension may be obstructed by failure to understand the literal meaning of words, failure to understand the author's allusions, and by confusion in regard to unusual sentence construction. Your first task is to clarify these external obstructions.

Find the meaning of unfamiliar words and allusions. Consult proper sources to determine their significance. Let us illustrate by referring to a specific poem.

SAFE IN THEIR ALABASTER CHAMBERS[1]

Emily Dickinson

 1 Safe in their Alabaster Chambers—
 2 Untouched by Morning—
 3 And untouched by Noon—
 4 Sleep the meek members of the Resurrection,
 5 Rafter of Satin—and Roof of Stone—

(version of April 1862)

 6 Light laughs the breeze
 7 In her Castle above them—
 8 Babbles the Bee in a stolid Ear,
 9 Pipe the Sweet Birds in ignorant cadence—
10 Ah, what sagacity perished here!

(version of 1859)

11 Grand go the Years,
12 In the Crescent above them—
13 Worlds scoop their Arcs—
14 And Firmaments—row—
15 Diadems—drop—
16 And Doges—surrender—
17 Soundless as Dots,
18 On a Disc of Snow.

(version of April 1862)

Though this poem would require an extended study of symbolic meanings for full understanding, you might gain some insight into the meaning by simply using the dictionary. You would find: *alabaster*—a substance which is cold, hard, white, and smooth; *sagacity*—a keenness of mind or perception; *row*—casting light downward (an archaic meaning probably intended here); *diadem*—a mark or badge of royalty worn on the head; *doge*—the chief magistrate of Venice and Genoa; *disc*—a flat surface. And consulting a reliable source to clarify the Biblical allusion, "meek members of the Resurrection," you would find that this is a reference to the Puritan

---

[1] Reprinted by permission of the publishers and the Trustees of Amherst College from Thomas H. Johnson, Editor, *The Poems of Emily Dickinson*, Cambridge, Mass.: The Belknap Press of Harvard University Press, Copyright, 1951, 1955, by The President and Fellows of Harvard College, pp. 151, 154.

faith in a literal resurrection after death. It is likely that this clarification of denotative meanings would be a necessary step for you to take *toward* understanding. After this you might find it helpful to use the meanings in a *general* paraphrase:

> The meek Puritans, with their faith in the resurrection of the dead, lie safely in their cold chambers. But they no longer have the perceptions to see and hear and feel; the breeze, the bees, the birds are lost to them. Their castle—the world —has given place to cold whiteness. Time passes; and while worlds make arcs in space and the heavens cast light down, crowns of royalty drop and magistrates surrender without noise like specks falling on a snow covered surface.

Find the subject–verb–object in difficult sentence constructions to clarify the relationship of words and phrases. You can have comprehension difficulties even when word meanings are clear. In some cases it is sensitivity to the relationship of words and phrases that is needed. The use of inversion and long complex-compound arrangements may obstruct meaning. Unless you have the knack for unraveling a twisted sentence, you may have difficulty with Shakespeare's meaning. Here is a speech from *Julius Caesar:*

> CASSIUS: I will this night,
> In several hands, in at his windows throw,
> As if they came from several citizens,
> Writings all tending to the great opinion
> That Rome holds of his name; wherein obscurely
> Caesar's ambition shall be glanced at;
> And after this let Caesar seat him sure,
> For we will shake him, or worse days endure.   (Act I, sc. 2)

To clarify this complex-compound sentence find the subject–verb–object of each of the main clauses:

> I will throw writings
> Ambition shall be glanced at
> Let Caesar seat him
> We will shake him—or
> (We will) endure worse days

The modifying phrases which tell how, what, and when now become less confusing:

> throw—in several hands, in at his window, as if they came from several citizens
> writings—tending to the great opinion that Rome . . .
> ambition glanced at—obscurely
> let Caesar seat him sure—after this

When you have clarified such details, you will be better prepared to understand the situation in the selection.

Determining the Situation

Find answers to the two questions:

Who is speaking—the author, a narrator, or a character outside the personality of the author?

Who is the listener—the reading (or listening) audience or a specific person?

To illustrate this and the other procedures we will use the following poem:

BREDON HILL[2]

A. E. Housman

In summertime on Bredon
  The bells they sound so clear;
Round both the shires they ring them
  In steeples far and near,
  A happy noise to hear.

Here of a Sunday morning
  My love and I would lie,
And see the colored counties,
  And hear the larks so high
  About us in the sky.

The bells would ring to call her
  In valleys miles away;
"Come all to church, good people;
  Good people, come and pray."
  But here my love would stay.

And I would turn and answer
  Among the springing thyme,
"Oh, peal upon our wedding,
  And we will hear the chime,
  And come to church in time."

But when the snows at Christmas
  On Bredon top were strown,
My love rose up so early
  And stole out unbeknown
  And went to church alone.

[2] From *A Shropshire Lad*—Authorized Edition from *The Collected Poems of A. E. Housman*. Copyright 1939, 1940, © 1959 by Holt, Rinehart and Winston, Inc. Copyright © 1967 by Robert E. Symons. Reprinted by permission of Holt, Rinehart and Winston, Inc.

They tolled the one bell only,
  Groom there was none to see,
The mourners followed after,
  And so to church went she,
  And would not wait for me.

The bells they sound on Bredon,
  And still the steeples hum.
"Come all to church, good people"—
  Oh, noisy bells, be dumb;
  I hear you, I will come.

The speaker in the poem is one of the lovers; we can assume this to be the boy and that he is a character outside the personality of the author. The speaker is addressing no specific person. He tells his story in the past tense as though he expected someone to be listening, so we can say that he is openly addressing the outside audience. The view is subjective until the last verse when there is a shift to the present. As the narrator addresses the church bells and speaks his inner thoughts, the view takes on an objective quality.

Charting the Movement of the Situation

This may be done by dividing the selection into units.

Unit 1 (or Act 1)

> The boy tells the situation and answers the bells.
> (His answering the bells is the high point of unit 1.)
> The purpose of this "act" is to introduce the characters and to set the scene.

Unit 2 (or Act 2)

> The girl goes to church alone.
> The bells toll once.   (structural climax)
> Mourners follow after.
> The purpose here is to tell what happens—to show the dramatic action.

Unit 3 (or Act 3)

> The bells call people to church.
> The boy answers.   (emotional climax)
> The purpose here is to show an emotional response toward the experience and to suggest the outcome.

Clarifying the Place and Time

In "Bredon Hill" there is an abrupt change in time and scene: it is a peaceful Sunday morning in summer, and the scene is the top of Bredon Hill (Shropshire, England); then it is winter at Christmas, and Bredon Hill is covered with snow.

Determining the Tone

Find answers to the two questions: What is the author's attitude toward his subject? and What is the author's attitude toward his audience?

In the first "act" of the poem the narrator's attitude toward the scene is evident through the visual and sound imagery: the sounds of the bells are a "happy noise to hear;" the sounds of the larks are "about us in the sky;" and the couple lies among "springing thyme" looking down on "colored counties." No elaborate description could make us sense so vividly the peace and beauty of the English countryside and the narrator's (and likewise the author's) feeling for this place. Here, too, the youth's attitude toward what is happening is confident and carefree: the bells call "her"— "but here my love would stay"; and he answers the bells in a rather light, merry tone: "Oh, peal upon our wedding, / And we will hear the chime, / And come to church in time."

But at the beginning of the second unit there is an abrupt change in time and mood: it is winter and the mood is dark, for the beloved has been snatched away by death. The author's economy of language and change in rhythm emphasizes the emotional connotations of the simple words: the long vowel sounds (long *o*) are dominant (in contrast to the short vowel sounds in the previous stanzas) in the terse descriptive phrases: "stole out unbeknown," "went to church alone," "tolled the one bell only." The youth's feelings of dejection and aloneness are strikingly evident in "groom there was none to see," and "And would not wait for me." The contrast in his attitude toward the bells in the first part of the poem and in the last part is significant: their "happy noise" is now a "noisy sound." This tells us that the youth is not consoled. His answer to the bells at the end is a cry of bitterness.

Determining the Theme

A story, a poem, or a play may have many meanings. To find the theme you must look for the underlying meaning, the meaning to which everything in the story relates. Clues may be found in the title, key words, and repetitions; in the movement of the situation, and in the conflict.

In "Bredon Hill" young lovers are separated by death. It is evident that this is the cause of the conflict. What is the outcome of this conflict? On first reading, one might impose a moral theme here because the speaker's attitude toward the experience at the end is not immediately clear. Is Housman pointing a moral? No, he is not saying that the boy, having learned a lesson, will now be good and go to church! The tone of the boy's words at the end is angry and bitter, for he suddenly sees the world as a dark riddle and life as intolerably cruel. What is the meaning of his cry, "Oh, noisy bells, be dumb; I hear you, I will come."? Could he be expressing a wish to die—to follow his love to the church in death? Or is he expressing his agony over a realization that man *accepts?* The church bells call all the good people to church as before; daily life goes on, and the dead are forgotten. If the latter interpretation is accepted, the poet is pointing the inconstancy of man's heart—a bitter discovery. While expressing sympathy for his subject, he leaves his readers with a troubled sense of life's uncertainties and man's inconstancy.

Considering the Aesthetic Effect

Consider the aesthetic effect of the whole selection. Ask: how has the author employed variety, balance, and unity? After an analysis of parts, you are better prepared to see how an author has achieved an aesthetic effect. Such a consideration gives you a means for judging the author's skill in handling his material and aids you in putting the parts back together, in seeing and projecting the whole.

Variety is created in "Bredon Hill" by the sharp contrasts in time and mood. Four stanzas are devoted to the happy summer mood; two tell of the tragedy, and only one stanza—or rather the last two lines—carry the weight of the emotional reaction to what has happened. But because the intensity of these lines is great, we feel no imbalance of the parts. The intensity tends to balance the length of what has preceded. Unity is achieved through a harmony in details concerning the place, the character, and the language. The experience is not made to appear merely local and individual, but universal and typical of all men's struggles with the uncertainties of life and inward conflict.

APPLICATION OF ANALYSIS IN ORAL READING

How can the silent reader's analysis of a given piece of literature assure a more successful *oral* interpretation of the selection? During the process of studying a selection for a clear grasp of an author's experience, the interpreter usually finds it a natural thing to identify a personal experience with the author's. As a result of this "relating," the recorded experience takes on a personal meaning for him which may give impetus to his vocal and physical response in performance. But there are certain controls of which he must be aware lest his responses overweigh the author's intent. Within the selection the student interpreter finds his clues for vocal and physical response. Words in action can be thought of as gestures that imply active responses. Let us be more specific in regard to the oral reading of "Bredon Hill."

It would be necessary to project the speaker's attitudes toward the situation as it changes and as he changes. Since the narrator tells his story in the past tense to the outside listener, you would tell his story directly to the audience; but your degree of direct eye contact with the audience would be influenced by the emotional and dramatic quality of the content. In this case the experience is both dramatic and personal. While maintaining contact with your audience you would not look directly into the eyes of your listeners; this would suggest a degree of withdrawal—of aesthetic distance. At times, you might suggest that the narrator is thinking out loud. At the end, when the tense changes and the narrator addresses the bells directly, your withdrawal from the audience would be increased even more.

The details of interpretation for the most part would be concerned with making contrasts in the two "acts" and in handling the abrupt transition in mood. Your voice and body tone should suggest the boy's attitude toward the beauty and peace of the first scene and his air of confidence in his near-possession of the girl. In this part a light tonal touch with a generally brisk tempo and conversational flow would heighten the heavy tone and slower tempo of the second part. Between the acts an extended pause—during which you see, in your own mind, the change of scene and the tragic happening—would make the transition less abrupt and the situation believable. You should give special attention to the reading of the last two lines, taking care not to be maudlin, but to suggest the boy's bitter cry at the end with appropriate intensity and restraint.

A surface analysis, such as the one above, might suffice for the oral reading of "Bredon Hill." However, for a full understanding and appreciation of some poems more would be required: an extended analysis of the author's symbolic meanings and an investigation of biographical and critical studies might be necessary.

EXTENDED ANALYSIS

Earlier in this chapter Emily Dickinson's poem "Safe in Their Alabaster Chambers" was used to illustrate the importance of understanding the allusions and denotative meaning of words within a selection. And although an investigation of the literal meanings of words of this poem are helpful in terms of a general clarification, this is only a step toward understanding this particular poem. Obviously there is a spiritual gap between literal language and poetic intention. To suggest further study of poetic intention, we will include a student's "extended analysis" of this poem.

"How Can You Print a Piece of Your Soul?"

From correspondence and some of her poems we find that E. D. [Emily Dickinson] wished to become a successful recognized poet. She enjoyed virtually no attention as a poet while she lived and after a gentle rebuff by one of her critics she raised the question which leads to this analysis, "How can you print a piece of your soul?"

In the formal analysis of poetry it is often a temptation to examine the author's biography for clues to understanding. With E. D. this is, at best, not a very reliable approach. E. D. is a conscious and able poet; her imaginative craftsmanship with language and thought and experience results in a kind of art which is not simply subjective autobiographical sentiment. She in effect describes or constructs an emotional–physical–spiritual condition whose essence relates, with varied degrees of intensity, to a common mass of human experience. To attach this short lyric to specific experiences in her life would no doubt limit its universality and inhibit understanding. One detail which has relevance in regard to this poem is that E. D. was born and reared in the college town of Amherst; her milieu was that of entrenched orthodoxy during the time of the opening debates between religion and science. It was a time of social and religious transition and if she conformed to the stringent dictates of family and society, her mind and art have the characteristics which lend it universality both before and beyond contemporaneous comment and situations. This poem may be considered characteristic of E. D.'s reaction to the flux around her; it is a speculative inquiry for her own satisfaction.

We have no evidence that the poem at hand was ever seen as a three-stanza unit by its author. From extant "Pony Express" notes exchanged with her sister-in-law and occasional critic, we do know that there was dissatisfaction over the first draft (stanzas I & II) which led E. D. to attempt further stanzas. Editors have since added one of these stanzas and placed the entire poem into a hymnodic metrical form. Though we will consider the three-stanza construction, metrically we will examine the stanzas as they were originally presented by the poet. Indeed, with the exception of the objective pronoun in line 12, the two stanzas are essentially self-containing.

If viewed as a whole, the poem is defensible and meaningful. The particular sensibility of the poet when writing in both instances appears to have been similar. In determining the central concern or theme we might remark the power through metaphor of words such as "alabaster," "resurrection," "stone," "stolid," "cadence," "perished" (which is perhaps intentionally made obvious), "drop," "surrender," "soundless," and "snow" in terms of their unifying relationship in this poem. Another unifying device is the sound imagery, the repetition of soporific "s" sounds cresting to an aesthetic climax through line 14, then falling through abrupt consonants in "drop," "dots," and "disc."

In the final stanza alone, one should note the shift from fluid language to broken rhythm at the end of line 14 effected through the poet's peculiar use of the dash. This indeed is not coincidental. Further, one might note throughout the patterns of vowel sounds, particularly the "o" which is restrained from becoming a moan so as not to disturb the effect of the "s."

Much of this detail is speculative and circumstantial; yet when considered in relation to the poem at hand the dominance of the death motif is believable. E. D. dealt with the ambiguity of life and in that scrutiny found much of worth. A result is the use of symbolic language; she is knowledgeable in the power and fine mutations of single words; her images and symbols are condensed and allusive.

The death motif, however, is at best the warp of the poem. In a similar analysis of language we find woven in themes of religion, social class consciousness, sentient experience, nature, time, and light—both physical and poetic. These ideas are variously spotted throughout the fabric and related independently and mutually through allusion whereby images and associations are made.

Language as the vehicle of organization through motifs may be briefly remarked by pointing out three more word groups: (1) religion is closely meshed with the death symbols through "meek members," "Resurrection," "cadences," "perished," and "firmament" (the latter three are more clearly understood as religious in allusion if seen as parts of the religious vernacular); class consciousness is seen through "meek members," "diadems," "castle," and "Doges"; the theme of light is both physical and spiritual vision as in lines 2–3 we note the absence of light then find it in "sagacity," "row," "Crescent" and "diadems," and the visual image in the last two lines.

We have noted the possible unity of the three stanzas through language, detail, and theme. In conclusion we must consider the matters of variety and particularly of balance. Each stanza is different in effect. Stanza I deals primarily with a view of temporal examples of physical—spiritual fatalism and decline. Stanza III is cosmic in reach but swings in closing to explore the eternity and undiscriminating, perhaps omniscient nature of death. The poet speaks of the variousness of death, an important part of which is the rejection or absence of sentient experience. In four lines (6–9) E. D. soars into examples of the possible vitality of life but consistently tempers even this departure with the pall of indifference albeit suspicious insensitivity. Across this fulcrum, which stanza II becomes, are two masses in balance; both are mutually complimentary in theme, language, tone and shape.[3]

EXERCISES FOR APPLICATION OF ANALYSIS PROCEDURES

The selections which follow are arranged to give attention to special problems as they appear in particular poems and prose selections. The attempt to classify selections under headings like "Language and Structure," and

[3] By Edward de Rosset.

"Language and Tone" is simply a device to give emphasis to what might be considered the most important elements in particular selections and to assist in making the best use of class time. For instance, when we consider Blake's use of language (allusions, imagery, and figures) in "The Scoffers," this is not to say that *form* does not play a part in the communication, but rather that the language devices are of particular importance here. The student should never lose sight of the fact that the total meaning of a piece of literature is dependent upon the use the author has made of all the elements working together.

The exercise may offer the opportunity for the student to apply his knowledge of analysis techniques and, at the same time, to share his insights with his fellow classmates in oral performance and discussion (see Project 1: Appendix II, p. 216).

ORAL ANALYSIS EXERCISES (Language)

1   Relationship of Words and Phrases

Problem   How does an analysis of the grammatical construction help the oral reader project the author's meaning in each of the following sentences?

a   Histories make men wise; poets, witty; the mathematics, subtle; natural philosophy, deep, moral, grave; logic and rhetoric, able to contend; *Abeunt studia in mores* [studies form manners].

b   This City now doth like a garment wear
The beauty of the morning; silent, bare,
Ships, towers, domes, theatres, and temple lie
Open unto the fields, and to the sky;
All bright and glittering in the smokeless air.
    (Wordsworth, "Composed upon Westminster Bridge")

c   It was as if the boy had already divined what his senses and intellect had not encompassed yet: that doomed wilderness whose edges were being constantly and punily gnawed at by men with plows and axes who feared it because it was wilderness, men myriad and nameless even to one another in the land where the old bear had earned a name, and through which ran not even a mortal beast but an anachronism indomitable and invincible out of an old, dead time, a phantom, epitome and apotheosis of the old, wild life which the little puny humans swarmed and hacked at in a fury of abhorrence and fear, like pygmies about the ankles of a drowsing elephant;—the old bear, solitary, indomitable, and alone; widowered, childless, and absolved of mortality—old Priam reft of his old wife and outlived all his sons.
    (William Faulkner, "The Bear")[4]

---

4 Copyright 1942 by Curtis Publishing Co. Copyright 1942 by William Faulkner. Reprinted from *Go Down, Moses*, by William Faulkner, by permission of Random House, Inc.

2 Allusions, Imagery, and Figurative Language

Problem   Identify the historical figures, Voltaire and Rousseau. Why does Blake feel that they are scoffers? What figure does the poet use to show the futility of the scoffer's mockery? Who were Democritus and Newton? In what sense does Blake consider them scoffers? What meaning is implied by the contrasts in imagery: "sands upon the Red Sea shore" and "Israel's tents" shining? In the whole poem what is Blake protesting against?

THE SCOFFERS

William Blake

Mock on, mock on, Voltaire, Rousseau,
   Mock on, mock on; 'tis all in vain;
You throw the sand against the wind
   And the wind blows it back again.

And every sand becomes a gem
   Reflected in the beams divine;
Blown back, they blind the mocking eye,
   But still in Israel's paths they shine.

The atoms of Democritus
   And Newton's particles of light
And sands upon the Red Sea shore,
   Where Israel's tents do shine so bright.

ORAL ANALYSIS EXERCISES (Situation)

3 Point of View and Language

Problem   Here is a sonnet written in 1619. Study the poem carefully to determine: Who is speaking? What can you learn about the speaker(s)? To whom are the words addressed? Give special attention to lines 9–14. What is the reference of the pronoun "his" in line 10 and "him" in line 14? Does this help to clarify what the poem is saying? What would be the interpreter's relationship with the audience while reading?

SINCE THERE'S NO HELP

Michael Drayton

Since there's no help, come let us kiss and part;
Nay, I have done, you get no more of me,
And I am glad, yea, glad with all my heart
That thus so cleanly I myself can free;
Shake hands forever, cancel all our vows,
And when we meet at any time again,

Be it not seen in either of our brows
That we one jot of former love retain.
Now, at the last gasp of love's latest breath,
When, his pulse failing, passion speechless lies,
When faith is kneeling by his bed of death,
And innocence is closing up his eyes,
Now, if thou wouldst, when all have given him over,
From death to life thou mightst him yet recover.

4   Situation and Language

Problem   What is the situation? Who is speaking? What happens? Do you
find any humor in the movement of the situation? If so—why?

A BOX TO HIDE IN[5]

James Thurber

I waited till the large woman with the awful hat took up her sack of groceries
and went out, peering at the tomatoes and lettuce on her way. The clerk asked
me what mine was.

"Have you got a box," I asked, "a large box? I want a box to hide in."

"You want a box?" he asked.

"I want a box to hide in," I said.

"Whatta you mean?" he said. "You mean a big box?"

I said I meant a box, big enough to hold me.

"I haven't got any boxes," he said. "Only cartons that cans come in."

I tried several other groceries and none of them had a box big enough for
me to hide in. There was nothing for it but to face life out. I didn't feel strong,
and I'd had this overpowering desire to hide in a box for a long time.

"Whatta you mean you want to hide in this box?" one grocer asked me.

"It's a form of escape," I told him, "hiding in a box. It circumscribes your
worries and the range of your anguish. You don't see people either."

"How in the hell do you eat when you're in this box?" asked the grocer.
"How in the hell do you get anything to eat?" I said I had never been in a box
and didn't know, but that that would take care of itself.

"Well," he said, finally, "I haven't got any boxes, only some pasteboard
cartons that cans come in."

It was the same every place. I gave up when it got dark and the groceries
closed, and hid in my room again. I turned out the light and lay on the bed. You
feel better when it gets dark. I could have hid in a closet, I suppose, but people
are always opening doors. Somebody would find you in a closet. They would
be startled and you'd have to tell them why you were in the closet. Nobody pays
any attention to a big box lying on the floor. You could stay in it for days and
nobody'd think to look in it, not even the cleaning-woman.

5 Copr. © 1935 James Thurber. Copr. © 1963 Helen W. Thurber and Rosemary Thurber Sauers. From *The Middle-Aged Man on the Flying Trapeze*, published by Harper &
Row. Originally printed in *The New Yorker*.

My cleaning-woman came the next morning and woke me up. I was still feeling bad. I asked her if she knew where I could get a large box.

"How big a box you want?" she asked.

"I want a box big enough for me to get inside of," I said. She looked at me with big, dim eyes. There's something wrong with her glands. She's awful but she has a big heart, which makes it worse. She's unbearable, her husband is sick and her children are sick and she is sick too. I got to thinking how pleasant it would be if I were in a box now, and didn't have to see her. I would be in a box right there in the room and she wouldn't know. I wondered if you have a desire to bark or laugh when someone who doesn't know walks by the box you are in. Maybe she would have a spell with her heart, if I did that, and would die right there. The officers and the elevator man and Mr. Gramadge would find us. "Funny doggone thing happened at the building last night," the door-man would say to his wife. "I let in this woman to clean up 10-F and she never come out, see? She's never there more'n an hour, but she never come out, see? So when it got to be time for me to go off duty, why I says to Crennick, who was on the elevator, I says 'what the hell you suppose has happened to that woman cleans 10-F.' He says he didn't know; he says he never seen her after he took her up. So I spoke to Mr. Gramadge about it. 'I'm sorry to bother you, Mr. Gramadge,' I says 'but there's something funny about that woman cleans 10-F.' So I told him. So he said we better have a look and we all three goes up and knocks on the door and rings the bell, see, and nobody answers so he said we'd have to walk in so Crennick opened the door and we walked in and here was this woman cleans the apartment dead as a herring on the floor and the gentleman that lives there was in a box." . . .

The cleaning-woman kept looking at me. It was hard to realize she wasn't dead. "It's a form of escape," I murmured. "What say?" she asked, dully.

"You don't know of any large packing boxes, do you?" I asked.

"No, I don't," she said.

I haven't found one yet, but I still have this overpowering urge to hide in a box. Maybe it will go away, maybe I'll be all right. Maybe it will get worse. It's hard to say.

5 Point of View and Time

Problem   What is this selection's place in time? What can you determine about the speaker and the person to whom the words are addressed? Would the reading of the selection demand changes in audience relationship? Explain in relation to aesthetic distance.

THE LABORATORY

Robert Browning

Now that I, tying thy glass mask tightly,
May gaze through these faint smokes curling whitely,
As thou pliest thy trade in this devil's smithy—
Which is the poison to poison her, prithee?

He is with her, and they know that I know
Where they are, and what they do; they believe my tears flow
While they laugh, laugh at me, at me fled to the drear
Empty church, to pray God in, for them!—I am here.

Grind away, moisten and mash up thy paste,
Pound at thy powder—I am not in haste!
Better sit thus, and observe thy strange things,
Than go where men wait me and dance at the King's.

That in the mortar—you call it a gum?
Ah, the brave tree whence such gold oozings come!
And yonder soft phial, the exquisite blue,
Sure to taste sweetly, is that poison too?

Had I but all of them, thee and thy treasures,
What a wild crowd of invisible pleasures!
To carry pure death in an earring, a casket,
A signet, a fan-mount, a filigree-basket!

Soon, at the King's, a mere lozenge to give
And Pauline should have just thirty minutes to live!
But to light a pastille, and Elise, with her head,
And her breast, and her arms, and her hands, should drop dead!

Quick—is it finished? The color's too grim!
Why not soft like the phial's, enticing and dim?
Let it brighten her drink, let her turn it and stir,
And try it and taste, ere she fix and prefer!

What a drop! She's not little, no minion like me—
That's why she ensnared him. This never will free
The soul from those strong, great eyes,—say, "no!"
To that pulse's magnificent come-and-go.

For only last night, as they whispered, I brought
My own eyes to bear on her so, that I thought
Could I keep them one half minute fixed, she would fall
Shrivelled; she fell not; yet this does it all!

Not that I bid you spare her the pain!
Let death be felt and the proof remain;
Brand, burn up, bit into its grace—
He is sure to remember her dying face!

Is it done? Take my mask off! Nay, be not morose,
It kills her, and this prevents seeing it close:
The delicate droplet, my whole fortune's fee—
If it hurts her, besides, can it ever hurt me?

Now, take all my jewels, gorge gold to your fill,
You may kiss me, old man, on my mouth if you will!
But brush this dust off me, lest horror it brings
Ere I know it—next moment I dance at the King's!

ORAL ANALYSIS EXERCISES (Movement of Situation)

6 Structure and Language

Problem   What are the unit divisions and the purpose of each? What is the
high point in each and the climax of the whole? Comment on the
symbols, sound symbolism, and rhythm of the language.

THE RIVER MERCHANT'S WIFE: A LETTER[6]

Ezra Pound

While my hair was still cut straight across my forehead
I played about the front gate, pulling flowers.
You came by on bamboo stilts, playing horse,
You walked about my seat, playing with blue plums.
And we went on living in the village of Chokan:
Two small people, without dislike or suspicion.

At fourteen I married My Lord you.
I never laughed, being bashful.
Lowering my head, I looked at the wall,
Called to, a thousand times, I never looked back.

At fifteen I stopped scowling,
I desired my dust to be mingled with yours
Forever and forever and forever.
Why should I climb the look out?

At sixteen you departed.
You went into far Ku-to-Yen, by the river of swirling eddies,
And you have been gone five months.
The monkeys make sorrowful noise overhead.

You dragged your feet when you went out.
By the gate now, the moss is grown, the different mosses,
Too deep to clear them away!
The leaves fall early this autumn, in wind.
The paired butterflies are already yellow with August
Over the grass in the West garden,
They hurt me. I grow older.

If you are coming down through the narrows of the river Kiang,
Please let me know beforehand,
And I will come out to meet you
    As far as Cho-fu-sa.

7 Structure and Language

Problem   What are the structural divisions? How does the structure rein-
    force the thought and emotional impact of the poem? How does the
    use of language reinforce the impact?

THE HARBOR[7]

Carl Sandburg

Passing through huddled and ugly walls
By doorways where women
Looked from their hunger-deep eyes,
Haunted with shadows of hunger-hands,
Out from the huddled and ugly walls,
I came sudden, at the city's edge,
On a blue burst of lake,
Long lake waves breaking under the sun
On a spray-flung curve of shore;
And a fluttering storm of gulls,
Masses of great gray wings
And flying white bellies
Veering and wheeling free in the open.

8 Structure and Language

Problem   What are the unit divisions and the purpose of each? Discuss the
    use of images, figures, symbolism, and sound symbolism.

THE BOMBARDMENT[8]

Amy Lowell

Slowly, without force, the rain drops into the city. It stops a moment on the
carved head of Saint John, then slides on again, slipping and trickling over his
stone cloak. It splashes from the lead conduit of a gargoyle, and falls from it in
turmoil on the stones in the Cathedral square. Where are the people, and why
does the fretted steeple sweep about in the sky? Boom! The sound swings

[7] From *Chicago Poems* by Carl Sandburg, Copyright 1916 by Holt, Rinehart and Winston, Inc. Copyright 1944 by Carl Sandburg. Reprinted by permission of Holt, Rinehart
and Winston, Inc.

[8] From *Men Women and Ghosts* (Boston: Houghton Mifflin Company). Reprinted by
permission of the publisher.

against the rain. Boom again! After it, only water rushing in the gutters, and the turmoil from the spout of the gargoyle. Silence. Ripples and mutters. Boom!

The room is damp, but warm. Little flashes swarm about from the firelight. The lustres of the chandelier are bright, and clusters of rubies leap in the bohemian glasses on the *étagère*. Her hands are restless, but the white masses of her hair are quite still. Boom! Will it ever cease to torture, this iteration! Boom! The vibration shatters a glass on the *étagère*. It lies there, formless and glowing, with all its crimson gleams shot out of pattern, spilled, flowing red, blood-red. A thin bellnote pricks through the silence. A door creaks. The old lady speaks: "Victor, clear away that broken glass." "Alas! Madame, the bohemian glass!" "Yes, Victor, one hundred years ago my father brought it—" Boom! The room shakes, the servitor quakes. Another goblet shivers and breaks. Boom!

It rustles at the window-pane, the smooth, streaming rain, and he is shut within its clash and murmur. Inside is his candle, his table, his ink, his pen, and his dreams. He is thinking, and the walls are pierced with beams of sunshine, slipping through young green. A fountain tosses itself up at the blue sky, and through the spattered water in the basin he can see copper carp, lazily floating among cold leaves. A wind-harp in a cedar-tree grieves and whispers, and words blow into his brain, bubbled, iridescent, shooting up like flowers of fire, higher and higher. Boom! The flame-flowers snap on their slender stems. The fountain rears up in long broken spears of dishevelled water and flattens into the earth. Boom! And there is only the room, the table, the candle, and the sliding rain. Again, Boom!—Boom!—Boom! He stuffs his fingers into his ears. He sees corpses, and cries out in fright. Boom! It is night, and they are shelling the city. Boom! Boom!

A child wakes and is afraid, and weeps in the darkness. What has made the bed shake? "Mother, where are you? I am awake." "Hush, my Darling, I am here." "But, Mother, something so queer happened, the room shook." Boom! "Oh, what is it? What is the matter?" Boom! "Where is Father? I am so afraid." Boom! The child sobs and shrieks. The house trembles and creaks. Boom!

Retorts, globes, tubes, the phials lie shattered. All his trials oozing across the floor. The life that was his choosing, lonely, urgent goaded by a hope, all gone. A weary man in a ruined laboratory, that is his story. Boom! Gloom and ignorance, and the jig of drunken brutes. Diseases like snakes crawling over the earth, leaving trails of slime. Wails from people burying their dead. Through the window, he can see the rocking steeple. A ball of fire falls on the lead of the roof, and the sky tears apart on a spike of flame. Up the spire, behind the lacings of stone, zigzagging in and out of the carved tracings, squirms the fire. It spouts like yellow wheat from the gargoyles, coils round the head of Saint John, and aureoles him in light. It leaps into the night and hisses against the rain. The Cathedral is a burning stain on the white, wet night.

Boom! The Cathedral is a torch, and the houses next to it begin to scorch. Boom! The bohemian glass on the *étagère* is no longer there. Boom! A stalk of flame sways against the red damask curtains. The old lady cannot walk. She watches the creeping stalk and counts. Boom!—Boom!—Boom!

The poet rushes into the street, and the rain wraps him in a sheet of silver. But it is threaded with gold and powdered with scarlet beads. The city burns. Quivering, spearing, thrusting, lapping, streaming, run the flames. Over roofs, and walls, and shops, and stalls. Smearing its gold on the sky, the fire dances, lances itself through the doors, and lisps and chuckles along the floors.

The child wakes again and screams at the yellow petalled flower flickering at the window. The little red lips of flame creep along the ceiling beams.

The old man sits among his broken experiments and looks at the burning Cathedral. Now the streets are swarming with people.

They seek shelter and crowd into the cellars. They shout and call, and over all, slowly and without force, the rain drops into the city. Boom! And the steeple crashes down among the people. Boom! Boom, again! The water rushes along the gutters. The fire roars and mutters. Boom!

ORAL ANALYSIS EXERCISES (Tone)

9   Tone and Language

Problem   Point out the imagery and the figurative language used by the poet to describe the scene and the feelings of its witnesses. What is the author's attitude toward the subject? What is the author's attitude toward his readers? What is the pervading tone?

AUTO WRECK[9]

Karl Shapiro

Its quick soft silver bell beating, beating,
And down the dark one ruby flare
Pulsing out red light like an artery,
The ambulance at top speed floating down
Past beacons and illuminated clocks
Wings in a heavy curve, dips down,
And brakes speed, entering the crowd.

The doors leap open, emptying light;
Stretchers are laid out, the mangled lifted
And stowed into the little hospital.
The bell, breaking the hush, tolls once,
And the ambulance with its terrible cargo
Rocking, slightly rocking, moves away,
As the doors, an afterthought, are closed.

We are deranged, walking among the cops
Who sweep glass and are large and composed.
One is still making notes under the light.

One with a bucket douches ponds of blood
Into the street and gutter.
One hangs lanterns on the wrecks that cling,
Empty husks of locusts, to iron poles.

Our throats were tight as tourniquets,
Our feet were bound with splints, but now
Like convalescents intimate and gauche,
We speak through sickly smiles and warn
With the stubborn saw of common sense,
The grim joke and the banal resolution.
The traffic moves around with care,
But we remain, touching a wound
That opens to our richest horror.

Already old, the question Who is innocent?
For death in war is done by hands;
Suicide has cause and stillbirth, logic.
But this invites the occult mind,
Cancels our physics with a sneer,
And spatters all we know of dénouement
Across the expedient and wicked stones.

10 Tone and Language

Problem To whom are the words addressed? Is the change in rhythm of
the last line significant? What is the poet's attitude toward his subject—
toward his readers? Which is more significant?

NEXT TO OF COURSE GOD AMERICA I[10]

e. e. cummings

"next to of course god america i
love you land of the pilgrims' and so forth oh
say can you see by the dawn's early my
country 'tis of centuries come and go
and are no more what of it we should worry
in every language even deafanddumb
thy sons acclaim your glorious name by gorry
by jingo by gee by gosh by gum
why talk of beauty what could be more beautiful than these heroic happy dead
who rushed like lions to the roaring slaughter
they did not stop to think they died instead
then shall the voice of liberty be mute?"

He spoke. And drank rapidly a glass of water.

11   Tone and Language

Problem   What meaning is suggested to you as you read this poem for the
first time? What do "rain," "night," "city light," "city lane," and "luminary clock" suggest? Why is he walking in the rain at night? Why is he
alone? Can you, from your ideas of what is suggested by the words,
arrive at a statement of what Frost is saying in the poem?

ACQUAINTED WITH THE NIGHT[11]

Robert Frost

I have been one acquainted with the night.
I have walked out in rain—and back in rain.
I have outwalked the furthest city light.

I have looked down the saddest city lane.
I have passed by the watchman on his beat
And dropped my eyes, unwilling to explain.

I have stood still and stopped the sound of feet
When far away an interrupted cry
Came over houses from another street,

But not to call me back or say good-bye;
And further still at an unearthly height,
One luminary clock against the sky

Proclaimed the time was neither wrong nor right.
I have been one acquainted with the night.

12   Tone and Structure

Problem   What do you think was Thurber's purpose in writing this fable?
What is his attitude toward his subject—toward his readers? Which
dominates? How does the structure reinforce the tone?

THE BEAR WHO LET IT ALONE[12]

James Thurber

In the woods of the Far West there once lived a brown bear who could take
it or let it alone. He would go into a bar where they sold mead, a fermented
drink made of honey, and he would have just two drinks. Then he would put
some money on the bar and say, "See what the bears in the back room will

---

11 From *Complete Poems of Robert Frost.* Copyright 1923, 1928 by Holt, Rinehart and
Winston, Inc. Copyright 1942, 1951, © 1956 by Robert Frost. Reprinted by permission of
Holt, Rinehart and Winston, Inc.

12 Copr. © 1940 James Thurber. From *Fables For Our Time*, published by Harper and
Row. Originally printed in *The New Yorker.*

have," and he would go home. But finally he took to drinking by himself most of the day. He would reel home at night, kick over the umbrella stand, knock down the bridge lamps, and ram his elbows through the windows. Then he would collapse on the floor and lie there until he went to sleep. His wife was greatly distressed and his children were very frightened.

At length the bear saw the error of his ways and began to reform. In the end he became a famous teetotaller and a persistent temperance lecturer. He would tell everybody that came to his house about the awful effects of drink, and he would boast about how well and strong he had become since he gave up touching the stuff. To demonstrate this, he would stand on his head and on his hands and he would turn cartwheels in the house, kicking over the umbrella stand, knocking down the bridge lamps, and ramming his elbows through the windows. Then he would lie down on the floor, tired by his healthful experience, and go to sleep. His wife was greatly distressed and his children were very frightened.

Moral: You might as well fall flat on your face as lean over too far backward.

13   Tone and Situation

Problem   How does the poet's manner of revealing the situation enable the reader to feel that what happens is credible? Where is the climax? What is the motive for the murder? What is the attitude of the murderer?

PORPHYRIA'S LOVER

Robert Browning

The rain set early in tonight,
   The sullen wind was soon awake,
It tore the elm-tops down for spite,
   And did its worst to vex the lake:
I listened with heart fit to break.
When glided in Porphyria; straight
   She shut the cold out and the storm,
And kneeled and made the cheerless grate
   Blaze up, and all the cottage warm;
Which done, she rose, and from her form
Withdrew the dripping cloak and shawl,
   And laid her soiled gloves by, untied
Her hat and let the damp hair fall,
   And, last, she sat down by my side
And called me. When no voice replied,
She put my arm about her waist,
   And made her smooth white shoulder bare
And all her yellow hair displaced,
   And, stooping, made my cheek lie there,
And spread, o'er all, her yellow hair.

Murmuring how she loved me—she
   Too weak, for all her heart's endeavor,
To set its struggling passion free
   From pride, and vainer ties dissever,
And give herself to me forever.
But passion sometimes would prevail,
   Nor could tonight's gay feast restrain
A sudden thought of one so pale
   For love of her, and all in vain:
So, she was come through wind and rain.
Be sure I looked up at her eyes
   Happy and proud; at last I knew
Porphyria worshipped me; surprise
   Made my heart swell, and still it grew
While I debated what to do.
That moment she was mine, mine, fair,
   Perfectly pure and good: I found
A thing to do, and all her hair
   In one long yellow string I wound
Three times her little throat around,
And strangled her. No pain felt she;
   I am quite sure she felt no pain.
As a shut bud that holds a bee,
   I warily oped her lids: again
Laughed the blue eyes without a stain.
And I untightened next the tress
   About her neck; her cheek once more
Blushed bright beneath my burning kiss:
   I propped her head up as before,
Only, this time my shoulder bore
Her head, which droops upon it still:
   The smiling rosy little head,
So glad it has its utmost will,
   That all it scorned at once is fled.
And I, its love, am gained instead!
Porphyria's love: she guessed not how
   Her darling one wish would be heard.
And thus we sit together now,
   And all night long we have not stirred,
And yet God has not said a word.

14   Tone and Language

Problem   Here is an example of seventeenth-century satire and wit. Comment on the author's use of irony; how does it compare to the irony found in contemporary poetry? What is the pervading tone?

TO HIS COY MISTRESS

Andrew Marvell

Had we but world enough, and time,
This coyness, lady, were no crime.
We would sit down and think which way
To walk, and pass our long love's day.
Thou by the Indian Ganges' side
Should's rubies find; I by the tide
Of Humber would complain. I would
Love you ten years before the Flood,
And you should, if you please, refuse
Till the conversion of the Jews.
My vegetable love should grow
Vaster than empires, and more slow;
An hundred years should go to praise
Thine eyes, and on thy forhead gaze;
Two hundred to adore each breast,
But thirty thousand to the rest;
An age at least to every part,
And the last age should show your heart.
For, lady, you deserve this state,
Nor would I love at lower rate.

But at my back I always hear
Time's wingèd chariot hurrying near;
And yonder all before us lie
Deserts of vast eternity.
Thy beauty shall no more be found,
Nor in thy marble vault, shall sound
My echoing song; then worms shall try
That long preserved virginity,
And your quaint honour turn to dust,
And into ashes all my lust:
The grave's a fine and private place,
But none, I think, do there embrace.

Now therefore, while the youthful hue
Sits on thy skin like morning dew
And while thy willing soul transpires
At every pore with instant fires,
Now let us sport us while we may,
And now, like amorous birds of prey,
Rather at once our time devour
Than languish in his slow-chapt power.
Let us roll all our strength and all
Our sweetness up into one ball,

And tear our pleasures with rough strife
Through the iron gates of life:
Thus, though we cannot make our sun
Stand still, yet we will make him run.

ORAL ANALYSIS EXERCISES (Theme)

15   Theme

Problem   Compare the two poems as to the importance of theme.

I LIKE TO SEE IT LAP THE MILES[13]

Emily Dickinson

I like to see it lap the Miles—
And lick the Valleys up—
And stop to feed itself at Tanks—
And then—prodigious step

Around a Pile of Mountains—
And, supercilious peer
In Shanties—by the sides of Roads—
And then a Quarry pare

To fit its sides—
And crawl between
Complaining all the while
In horrid-hooting stanza—
Then chase itself down Hill—

And Neigh like Boanerges—
Then—prompter than a Star
Stop—docile and omnipotent
At its own stable door—

LONDON

William Blake

I wander through each chartered street,
Near where the chartered Thames does flow,
And mark in every face I meet
Marks of weakness, marks of woe.

[13] Reprinted by permission of the publishers and the Trustees of Amherst College
from Thomas H. Johnson, Editor, *The Poems of Emily Dickinson,* Cambridge, Mass.: The
Belknap Press of Harvard University Press, Copyright, 1951, 1955, by the President and
Fellows of Harvard College. Pg. 65.

In every cry of every man,
In every infant's cry of fear,
In every voice, in every ban,
The mind-forged manacles I hear:

How the chimney-sweeper's cry
Every blackening church appalls,
And the hapless soldier's sigh
Runs in blood down palace-walls.

But most, through midnight streets I hear
How the youthful harlot's curse
Blasts the new-born infant's tear,
And blights with plagues the marriage-hearse.

WRITTEN ANALYSIS EXERCISE (Theme)

16 Theme

Problem   Give special attention to the meaning of the last two lines of this
sonnet. To what does "that" refer? Which of the statements do you
think is nearer to what the poet is saying in essence?

SONNET 73

William Shakespeare

That time of year thou mayst in me behold
When yellow leaves, or none, or few, do hang
Upon those boughs which shake against the cold,
Bare ruined choirs, where late the sweet birds sang.
In me thou seest the twilight of such day
As after sunset fadeth in the west;
Which by and by black night doth take away,
Death's second self, that seals up all in rest.
In me thou seest the glowing of such fire,
That on the ashes of his youth doth lie,
As the death-bed whereon it must expire,
Consum'd with that which it was nourished by.
　　This thou perceiv'st, which makes thy love more strong,
　　To love that well which thou must leave ere long.

a   You know that I am growing old; therefore, you love me more since I
must leave you.
b   You see the death of my youth, and it makes your love for life and
youth more strong because you too must grow old.

Write a summarizing statement of your own.

ADDITIONAL EXERCISES

17   Aesthetic Effect

Problem   Read D. H. Lawrence's poem "Snake." How does the poet's use
    of variety, balance, and unity contribute to the total effect of the poem?

18   Theme and Research

Problem   Read "The Parsi Woman" by Edna St. Vincent Millay. Through
    research discover all you can about the Parsi woman and the culture of
    which she was a part. Is the full meaning of this poem dependent upon
    this knowledge?

Part Three

TECHNIQUES FOR
ORAL COMMUNICATION

5 TECHNIQUES FOR
PROJECTING MEANING

Oral reading is an activity which requires a high degree of concentration and integration of body, voice, and mind. The oral interpreter's success in arousing a meaningful response from an audience depends upon his ability to properly control these three factors during the reading performance. It may be that comparatively little attention needs to be paid to these controls (the "hows"). If a reader understands what he is reading aloud and if he has the *desire* to have his audience comprehend the ideas and participate in the emotional aspects of the literary experience, he may have the necessary skills. Unfortunately in the case of the student reader, this is not always true. As a result of long-established bad habits in his use of voice or body he may need to employ techniques consciously for a time.

In this and the next three chapters we will discuss certain means by which the student may control his voice, body, and mind. The two to be considered in this chapter are (1) the control of speech rhythm for projecting logical meaning and (2) the control of psychological inhibitions for projecting emotional meaning.

TECHNIQUES FOR PROJECTING LOGICAL MEANING

Rhythm, a regular recurrence of similar features, is one of man's basic needs; we see it in all forms of nature, and it seems to be intuitive in man. Each person has a characteristic rhythm evident in the flow of his speech and in the movement of his body. Habits of speaking in a rapid, choppy, broken rhythm or in a slow, pedantic pattern are not easily broken, but better speech patterns can be learned. The oral reading of good literature, especially poetry, is perhaps the best way to become more aware of language rhythms.

Both prose and poetry have distinctive rhythms, and it is important for the oral interpreter to recognize these and to adjust his speech rhythm to the rhythm inherent in the writing.

Conversational Speech Rhythm

In prose writing and in some poetry as well modern authors capture the pattern of conversational speech. This should be easy for the oral reader. All he has to do is to project the logical meaning of the author's words in a natural conversational flow of speech. But many persons, instead of reading naturally as they talk, impose a pattern that has little relation to conversational rhythm.

What do we do in good conversational speech? We communicate ideas by blending words together into idea groups. We do not say: She - is - coming - today, but rather: Sheiscomingtoday. In saying an idea group, we tend to blend the sound from one word into the next word in a continuance of sound, and we *pause* at the end of each blended word group: Sheiscoming today / at noon. We use a falling or rising inflection at the end of these blended word groups to suggest a closed or continuing thought: She'scoming (falling); She'scoming (rising) / ifatallpossible (rising) / today (falling). We emphasize the words that carry the intended meaning, and we subordinate the others: She'scomingto*day* (today, not tomorrow); *She's*coming today (she, not he).

These observations point three techniques which we will consider in more detail: (1) grouping, (2) inflectional endings, and (3) emphasis and subordination. The proper control of these three factors may result in a natural conversational pattern.

Grouping (or Phrasing)

This technique is closely allied to analysis for understanding. Students who understand the sense of what they are reading and who read ideas instead of words have no difficulty, but others must give special attention to the correct grouping of words before they can communicate ideas clearly.

Grouping is simply speech punctuation. In silent reading punctuation marks help with understanding and are adequate guides to the intended meaning; in *oral* reading punctuation marks are helpful, but they are inadequate. The reader must supply additional speech punctuation. How do we group words? Are there any rules to govern this?

Words should be grouped together that make up a unit of thought. A sentence is a complete unit of thought, but within the sentence there may be smaller units—a clause, a phrase, or even a word. A pause between these idea or thought units serves to show relationships and to clarify meaning.

Guides for grouping. If you try to lift the thought of a sentence from the page and to say it as you would in conversation, you find you have broken the sentence into word groups with pauses between the groups. We seem to do this automatically in conversational speech. Read the poem we analyzed in two ways:

> 1 Others because / you did not / keep
> That / deep-sworn vow have been / friends of mine; /
> Yet always when I / look death / in the face, /
> When I clamber to / the heights of sleep, /
> Or when I grow / excited with wine,
> Suddenly / I meet your face.

This does not make sense because the pauses come in the wrong places; the word groups do not make sense. Now read the poem with these pauses:

> 2 Others / because you did not keep →
> That deep-sworn vow / have been friends of mine; /
> Yet always / when I look death in the face, /
> Or when I grow excited with wine, /
> Suddenly / I meet your face.

This makes sense because each group is an idea unit that contributes to the whole meaning. "Others," though one word, is an idea unit because we can hold its meaning in our consciousness; it is an idea. Notice that the speech punctuation follows the written punctuation except that there are additional pauses than those indicated by the punctuation marks.

Read (2) aloud again, concentrating on the thoughts of the speaker. If you were thinking, the pauses after "vow," "always," and "suddenly" were probably longer in length. Timing (the use of pause and duration) plays an important part in conversational rhythm. This will be discussed in detail in regard to vocal variety (see p. 112).

EXERCISE FOR GROUPING

Using a slash mark (/) indicate, according to your judgment, the idea groups that best project the logical meaning of the sentences. What do you learn about grouping in relation to punctuation?

1 The teacher says the student is a fool.

2 Jesus went up on the mountain and spoke.

3 And now there remain faith, hope, and love, these three; but the greatest of these is love. (Bible: I Corinthians xiii: 13)

4 She was, however, in the realization of what might happen, disturbed by his statement.

5   There is so little good in the best of us and so little bad in the worst of us
    that it ill behooves the most of us to speak about the rest of us.

6   If to do were as easy as to know what were good to do, chapels had been
    churches, and poor men's cottages princes' palaces.
                         (Shakespeare, *The Merchant of Venice*, Act I, sc. 2)

7   To-morrow, and to-morrow, and to-morrow,
    Creeps in this petty pace from day to day,
    To the last syllable of recorded time,
    And all our yesterdays have lighted fools
    The way to dusty death.   (Shakespeare, *Macbeth*, Act V, sc. 5)

8   Listen to the recording of Hamlet's soliloquy "To Be, or Not To Be," as
    read by two British actors, John Gielgud and Maurice Evans. Note the dif-
    ferences in grouping as marked.

    John Gielgud:[1]

    To be, // or not to be: // that is the question: //
    Whether 'tis nobler in the mind // to suffer
    The slings and arrows of outrageous fortune, /
    Or to take arms against a sea of troubles,
    And by opposing end them? // To die: // to sleep: //
    No more; // and by a sleep to say we end
    The heart-ache and the thousand natural shocks
    That flesh is heir to, / 'tis a consummation
    Devoutly to be wish'd. // To die, // to sleep; //
    To sleep: perchance to dream: ay, there's the rub; //
    For in that sleep of death what dreams may come
    When we have shuffled off this mortal coil, /
    Must give us pause.

    Maurice Evans:[2]

    To be, or not to be: // that is the question: //
    Whether 'tis nobler in the mind to suffer
    The slings and arrows of outrageous fortune, /
    Or to take arms against a sea of troubles,
    And by opposing / end them? // To die: // to sleep: /
    No more; // and by a sleep to say we end
    The heart-ache and the thousand natural shocks
    That flesh is heir to, // 'tis a consummation
    Devoutly to be wish'd. // To die, // to sleep; //
    To sleep: / perchance to dream: // ay, there's the rub; /
    For in that sleep of death what dreams may come
    When we have shuffled off this mortal coil, /
    Must give us pause.

[1] John Gielgud gives an interpretation of this selection in an album of readings from
Hamlet: Victor L M 6007.

[2] Maurice Evans gives an interpretation of this selection in an album of readings from
Hamlet: Columbia Masterworks Set M-340.

Vocal Inflectional Endings

This technique relates to the direction the pitch of the voice takes at the end of idea groups. Some thought groups are complete, but others are part of a larger thought unit. In the poem "A Deep-Sworn Vow," the first complete thought ends with "have been friends of mine," but there are three other idea groups contributing to the complete thought. If, when reading this aloud, you ended each of these idea groups with a distinct falling vocal inflection, the sequence of the complete thought would probably escape the listener. Try it.

> Others ⬂
> because you did not keep ⬂
> that deep-sworn vow ⬂
> have been friends of mine; ⬂

This should make clear the importance of inflectional endings in showing proper relationships.

Guides for inflectional endings. It is difficult to make rules about anything as subtle as vocal inflection, but a few general statements can serve as guides:

When the word group expresses a complete thought or when the word group completes a series, the pitch drops. The vocal inflection suggests finality; the thought is complete, "closed."

When the idea group is only a part of a complete thought, the pitch rises, suggesting that there is something to follow. This is the "open" ending.

The open ending may be of two kinds: (1) the open ending, which says (by means of pause and upward inflection) that more follows, and (2) the carry-over ending where the vowel sound in the last word in a line of poetry is prolonged and carried over to the first word in the next line (more will be said about this in the chapter on poetry).

The rising inflection should be varied in pitch levels, stress, and duration. An insertion is an example of the stressed inflection:

> We forgot, ⬈ and that is the real test, ⬈ who he was.

In a series of images the upward inflection need not be so strong, but it should be held longer to give the listener time to see the images:

> Here are workers, ⬈ loafers, ⬈ thinkers ⬈ and dreamers. ⬂

There are countless combinations of vocal means to point relationships. What should be avoided is overuse of either the rising or falling inflection. In some areas of the United States the speech pattern is marked by falling inflections. This tends to give the speech a dull and monotonous pattern. Rising inflections may, at times, indicate indecision, but they can also suggest liveliness—a much needed sound.

EXERCISE FOR INFLECTIONAL ENDINGS

Read aloud:

1   A gun that breaks its mooring becomes suddenly some indescribable super-natural beast. It is a machine which transforms itself into a monster. This mass turns itself upon its wheels, has the rapid movements of a billiard-ball; rolls with the rolling, pitches with the pitching, comes, pauses, seems to meditate; resumes its course, rushes along the ship from end to end like an arrow, circles about, springs aside, evades, roars, breaks, kills, exterminates.
                                             (Victor Hugo, "Ninety-Three")

2   Frigid and yet friendly, frank yet cautious, shrewd yet credulous, positive yet sceptical, confident yet shy, extremely intelligent and extremely good-humored, there was something vaguely defiant in its concessions and some-thing profoundly reassuring in its reserve.   (Henry James, *The American*)

3   He finds his house in ruins, his farm devastated, his slaves free, his stock killed, his barns empty, his trade destroyed, his money worthless; his social system, feudal in its magnificence, swept away; his people without law or legal status; his comrades slain, and the burdens of others heavy on his shoulders. Crushed by defeat, his very traditions gone: without money, credit, employment, material or training; and besides all this, confronted with the gravest problem that ever met human intelligence—the establishing of a status for the vast body of his liberated slaves.
                                             (Henry W. Grady, "The New South")

4   Whenas in silks my Julia goes,
     Then, then, methinks, how sweetly flows
     The liquefaction of her clothes!

     Next when I cast mine eyes and see
     That brave vibration each way free,
     —O how that glittering taketh me!   (Herrick, "Upon Julia's Clothes")

5   If all be true that I do think,
     There are five reasons we should drink:
     Good wine—a friend—or being dry
     Or lest we should be by and by—
     Or any other reason why.
                    ("Causae Bibendi," by John Sirmond; Trans. Henry Aldrich)

Emphasis and Subordination

Emphasis is regarded by many readers as the all important thing: but it is really the least important. Any untrained voice can emphasize. The difficult thing to do well is the opposite of emphasis—the slighting of certain subordinate parts of discourse.[3]

This is important. The task of the oral interpreter is to find the words that carry the central thought of a passage or sentence, to emphasize these key words and to learn to subordinate the others. The interpreter's guide for emphasis and subordination is his analysis of meaning and structure.

What to emphasize and what to subordinate. In regard to the selection as a whole:

The highest point of interest (or climax) should be emphasized.

The focal points within the parts (or units) should receive emphasis, the degree determined by their relation to the climax. Naturally, low parts between focal points are subordinated.

In regard to sentences:

Emphasize words that point the main idea of the sentence.
Emphasize words that point contrast.
Emphasize words that introduce new ideas.

Words and parts of sentences frequently requiring subordination are: articles, conjunctions, prepositions, and (sometimes) pronouns.

How to emphasize and subordinate. Don't expect to learn new ways to emphasize and subordinate by reading about how to do it; you can only learn through doing. Begin with a simple sentence: "She is coming today." If the idea you want to convey is that she, not he, is coming, you would say: *She*iscomingtoday. What happened when you emphasized *she?* You probably said this word in a louder voice (more volume); you used a higher pitch, and you took longer to say it (more duration). If, one the other hand, you wanted to suggest that a man was involved and that *she* would not allow *him* to come, the "she" would be emphasized with a different quality of tone and, perhaps, with a circumflex inflection to suggest sarcasm. Remember that emphasis is achieved by a change in manner of utterance. These changes have to do with the variable attributes of voice: pitch, quality, volume, and timing (refer to pp. 106–14). A change in any one of these variable attributes or any combination of them will emphasize. The best way to correct overemphasis is to learn how to subordinate. Subordination in the sentence may be acquired by:

—"throwing away" words and phrases by using weak forms (refer to p. 104);
—saying the words and phrases to be subordinated more rapidly;

[3] From *Aims of Literary Study* by Hiram Carson.

—using an upward inflection before and at the end of a group of words that should be subordinated:

Two women ↗ (coming from opposite cultures) ↗ faced each other.

—saying a difficult sentence as if you were saying it in conversation and then trying to read it in the same way.

EXERCISE FOR EMPHASIS AND SUBORDINATION

Read the following sentences aloud, emphasizing the key words and subordinating others. What vocal means did you use to emphasize, to subordinate?

1 Four of them were included; one of the four was a dancer.

2 Two of them were included; one was a dancer, the other a singer.

3 A house should be of the hill, not on the hill.

4 If you prick us, do we not bleed? If you tickle us, do we not laugh? If you poison us, do we not die? And if you wrong us, shall we not revenge?
(Shakespeare, *The Merchant of Venice,* Act III, sc. 1)

5 Good morrow, Kate: for that's your name, I hear.
(Shakespeare, *The Taming of the Shrew,* Act II, sc. 1)

6 A thing that hath been, it is that which shall be; and that which is done is that which shall be done; and there is no new thing under the sun.
(Bible: Ecclesiastes i: 9)

7 Four things on earth are small but they are exceeding wise: the ants are a people not strong, yet they provide their food in the summer; the badgers are a people not mighty, yet they make their homes in the rocks; the locusts have no king, yet all of them march in rank; the lizard you can take in your hands, yet it is in kings' palaces. (Bible: Proverbs 30: 24–28)

8 The grass withereth, the flower fadeth, because the spirit of the Lord bloweth upon it: surely the people is grass. The grass withereth, the flower fadeth: but the word of our God shall stand forever. (Bible: Isaiah 40: 7–8)

9 As subordinating phrases are added to the sentence try to subordinate smoothly:

A sense of timing is a determining factor in our lives.

A sense of timing, an element of luck, is a determining factor in our lives.

A sense of timing, an element of luck, affecting every successful person— artist or businessman, writer or politician—is a determining factor in our lives.

A sense of timing, an element of luck, but at the same time, the ability to sense and seize the right moment without faltering, affects every successful person—artist or businessman, writer or politician; and without this he is likely to shine briefly and then fade from the scene.

In this part of the chapter we have recognized conversational rhythm as the basic pattern for communicating *logical meaning* from the printed page. In the chapter on poetry, we will extend this discussion by examining various rhythm patterns and ways of handling them effectively in oral reading.

Now let us consider another basic problem that may block the oral reader's projection of *emotional meaning*.

DIRECT TECHNIQUES FOR PROJECTING EMOTIONAL MEANING

In reading aloud, a person may express logical meaning clearly in a pleasing conversational flow of speech, but unless the listener catches the emotional tones that suggest the feeling or attitude behind the words the full meaning is not conveyed.

It is always important to *control* emotional expression in reading: the reader, in contrast to the actor, is re-creating, not creating. But before the finer controls are considered, the reader must be sure that he has "something" to control. Is he free enough to express emotional meaning? Sometimes a student reader shies away from any expression of emotion, or else he feels the emotion intensely but lacks the freedom or skill to express it. When this is the case, certain "exaggerated" techniques may be helpful.

The psychology on which the first exercise is based is the James-Lange theory which maintains that emotion is an awareness brought on by a muscular change in the body which is identified with a similar change experienced in the past. In our application of the theory, a physical muscular response, peculiar to a certain emotion, is believed to result in the production of that emotion. In other words, if a person assumes the muscular body tensions of anger as he remembers an actual experience of anger, this assumed body response will tend to make him feel angry. The theory is no longer held in high esteem among psychologists, but, used as an exercise for emotional response, there is some validity in its application.

Expression of Mood or Attitudes

If you have difficulty feeling a certain mood or attitude within a selection, try deliberately to arouse and energize this emotion. Do this by using your body as if you were in the mood. If the mood is anger, look angry, stand angry, move and gesture angry, and speak angry! Use the whole body and exaggerate the mood in any way you can think of as you read. You might grip the floor with your toes, bang the lectern, stamp your foot, and spit out the lines, making the sounds in the words harsh and biting. After this deliberate focus on the emotion, you should gradually change your focus to the *cause* of the emotion as evidenced in the selection.

EXERCISES FOR AROUSING OVERT BODILY EXPRESSION

Select one of the following examples (or a section from any previously studied material) and deliberately try to arouse the emotion.

1   Exaggerate the woman's jealousy and bitterness in "The Laboratory":

> He is with her, and they know that I know
> Where they are, what they do: they believe my tears flow
> While they laugh, laugh at me, at me fled to the drear
> Empty church, to pray God in, for them!—I am here.

2   The young lover's anguish in "Bredon Hill":

> Oh noisy bells be dumb
> I hear you. I will come.

3   The attitude of the speaker in "A Box to Hide In":

> "It's a form of escape," I told him "hiding in a box. It circumscribes your worries and the range of your anguish. You don't see people either."

4   Blake's attitude in "The Scoffers":

> Mock on, mock on, Voltaire, Rousseau,
> Mock on, mock on; 'tis all in vain;

Overt Character Actions

In preparation for "suggesting" a character in a story, a play, or a poetry reading, it is sometimes helpful to act out a character's physical movements and "business" as if you were portraying the character in a play. Before trying this "play-acting" exercise, you should analyze the characters in a scene. This accomplished, you proceed to go through each character's lines using overt movements and gestures. Assuming the character's posture, walk, and vocal characteristics, you enter and exit as the character would do in a play. Working in this way you get a clear external image and "feel" for the character that can be useful later when you only suggest the character.

Let us use the character who speaks in "The Laboratory" to illustrate this exercise. An analysis of what the character does and says would reveal a complex creature of medieval times, a "lady" in appearance who, in a jealous rage, is plotting the murder of her rival. Her hatred has been intensified by her jealousy of the rival's beauty and by the mocking attitude of the lovers toward her. You would first try to get a body feel for the proud, cruel, little woman; then you would go through the lines with overt movements and gestures to represent her outward appearance and inner state of mind. The text as your guide, you would find general actions: tying on the mask, moving about the shop inspecting the "devil's smithy," moving toward the old man when speaking directly to him, sitting and rising, allowing the old man to remove the mask, taking off the jewels, offering her lips to be kissed, and brushing dust from her dress.

Arousing Vocal Response

Oral Paraphrasing. Start with a part in a selection where the emotional response is difficult for you and talk about it, in your own words, aloud—in emotional terms; and then read the part immediately. The color of tone you use in your paraphrase should be transferred or copied, in some degree, when you read the line in the text. In *practice* these talking phrases may be used in transitions to help convey a change of time or place. Read "A Deep-Sworn Vow" again supplying these oral paraphrases or additions:

> Yet always (yes, it's happened every time!)
> When I look death in the face (your face—I saw it so clearly)
> When I clamber to the heights of sleep (it was as though I had to reach you),
> Or when I grow excited with wine (how gay I was and how I talked!)
> Suddenly (a flash) I meet your face (and I know).

These additions should make your pauses longer and more meaningful and help to convey the emotional overtones. First as you rehearse, say the additions aloud, and then say them silently between the lines.

Practice this transitional paraphrase and make up another for other transitions in the poem:

> Now that I tying thy glass mask tightly,
> May gaze through these faint smokes curling whitely,
> As thou pliest thy trade in this devil's smithy—
> Which is the poison to poison her, prithee?
>
> (Yes, a poison that will kill the beautiful creature who is with my love at this moment!)
>
> He is with her, and they know that I know
> Where they are, what they do . . .

Word Coloring. Charles A. Dana, the renowned nineteenth-century journalist, said this about words:

> Words seem to be little vessels that hold in some puzzling fashion exactly what is put into them. You can put tears into them, as though they were so many little buckets; and you can hang smiles along them, like Monday's clothes on the line; or you can starch them with facts and stand them up like a picket fence; but you won't get the tears out unless you first put them in.

If you have trouble coloring words with their emotional meanings, take the time to consider them separately. In rehearsal, exaggerate the feeling in the words: let the happy words laugh, the sad words cry, the sarcastic words mock, and the angry words pierce.

In the following poem color the words and sounds to suggest the surf, tow, and wind.

FOREBODING[4]

Don Blanding

    . . . . zoom . . . zoom . . . zoom . . .
    that is the sound of the surf . . .
as the great green waves rush up the shore
with a murderous thundering ominous roar
and leave drowned dead things at my door
    . . . zoom . . . zoom . . . zoom . . .

    . . . suish . . . suish . . . shui-s-h . . .
    that is the sound of the tow
as it slips and slithers along the sands
with terrible groping formless hands
that drag at my beach house where it stands
    . . . suish . . . shis-s-h . . . shuis-s-sh . . .

    eeeie . . . eeeie-u-u . . . eeeie-u-u . . .
    that is the sound of the wind
it wails like a banshee adrift in space
and threatens to scatter my driftwood place.
it slashes the sand like spite in my face
    eeie-u-u-u . . . eeie-u-u . . . . eeie-u-u . . .

    Surf . . . tow . . . or the wind . . .
    which of the three will it be . . .
the surf . . . will it bludgeon and beat me dead
or the tow drag me down to its ocean bed . . .
or the wind wail a dirge above my head . . .
    zoom . . . suis-s-h . . . eeie-u-u . . .

These exercises may not work the same for everyone, but for some students they have proven to be an effective means of letting go and of breaking down inhibitions.

---

[4] Reprinted by pemission of Dodd, Mead & Company, Inc. from *Vagabond's House* by Don Blanding. Copyright 1928, 1956 by Don Blanding.

6 TECHNIQUES FOR VOICE AND SPEECH

The voice mechanism has two distinct functions: producing tone and producing words. The two functions are closely related and, at the same time, distinct. We use vocal tone instinctively. Speech is an acquired habit. The child cries instinctively, but he must learn certain movements of the tongue and lips before he sets up the habits for producing words. Voice is the tone produced by the speaker which is dependent upon the vocal instrument he was fortunately, or unfortunately, born with. This tone can, to some extent, be improved by the use of good technique. The utterance of words, however, can be greatly altered by the knowledge and practice of correct speech sound production. Every voice is basically different from every other voice, but whole regional groups have certain identical speech habits. New habits (correct speech sounds or more pleasant ones) can replace old speech habits, but this takes interest on the learner's part and much time and effort. The professional actor is required to learn stage speech and to take every possible step toward perfecting his voice. In everyday life these demands are not made, but it is generally agreed that improvement of unpleasant voices and careless speech is an urgent need. Certainly, the sharing of literature for the pleasure of others demands a pleasing tone and clear, distinct speech. Even the most intellectual grasp of an author's ideas and emotions are of no use to the interpreter without the adequate vocal means to convey that meaning.

The aim of this chapter is to lead the student to a new awareness of voice and speech and to give him a basic technique for voice and speech improvement.

VOICE PRODUCTION

Since no amount of explanation of the vocal organs can insure their proper use, no detailed explanation of the anatomy of the vocal mechanism will be included here. Instead, our emphasis will be on guiding the student toward gaining a sense of the "feel" of the correct use of the vocal instrument. For this approach our discussion will include the steps for voice production with practice procedures and basic exercises.

There are three distinct factors that control voice production: the motor, or "exciter" of the energy for tone, the vibrator, and the resonator. A man-made instrument, such as the violin or trombone, may be compared to the human instrument since these same factors must function in both.

The *motor* is the part of the instrument that supplies the force or energy for tone. In the case of the violin it is the arm movements of the violinist which supply the energy; the trombone player supplies breath; man uses the air exhaled from the lungs to initiate sound. The exhaled air may leave the lungs, as it entered them, as breath, or it may be vocalized in the larynx.

The *vibrator* is the part of the instrument to which this energy is transferred: the strings of the violin, the mouth plates of the trombone, or the vocal cords of man. The vocal cords cause the exhaled air to be cut up into a series of waves which set up the fundamental tone and overtones. These sound waves are inherently weak and require additional means to build up the sound into full tones.

The *resonator* is the part of the instrument which amplifies the fundamental tone and overtones: the wooden box beneath the strings of the violin; the pipes of the trombone; the mouth, the pharynx, and the nose cavities of man.

Control of Breathing

When words are to be heard at a distance, or when a long phrase is attempted in reading, it becomes apparent that more breath is needed than in the usual conversational situation. The untrained speaker invariably obtains this additional breath incorrectly and is unable to effectively control the outgoing breath with the consequent bad effect on tone quality. Practice procedures for correct breathing should focus on three objectives: relaxation, adequate breath supply, and good breath control.

Relaxation. Correct breathing can only be obtained in a well poised body free of muscular tensions; no exercise can be helpful when the body is tense. First, relaxation of large muscles controlling posture should be achieved in order to bring about relaxation in the smaller muscles concerned in voice production. It is always wise to begin voice exercises with relaxation exercises.

Breath supply. In breathing for life, the cycle is a reflex consisting of a slow intake of breath and a quick release followed by a pause; for speech, the *outgoing* breath takes longer than the intake, and the pauses are according to the demands of the material being spoken. This means that through exercises you must become consciously aware of a change in the timing of the movements in breathing. First, it is important that the intake of breath, the supply, be sufficient. To insure this, you should become aware of proper control of the diaphragm.

Breath control. The next step is toward developing control of the outgoing breath. Through exercises you become conscious of quickening inhalation and *slowing* exhalation.

EXERCISES FOR BREATHING

1 For Relaxation

   a Stretch and yawn. The stretching should be intense but the yawning relaxed.

   b Sit very erect and rigid. Tense the body and then, beginning with the head, relax each part of the body. Let the head fall forward and the arms dangle loosely.

   c Standing, tense the muscles of the whole body; then, beginning with the head, relax each part of the body until you feel like a loose-jointed puppet.

   d Apply the pattern of tension followed by relaxation to the head, face, jaw, lips, tongue, palate, and throat.

2 Basic Exercise for Inhalation

Place the fingers of each hand on the ribs above the waist just in front of the armpits with the thumbs pointing toward the spine. As air is drawn in, see that the ribs move *outwards*. Start the movement at the back where the thumbs are placed. Keep trying this until you begin to sense this lateral movement of the ribs. Avoid the sensation that the ribs move outward in front; sense, instead, that the *back* widens.

3 Exercise for Control of Exhalation

In the exercise above, the inhalation and exhalation are of equal duration. Now, try to quicken inhalation and to *slow* exhalation. Gradually increase the exhalation count:

      in–2–3   hold–2–3   out–2–3
      in–2–3   hold–2–3   out–2–3–4
      in–2–3   hold–2–3   out–2–3–4–5

Keep increasing the exhaling count to 10 or 15, sensing the control of this outgoing breath.

4   Exercise for Controlled Breathing in Reading

The transition from breathing, as a technical exercise, to using controlled breath in reading aloud should be made gradually. Consciously using lateral breathing and consciously controlling outgoing breath, test your control by breathing only where the marks // indicate:

> This is the house that Jack built //
> This is the malt that lay in the house that Jack built //
> This is the rat that ate the malt that lay in the house
>   that ate the malt that lay in the house that Jack built //
> This is the cat that caught the rat that ate the malt
>   that lay in the house that Jack built //
> This is the dog that worried the cat that caught the rat
>   that ate the malt that lay in the house that Jack built //
> This is the cow with the crumpled horn that tossed the dog
>   that worried the cat that caught the rat that ate the malt
>   that lay in the house that Jack built //

> Rats! //
> They fought the dogs and killed the cats
> And bit the babies in the cradles,
> And ate the cheeses out of the vats,
> And licked the soup from the cooks' own ladles, //
> Split open the kegs of salted sprats,
> Made nests inside men's Sunday hats,
> And even spoiled the women's chats
> By drowning their speaking
> With shrieking and squeaking
> In fifty different sharps and flats. //
>   (Robert Browning, "The Pied Piper")

Although we have been considering the breath as though it existed apart from the other voice factors, we know this is not true. Each factor is dependent upon the other, and it is only for the purpose of pointing the logical order in which they relate that we attempt to discuss them separately.

The phonation of the breath is logically the next factor to consider after breathing; but it is most difficult to discuss or practice improvement of phonation separately from resonance, since the fundamental sound produced by the vibration of the vocal cords must, of necessity, be amplified by the resonators before we hear the resulting tone. For this reason, these two factors of voice should be considered in close relationship.

Control of Phonation (Vibrator)

When the impulse to speak comes, the pressure of the exhaled breath forces the vocal cords in the larynx to vibrate, thus producing the fundamental sound. The term "vocal cords" is misleading. They are not, as the term might imply, strings stretched across the windpipe; they are strips or bands of tissue that appear from above to be flat folds of muscle with thin inner edgings. These two edgings, composed of elastic tissue, are the vocal cords. When we breathe out they move closer together, and when we vocalize they meet, closing the opening completely. This closing action hinders or "bottles up" the air, but pressure of the exhaled air forces them apart. Air escapes and causes the bands to vibrate. The opening and shutting of the opening cuts the breath stream up into a series of puffs or waves that makes sound.

The degree of tension responsible for the rate of this vibrating action determines the pitch of the voice. A high degree of tension produces rapid vibration and a high pitch; less tension produces slower vibration and a lower pitch. The length and thickness of the cords determine the voice type; the longer and thicker cords of the man account for the difference between the voices of men and women.

The vibrating action in the larynx is instinctive. When we desire to speak or sing, the vocal cords come into the closed position. We should make no attempt to feel the movements in the larynx; in fact, there is little direct control we can, or should, exert over this part of the mechanism. Nature has provided the vocal cords, and structural differences cannot be changed. The best control that can be obtained is relaxation in the throat area. Working for throat *resonance* is, perhaps, the best exercise for producing a clear, free fundamental tone.

As you work on voice exercises, remember that a keen sense of hearing is important. At first you may not be able to hear what your teacher hears in your tone production, but your ability to hear fine shadings and gradations will improve. Learn to listen sharply and to compare your own voice recording with those of your classmates; learn to listen to the recordings of professional readers, not to imitate, but to hear more and more clearly the finer gradations in the vocal control of the artist.

Practice procedures for improving the fundamental tone produced by the vibrator should focus on these two objectives: to produce a free, clear tone, and to increase flexibility by extending the range of voice within the limits of that particular voice.

Production of a clear fundamental tone. As we have said, the best "feel" of control of the vibrator is that of relaxation in the throat area. Exercises for open throat are not only necessary for good pharynx resonance but are the best exercises for relaxing the throat for the production of a clear fundamental sound.

Tension or poor timing between the breathing muscles and the muscles in the larynx will result in what is called the "glottal attack." This is a sudden, rather violent opening of the cords that produces a grating harsh sound. A glottal attack is sometimes substituted for, or inserted before, an explosive consonant; and it is often used as a prefix to an initial vowel (heard when *a* is in an initial position). It is an ugly harsh clicking sound that should be eliminated. Awareness of the fault and vocalization exercises can help.

Vocal range control. The best pitch is one which lies toward the middle of the speaker's range. The center or optimum pitch may be found by singing down the scale until the lowest note which can be sung without tension can be reached. An octave above this will give a note toward the middle of the voice range and this, or one slightly below, should be the point from which to work. Practice scale exercises to increase the range above and below this middle point. Keep the tone forward in the mouth, and keep the throat open and relaxed.

EXERCISES FOR CONTROL OF PHONATION

5 Exercises for Open Throat

   a Take the open, free position for the "ah": jaw free and open teeth at least one inch apart, tongue flat on the floor of the mouth with tip touching inner surface of lower front teeth, and soft palate raised. Start, but do not complete, a yawn. Repeat this until you are able to feel the openness without the actual yawn. Memorize this feeling. Practice until you can easily produce this open throat.

   b Maintaining this relaxation and openness:

      whisper: HAH   HO   WHO   then vocalize
      whisper: WHO AM I   then vocalize

      Maintaining this relaxation and openness and directing sounds forward to the lips, read aloud:

      Most men want poise.
      "God of our Fathers known of old."
      "Roll on, thou deep and dark blue ocean, roll."
      "Double, double, toil and trouble;
      Fire burn and cauldron bubble."

6 Exercise for Extending Range of Pitch

   a Find center or optimum pitch. Practice singing the scale with vowels (above) down from center pitch, a note at a time, as low as you can with comfort. Whisper the vowel and then sing it.

b   Begin at center pitch level and count down a tone at a time:

   1
     2
       3
         4
           5 . . . Reverse, and count up.

c   Step down the pitch on each word:

The boy fell down
             down
                    down
                           down

Step up the pitch on each word:

                         up
                   up
             up
The girl felt lifted up

Step the pitch up and down with:

I am John Jones   I am John Jones
  I am John Jones   I am John Jones
    I am John Jones

The basic pitch of a voice can rarely be changed; a high voice cannot become a low voice however much this may be desired. When a voice is too high something can be done to give the impression of lowness: give attention to resonance. Effective use of resonance will add body and depth to the sound. For this, the best exercise is number 5 on page 88.

Control of Resonance

The resonator consists of three principal cavities: the pharynx (throat), the mouth, and the nose. These three cavities reinforce and amplify the fundamental tone and the overtones produced in the larynx. The tone quality of a voice is at its best when each part of the resonator contributes equally (more or less) to produce the total effect of the general voice quality. The use of too much nasal resonance results in an unpleasant nasal quality; over use of the pharynx results in a heavy, dull tone; excessive use of the mouth without enough use of the pharynx produces a thin, colorless tone. Practice procedures for improving the use of the resonator should focus on: awareness of full use of pharynx resonance, full use of mouth resonance, and proper use of nasal resonance.

Pharynx resonance. The pharynx functions best as a resonator when it is relaxed and open. Open throat, an open relaxed "feel," is essential to full pharynx resonance and good general tone quality.

Mouth resonance. The mouth resonator is readily subject to voluntary control, but as the shape of the mouth resonator is changed to make the different vowel sounds, the size of the resonator is altered, and, as a result, the general tone quality may be impaired. This can be corrected by thinking of the open jaw, the forward tongue positions, and controlled breathing as ever present factors. It is helpful to think of the positions of all the vowels as related to the "ah" position (the most open sound) and each vowel differentiated from another only by the degree of lip rounding and tongue movement required to make the sound.

Nasal resonance. The nasal resonator must never be allowed to dominate; but when the two cavities of mouth and throat are fully used, nasal resonance may add richness and vibrant carrying power. In making the three nasal sounds—*m*, *n*, and *ng*—feel that the closed lips block the air channel through the mouth and that the soft palate is lowered, allowing the vocalized breath to go through the nose.

EXERCISES FOR RESONANCE

For pharynx resonance use **Exercise 5** on page 88.

7   Exercise for Maintaining Tone While Forming Vowels

    a   Take basic "ah" position (refer to Ex. 5). Maintaining jaw in open position, round lips to size of lead pencil on ōō (u) sound. Alternate these two positions until lip movement for ōō can be taken with minimum jaw movement.

        h ah   h ōō   (u)   h ah   h ōō   (u)
        h ah   h ē   (i)   h ah   h ē   (i)

    b   Keep the jaw open, lips in the *ah* position, altering only the position of tongue or lips as required. Use increase in rate and rhythm change when the ability to direct the movements has been acquired. Add other vowel sounds: *o* and *aw*.

        HAH   HEE   HAH   HOO,   HAH   HOO   HAH   HEE,
        HAH   HEE   HAH   HOO

8   Exercise for Nasal Resonance

    a   Cup hands over mouth and nose. Alternate the sounds *m* and *ah.* There should be no break in the sound.

        M AH   M AH   M AH   M AH   M AH   M AH

The vibrations for the consonant should be felt strongly on the fingers. Only the faintest trace of nasal resonance should be heard on the vowels.

b   Hum *m*, change it suddenly to *b*. Try to feel the two actions of the soft palate (lowered for *m* and raised for *b*). Hum *n* and change quickly to *d;* hum *ng* and change to *g*.

c   Pause before the final nasal; gradually shorten the pause seeing that no nasality is heard until the final nasal.

> ti . . . me   ti . . . me   time
> ni . . . ne   ni . . . ne   nine

d   Articulate the following with prolonged nasal resonance, but avoid nasalization of vowels and diphthongs:

> Ninety nine times.
> Zoom—went the sound.
> Advancing and prancing and glancing and dancing,
> Recoiling, turmoiling, and toiling, and boiling.
>
> The mountains were said to be in labor, and uttered most dreadful groans. People came together far and near to see what birth would be produced; and after they waited a considerable time in expectation, out crept a mouse.   (Aesop's Fables)

WORD PRODUCTION

The pronounciation of words varies in different localities. This is due, primarily, to the differences in the habits of forming separate speech sounds and the connecting and combining of the sounds: eastern and southern Americans usually say "he-uh" for the word "here," while westerners say "heer"; most Americans say "haus" for the word "house," but most Virginians say something like "heoos."

This raises the question of standard pronunciation. What are the standards for speech utterance? Generally speaking, your standard should be the speech used by effective and cultured speakers in your own area. Each region in America has its own peculiar sound characteristics that give a natural "flavor" to an individual's speech; and when these characteristics do not call *undue* attention, they should be retained. Certainly, nothing is more painful than the efforts of someone trying to imitate "English" or stage speech, for this effort usually results in a strained and inconsistent affectation. If you keep the cultivated speech of your own locality as a standard, your speech will not draw attention to the speaking itself; but, at the same time, it will be free of undue provincialism and carelessness.

Your work in improving your speech in oral interpretation should be focused on correcting those sounds in your speech which interfere with effective communication. An audience's attention should always be directed to the content of the reading rather than to the manner in which it is being read. Your work in word production should be aimed toward correcting the placement of vowel sounds which interfere with pleasant tone quality, correcting the careless production of consonant sounds for more clarity and distinctness, and improving the flow of speech in reading.

Vowel Sounds

If a vowel is incorrectly made in the mouth, it is only the frequent repetition of a newly acquired position together with the concentrated effort to hear the sound which will make possible any improvement. Remember, too, that it is the position of the tongue that is principally responsible for changing the size and shape of the mouth resonator to form the vowels. These conditions should be present when working with the exercises: good diaphragmatic breathing, mouth and throat passages open and free of tension, flexible use of jaw and lips, and direction of the tone toward the front of the mouth.

We will consider each vowel individually, describing briefly the position of the principle articulators and calling attention to the most common errors associated with the production of the specific vowel. The phonetic symbols will be used to help you become aware of using the sound in words and sentences.

Front Vowels

ē (i) This vowel is heard in weed, police, receive.
The front of the tongue is raised and tensed in the front and top of the mouth, but there should be no movement of the tongue while saying the sound. Do not tense the lips. This vowel is diphthongized by many people (field becomes fe-uh-ld). Avoid this.

Practice material:

> even, each, eel, green, receipt, conceivable, see, we, lead, illegal, believe, esteem, machine, three, trees, police, field

> Please do not tease or sneeze—be discreet.
> The scene to be believed should be seen.
> Sea gulls weave and screech.
> The meek and the weak kneel speechless and three chiefs lead.

ĭ (ɪ) This vowel is heard in tin, guild, pity.
The front of the tongue is slightly lower and farther back than for ē. Make the sound short and clean. Be careful not to relax the tongue so much that

a neutral sound is made instead (st ɪl becomes stəl). Foreigners often substitute ē for the sound (ɪt becomes it). In unaccented syllables the ē sound
is reduced to ĭ (in city and coffee the *y* and *ee* should be pronounced ĭ,
not ē).

Practice material:

> *i*nn, *i*ll, *i*t, *i*tch, hymn, w*o*men, b*u*siness, s*i*eve, unt*i*l, beg*i*n, inst*i*ll, c*i*ty, tr*i*p,
> s*i*x, sl*i*ps

> The little tom-tit sang "Willow, titwillow, titwillow."
> "That he is mad, 'tis true; 'tis true tis pity and pity 'tis 'tis true."

ĕ (ɛ) This vowel is heard in l*e*d, s*ai*d, and spr*ea*d.
The front of the tongue is slightly lower than for ĭ. Do not spread the lips
and keep the tip of the tongue back of the lower teeth. Avoid substituting ĭ:
pen becomes pin, get becomes git. Other substitutions include: egg becomes aig, bury (beri) becomes buri. Also avoid prolonging this sound into
a drawl: fell becomes fe-uh-l.

Practice material:

> *e*lf, *e*nd, *e*nter, gu*e*ss, r*e*ady, m*ea*nt, p*e*nny, h*ea*d, t*e*n, fr*e*t, inst*ea*d, int*e*nd,
> att*e*ntion, b*u*ry, sh*e*lls, g*e*t

> Get the ten best dressed men.
> "It is a knell that summons thee to heaven or to hell."

ă (æ) This vowel is heard in gl*a*d, *a*dd, s*a*t.
The front of the tongue is low; the mouth more open than for ĕ. This vowel
is frequently produced with a flat, nasal quality or a glottal attack. Avoid
strain in any region of throat or mouth. Do not arch tongue toward hard
palate or stiffen jaw or prolong. Avoid diphthongization or excessive tension with nasality. Keep the sound soft.

Practice material:

> c*a*t, b*a*nd, m*a*n, s*a*d, f*a*ct, c*a*rry, l*a*nd, p*a*ct, *a*ction, C*a*mpus, c*a*mp, *a*tomic,
> bl*a*st, r*a*ndom, f*a*cts, m*a*rriage

> His mad fancy and random facts made him a sad sack.
> Put the cat in the family rag bag.

ȧ (a) This vowel is sometimes heard in b*a*th, cl*a*ss, *a*sk.
This intermediate vowel lies midway, theoretically speaking, between ă in
*a*dd and ä in f*a*ther. The front of the tongue is still lower than for ă but not
as low as for the low back ä.

Practice material:

> h*a*lf, b*a*th, cl*a*ss, d*a*nce, l*a*ugh, p*a*th, m*a*st, *a*sk

> After the dance she looked in the glass and asked for a bath.
> Ask half the class to have a last chance at the task.

Middle Vowels

û (er) (ɝ) This vowel is heard in h*ea*rd, n*u*rse, c*u*rl.
The middle portion of the tongue is raised toward the hard palate. The lips
are open, but relaxed; the tongue tip is behind the lower teeth (do not make
with tip of tongue turned back). The sound (ɜ) used in Southern and New
England speech is essentially the same except the *r* sound is only suggested;
in (ɝ) the *r* is blended with the sound. The tendency to diphthongize the
sound (bird becomes something like bur-uh-d) should be avoided. In some
metropolitan areas a substitution is heard: bird becomes boid. Also avoid
hardening and prolonging the sound.

Practice material:

> c*u*rl, f*i*rst, t*e*rse, det*e*rmine, conc*e*rn, det*e*r, w*o*rld, th*i*rd, ch*u*rch, best*i*rred,
> reh*ea*rse, l*ea*rn, b*i*rd

> The early bird was concerned by the curled worm.
> Learn to earn and to serve a certain purpose.

uh (ə) This sound is heard in *a*bout, sof*a*, nat*io*n.
This vowel, known as the neutral vowel, is produced with a relaxed tongue
in a position slightly lower than for (ɝ). It occurs only in unstressed syllables. It is probably the most frequently used vowel in American-English
speech because many vowels in unstressed positions are changed to this
sound: the (ði) becomes (ðə); dent and ment endings become (dənt) and
(mənt).

er (ɚ) This vowel is heard in pow*er*, p*er*form, moth*er*.
This sound is a blend of the neutral with *r* (ɚ). It is used in unstressed
syllables only and is the unstressed form of *û* (ɝ).

Practice material for neutral (ə) and neutral with *r* (ɚ):

> sod*a*, *a*llow, *a*dult, pres*e*nt, fash*io*n, pap*er*, occ*ur*, oth*er*

> The woman on the sofa is more aware than the other adult.
> The older brother allows the younger brother to salute.

ŭ (ʌ) This vowel is heard in c*u*p, y*ou*ng, d*u*mp.
The middle of the tongue is held quite low and the lips are slightly more
open than for (ə). The sound is heard only in stressed syllables and is the
same as the neutral except for this stress.

Practice material:

> bl*oo*d, cl*u*b, d*oe*s, l*o*ve, t*o*ngue, beg*u*n, c*u*t, spr*u*ng

> A flood of money covered the ugly rug.
> You make your trouble double trouble when it's just a bubble.

Back Vowels

ōō (u) This vowel is heard in l*oo*se, tr*u*e, thr*ough*.
This is the highest of the back vowels. The back of the tongue is high in the mouth, the lips rounded and protruded. It has a greater amount of lip rounding than any of the other vowels in American speech. The lips should assume the correct position or a diphthong may result.

Practice material:

doom, group, rude, prudent, ruler, troupe, tooth, brew

The fool threw the food at the troupe.
The blue mood flower blooms in the afternoon.

ŏŏ (ʊ) This vowel is heard in c*ou*ld, w*oo*d, p*u*ll.
The back of the tongue is slightly lower and the lips are slightly less rounded than for ōō (ʊ). Avoid substituting *ŭ* (ʌ): gŏŏd becomes (gʌd), put becomes (pʌt).

Practice material:

pull, took, bush, would, sugar, woolen, butcher, crooked

The cook took a look at her cookbooks.
Put the good bullets behind the bush.

ô (aw) (ɔ) This vowel is heard in l*aw*, c*au*ght, c*a*ll.
The tongue should be in a low position with the tip touching the floor of the mouth below lower gums and the extreme back elevated toward the soft palate. The lip rounding should not be extreme. The sound is liable to throaty production as a result of tension of the tongue. In many words the vowels (ɒ) or *ä* (ɑ) may be heard instead of *aw*.

Practice material:

call, taught, wall, outlaw, law, shawl, corn, lawn, stall

He caught the ball in the hall when she called.
The auto was bought in August and was just what he sought.

ŏ (ɒ) This vowel is heard in cl*o*g, cl*o*ck, h*o*t.
The rear of the tongue is slightly lower than for *aw* and more relaxed. The lips are only slightly rounded. The sound is not consistently used in the United States: *aw* (ɔ) or *ah* (ɑ) are often used instead.

Practice material:

clog, not, hot, honest, odd, policy, collar, doll, cloth

The mob shot the robber in the forest.
The frog looked odd on the log.

ä (ah) (ɑ) This vowel is heard in c*a*lm, f*a*rm, f*a*ther.
The tongue is low and flat with tip against lower teeth; the jaw and lips are relaxed. This is the most open of the sounds.

Practice material:

artist, c*a*r, b*a*rn, f*a*ther, c*a*lm, dis*a*rm, h*a*rbor

The alarm was heard by the army sergeant.
The far star was clear in the calm harbor.

Diphthongs

A diphthong is a compound vowel, a rapid blending together of two vowels. The simple vowels demand a fixed and stable position throughout their utterance. In compound vowels the articulators start in one position and immediately move in the direction of the second sound. The first vowel receives the greater stress.

ī (aɪ) Diphthong heard in sk*y*, h*igh*, b*uy*.
The tongue starts from the *ă* (a) or *ä* (ɑ) position and moves toward the *ĭ* (ɪ) position. It is often nasalized, and some fail to take the second position and it becomes *ă*.

Practice material:

*ai*sle, b*uy*, h*ei*ght, t*i*me, inv*i*ting, s*i*gning, l*i*fel*i*ke

Night light seemed to pile in the aisle.
The wise use other's hindsight for their own foresight.

au (aʊ) Diphthong heard in cl*ou*d, n*ow*, b*ough*.
The starting place for this vowel is somewhere between (a) and (ɑ). Pronounced with "ah" it may sound exaggerated and affected. This sound is often nasalized, and sometimes *ă* (æ) or *ĕ* (ɛ) is substituted for the first element and the word "house" becomes either "haoos" or "heoos."

Practice material:

t*ow*n, *ow*l, pr*ou*d, prof*ou*nd, ab*ou*t, c*ow*, th*ou*, c*ou*nty

How, now, brown cow—are you bound for the town?
I vow that brown house will be found.

oi (ɔɪ) Diphthong heard in c*oi*l, *oi*l, t*oy*.
Southerners tend to omit the second element, lengthening the *aw* sound.

Practice material:

t*oi*l, ch*oi*ce, b*oy*, p*oi*son, *oy*ster, j*oy*, p*oi*se, s*oi*l

The noise annoys the oyster.
The boy enjoyed the toy.

ā (eɪ) Diphthong heard in nail, pray, lace.
This sound may sometimes be heard as a pure vowel (e) in unstressed syllables (chaotic), but in stressed positions the two elements should be present.

Practice material:

age, ail, bail, dame, deign, lazy, caged, raged

Angel cake is good date bait.
The tame ape ate the hay in the rain.

ō (oʊ) Diphthong heard in toe, home, coal.
A protrusion and rounding of the lips is required to make *o*. In stressed
positions the second element is added to make it a diphthong; in unstressed
positions it is a pure vowel (o) and the second element is omitted. In
"hotel" the pure vowel is used (ho-'tɛl) not ('hoʊ-təl).

Practice material:

row, oh, own, beau, moan, slow, woe, below, toe

Sticks and stones may break your bones.
The precocious Joe slowly rowed the old boat to the owner.

(ɛɚ) Diphthong heard in their, fair, pear.
The starting place is *ĕ* (ɛ) or slightly lower; it must never be as low as *a*.
The second element, the neutral, should not be allowed to become the low
ah. It is used with the *r* (er) or without it (ɛə).

Practice material:

air, care, fair, their, declare, prepare

Women despair in the care of their hair.
The heiress was beyond compare in the affair.

(ɪɚ) Diphthong heard in ears, pier, dear.
The first element is *ĭ* as in bit. The second element may be the neutral with
or without the *r* (ɪɚ) or (ɪə).

Practice material:

dear, fear, cheer, bier, year, here, eerie

Don't fear the timid deer.
With queer, bleary leers he steers the tearful dear.

(ʊɚ) Diphthong heard in tour, sure, poor.
The first position is that of *ŏŏ* (ʊ); the second, the neutral with or without
the *r*. Care should be taken that no intrusive *w* be heard (as poor—poower).

Practice material:

cure, moor, pure, poor, boor, alluring

The poor seek a cure.
He must endure the tour.

(oɚ) Diphthong heard in soar, pour, ore.

In some words (ɔɚ) is used instead of (oɚ). Except in the New York City area most Americans are likely to use (ɔɚ) for "horse" and "for" and (oɚ) for "hoarse" and "four."

Practice material:

cord, course, import, lord, four, horse, hoarse, for

The performance was over at four in the morning.
The horse will not run the course; he is hoarse.

ū (ju) Diphthong heard in use, dew, new.

In certain words take care not to substitute ōō (u) for ū (ju): "dew" should be (dju) not (du).

Practice material:

new, dew, student, Tuesday, beauty, tune, mused

The view is new, due to a few subdued hues.
Tuesday's music students mused on the unique beauty of the tune.

Consonant Sounds

When the outgoing breath stream is diverted, obstructed, or stopped in the mouth resonator, the resulting sound is a consonant. Vowels should be produced without muscular force or tension in the resonators; the clarity of the consonants, on the other hand, depends upon the muscular energy with which the articulators move from one position to another making changes with precision. This means that even more effort must be made to keep this energetic movement from interfering with the production of good tone.

Consonants fall into two general classes: voiced and voiceless. In the voiced consonants the release of the breath is accompanied by actual vibrations of the vocal folds; in the voiceless consonants, the air stream is released without the vibration of the vocal folds.

Plosives

A plosive is a "little explosion." The air stream is temporarily blocked by the articulators and then suddenly released. Plosives are voiced and voiceless.

VOICELESS PLOSIVES	VOICED PLOSIVES
p (lips together, air is released suddenly and sharply)	b (produced as p except there is vibration of vocal cords)

VOICELESS PLOSIVES	VOICED PLOSIVES
t (tip of tongue makes firm contact with upper gum ridge; breath is released sharply as tongue is lowered)	d (produced as t except there is vibration of vocal cords)
k (rear of tongue elevated to touch firmly raised soft palate; breath released sharply as tongue lowered)	g (produced as k except there is vibration of vocal cords)

Errors in the production of t and d are very common: in forming the t and d, if the tip of the tongue is allowed to fall against the teeth instead of the gum ridge, the resulting sound may resemble th (ð) or th (θ); if the t and d are omitted or swallowed in the medial position "little kitten" will sound something like 'li'l ki'n.'' The t in the medial position is sometimes distorted by voicing: "Betty went to the party" becomes "Bedy went to the pardy." T and d at the end of words are often completely dropped: "Fred and Mary kept their pact" becomes "Fre' and Mary kep' their pac."

Fricatives

A fricative is produced when the breath is forced through a relatively small, narrow opening. This may take place as a result of a grooving of the tongue or by having other organs of articulation come close together. Fricatives should be clear and clean-cut, but they should not be prolonged or otherwise emphasized. Like the plosives, fricatives may be voiced or voiceless.

VOICELESS FRICATIVES	VOICED FRICATIVES
f (upper front teeth make a light contact with lower lips)	v (produced as f except that breath is vocalized)
th (θ) (tip of flattened tongue elevated, protruded to make contact with lower edges of upper teeth)	th (ð) (produced as (θ) except that breath is vocalized)
s (tip of tongue behind upper teeth—not touching; outgoing voiceless breath forced over grooved tongue and edges of upper and lower front teeth)	z (produced like s except that there is vocalization)
sh (ʃ) (tongue drawn back and broadened; breath forced over broad surface rather than narrow groove)	zh (ʒ) (produced as sh except that breath is vocalized)

VOICELESS FRICATIVES	VOICED FRICATIVES
hw (ʍ) (lips rounded and voiceless; air passes through; tongue lowered and relaxed)	*w* (produced as *hw* except that breath is vocalized)
h (articulating organs take up position for following vowel before *h* is heard)	*j* (voiced breath forced through narrow space between arched tongue and soft palate)
tsh (tʃ) (blend of *t* and *sh;* as tip of tongue lowered breath released)	*dzh* (dʒ) (produced as (tʃ) except that breath is vocalized)

Tsh and *dzh* are know as fricatives; *h* is known as a glottal aspirate; *w* and *j* are often classified as glides because they result from a gliding uninterrupted movement of the articulators; *l* and *r* are referred to as semivowels because of their vowel-like characteristics; *l* is known as the lateral continuant.

l (tongue tip in contact with upper gum ridges; vocalized breath passes laterally over the sides of tongue) If *l* precedes a front vowel it is generally referred to as a clear or light *l* (leap, lip, lad). If *l* precedes a consonant, occurs in the final position of a word, or is used to form a syllable it is generally referred to as dark (all, rule, little). Care should be taken not to allow the *l* to become too dark and muffled.

r (tongue tip close but not touching gum ridge and air forced over tongue tip; when it occurs after a voiceless sound (three, tree) it may be partly unvoiced).

Errors in the production of some of these consonants are often heard but can be avoided. In the production of *s* avoid having the tip of tongue touch either upper teeth or gum ridge. The tongue tip should not protrude between the teeth; this will produce a *th* lisp. Do not use too much breath for *s* or prolong it. There is a tendency to substitute voiceless *s* for *z;* this interferes with distinction between words: pays–pace, as–ass, prize–price. If the tongue is lazy *l* becomes indistinct, sounding something like *oo:* milk becomes miook, bell becomes beoo. Avoid a mushy *r*. A flexible active tongue with a minimum of lip movement is needed for a clear-cut *r*.

Nasals

There are three nasal consonants: *m, n,* and *ng*. For making these sounds you should feel that the soft palate is lowered, the air channel through the mouth blocked by closed lips, and the outgoing vocalized breath is sent into the nasal cavities.

m (lips should meet lightly with teeth apart, the jaw open, tongue flat and forward and *soft palate lowered*)

n (tongue comes forward and upwards, the tongue tip in contact with the upper gums. The jaw should be open, lips slightly closed with soft palate lowered)

ng (ŋ) (back of tongue is in contact with the lowered soft palate) Errors made with nasal sounds are often heard. The *m* is sometimes muffled. Avoid closing the jaw and bunching the tongue up in the mouth. The sound needs duration. The sensation of forward production for the nasals is important. Feel that the sound is directed toward the lips, not toward the soft palate. If given duration, the nasals may add beauty to tone quality. Unpleasant nasality is heard when the voiced air producing other sounds is allowed to pass through the nose.

EXERCISES ON PLOSIVE CONSONANTS

1 Practice discriminating between *t* and *d:*

latter–ladder	wetting–wedding
better–bedded	tenting–tending
butting–budding	rating–raiding
heated–heeded	written–ridden

Practice *t* followed by *l* or *n:*

little	battle	bottle	glottal	brittle
button	cotton	mountain	written	gotten

Practice the right duration to distinguish between:

wrap ten—wrapped ten, pastimes—past times,
cook dinner—cooked dinner

Practice for precision of *t* and *d:*

In tooting two tutors astute,
Tried to toot to a Duke on a flute,
But duets so gruelling
End only in duelling
When tutors astute toot the flute.

2 Practice for precision of other plosives:

Wipe up the pepper from the carpet.
Her job was to place tubing on the table in the lab.
The dog dug for the frog under the log; the big pig tried to take two little pigs into the bog.

EXERCISE ON FRICATIVE CONSONANTS

3   Practice material for *f, v, th:*

> The rough tough was footloose and fancy-free.
> If I leave, I believe you will grieve, my love.
> The breath of the moth meant death to the cloth.
> Tell them that these and those are theirs.

4   Distinguish between *th, t,* and *d:*

thank–tank	they–day	tithe–tide
oath–oat	there–date	bath–bat
then–den	thought–taught	though–dough
then–tin	thine–dine	

5   Practice material for *s* and *z:*

Adjust the tongue for correct *s.* Prolong *s* and *z* before and after vowel sounds. Gradually lessen the duration:

s...ē	z...ē	ē...s	ē...z
s...ĭ	z...ĭ	ĭ...s	ĭ...z
s...ĕ	z...ĕ	ĕ...s	ĕ...z
s...ă	z...ă	ă...s	ă...z

Pronounce without too much prolonging of *s* or *z:*

> eats, its, hats, lets, wets, hoots, ruts, forts, pots, notes, coats, sing, city, salt, scoff, wistful, statesman, asleep, beast, sinister, sunset, firsts, ghosts, hosts, mists, asks, crisps, as, jazz, raze, hers, raise

Distinguish between *s* and *z:*

bays–base	raise–race	hers–hearse
lazy–lacy	lost–loose	prizing–pricing

Read, taking care to distinguish *s* and *z* but giving neither too much prominence:

> My gentle Puck, come hither. Thou remember'st
> Since once I sat upon a promontory,
> And heard a mermaid, on a dolphin's back
> Uttering such dulcet and harmonious breath,
> That the rude sea grew civil at her song,
> And certain stars shot madly from their spheres,
> To hear the sea-maid's music.
>   (Shakespeare, *Midsummer Night's Dream*)

6   Practice material for *sh* (ʃ) and *zh* (ʒ):

she, ship, shoe, dish, wash, machine, notion, punish, azure, casual, seizure, usual, vision, rouge, garage

She should be sure and measure her pleasure.
The decision to wash the shoes was an intrusion.

7   Practice material for *tch* (tʃ) and *dzh* (dʒ):

Distinguish between *tch* (tʃ) and *ch* (ʃ):

chew–shoe, chair–share, chip–ship, ditch–dish

Eschew shoe-chewing.

Distinguish between *tch* (tʃ) and *dzh* (dʒ):

cheer–jeer, chump–jump, chin–gin, britches–bridges, rich–ridge

Share a chair and watch your cash.
The judge sent Madge to a rich college.

8   Exercises for *l* and *r:*

leap–peal	lip–pill	lap–pal	lane–rail
look–pull	lie–isle	allow–oil	law–wall

The lonely land is a wild isle.
Listen to the lively, lilting lyrics in Lulu's style.

proud, press, bring, bread, crayon, grim, groan, trip, train, tree, thrill, through, thrift, drown, dry, drip, squirrel, arrow, merrier, herring, fairy, fury, dare I, dire act, dear aunt, for a time, law and order

The train trip through three states made the crew groan.
Red roses with green leaves grew in brown earth.

Exercises for *nasal resonance* (on pp. 90–91) should be used again.

FLOW OF SPEECH

In connected speech, speech sounds influence each other. Dropping sounds or changing sounds in connected speech is not always careless speech; this may be an accepted pronunciation. The acceptance of such changes in connected speech has been due to the need for economy of effort in speech, continued use over a period of time, and the popularity of the conversational mode. Overprecise, pedantic speech interferes with smooth, varied, and natural conversational speech. We will consider three ways to acquire a more natural conversational flow of speech: the use of weak forms, the use of assimilation, and clarity in a more rapid speech flow.

Weak Forms

An outstanding characteristic of American-English speech is the general
use of weak vowels in unstressed syllables of polysyllabic words. For example: in the word "city" the *y* or *ē* sound is reduced to a weaker one, *ĭ* (ɪ); in
such words as "add*e*d," "nos*e*s," "beaut*i*ful" *ĭ* (ɪ) replaces *ĕ* (ɛ) or *ē* (i) in
the unstressed syllables. The neutral (ə) is, of course, the vowel most frequently used to replace another vowel in unstressed syllables. For example:
"to-day" becomes tə-day, "wo-man" becomes wo-mən, "con-clude" becomes
cən-clude, "pit-i-ful" becomes pit-i-fəl or pit-ə-fəl.

Connecting words: articles, pronouns, prepositions, conjunctions, and
auxiliaries (unless stressed for some special reason) are generally used in
their weak forms in connected speech: the (ði) becomes (ðə), *ā* (eɪ) becomes *uh* (ə).

Assimilation

Assimilation is the term used to identify the phonetic change that takes
place when a sound is modified as the result of the influence of a neighbor-
ing sound. This is a large subject that cannot be dealt with in any detail
here, but let us point a few assimilative changes which are really simplifications of articulations considered as correct after long use.

The most frequent assimilative change occurs in the omission of sounds
when two or more consonants are in juxtaposition. Thus the italicized
sounds are omitted from: Chris*t*mas, han*d*kerchief, han*d*some, sof*t*en,
of*t*en. In the pronunciation of "clothes," the *th* is dropped because it is too
difficult to say the *th* before the *z* sound.

Not all plosive consonants should be completely articulated. When one
is followed by another, only the stop of the first and the release of the
second should be heard (ro-bd—robbed). The same situation occurs when
final and initial plosives are in juxtaposition: hot dog, black gloves, sit
tight, glad day. Only one of the consonants is exploded; it is the length of
the silence which gives the impression of two sounds. The stop, its duration, and its release must all be observed, otherwise the impression is of one
sound only. Compare: red ear and red deer. The only difference between
the two pairs is the length of the stop. To articulate both *d*'s would make
for overprecise, pedantic speech.

In conversational speech the natural flow brings natural assimilative
changes in phrases. We say: bread 'n' butter, cup 'n' saucer, and these
simplifications are acceptable. Not all assimilation that we hear is acceptable, however. There is a tendency for many people to nasalize a vowel
before or after a nasal sound and thus nasalize the word: penny, nice, my,

mountain, man, known. In careless speech we hear many omissions, substitutions, and additions which are not acceptable: acts becomes axe, fifths becomes fifs, texts becomes teks, hunting becomes huntin, picture becomes pitcher, length and strength become lenth and strenth, "I'll meet you" becomes "I'll meechoo," "Would you mind?" becomes "Woojoomind?"

Clarity in Rapid Speech Flow

A general handicap in interpretation is the inability of students to articulate sounds rapidly and still be understood. Listen to recordings by professional readers such as John Gielgud, Judith Anderson, and others, and note their ability to articulate distinctly and with great rapidity. Exercises to develop the power of speaking clearly at a more rapid pace are most helpful.

EXERCISES FOR ASSIMILATION AND RAPID SPEECH FLOW

1 Pronounce words and phrases pointing use of weak forms and assimilation: president, Detroit, precedence, precedents, theatre, accident, civil, blossom, radiance, better, labor, murmur, ham and eggs, bread and butter, the girl and the boy, hot dog, red deer, black gloves, sit tight, glad day.

2 Stimulate movements of lips and tongue:

PPPPPP PAH	PPPPPP PAY	PPPPPP PEE
BBBBBB BAH	BBBBBB BAY	BBBBBB BEE
TTTTTT TAH	TTTTTT TAY	TTTTTT TEE
DDDDDD DAH	DDDDDD DAY	DDDDDD DEE

3 In these exercise passages, whisper first, trying to convey meaning by means of the clarity of articulatory movements alone; then add voice, concentrating on the light forward articulation. Gradually increase the volume and pace.

Turn to page 86 and use the passage from Browning's "Pied Piper."

> You're a regular wreck, with a crick in your neck,
> And no wonder you snore, for your head's on the floor,
> And you're needles and pins from your soles to your shins,
> And your flesh is a-creep, for your left leg's asleep, . . .
> And some fluff in your lung, and a feverish tongue,
> And a thirst that's intense, and a general sense
> That you haven't been sleeping in clover.
>
> (W. S. Gilbert, *Iolanthe*)

O, then, I see Queen Mab hath been with you.
She is the fairies' midwife; and she comes
In shape no bigger than an agate-stone
On the fore-finger of an alderman,
Drawn with a team of little atomies
Over men's noses as they lie asleep; ...
                    (Shakespeare, *Romeo and Juliet*, Act I, sc. 4)

VOCAL VARIETY

Ideally, vocal variety should be controlled by the reader's concentration on thought and feeling within a selection. But we know that this ability, however desired, is not always present. Vocal monotony is a common, ever disturbing fault in reading aloud. The interpreter must have an understanding of the variable attributes of voice: volume, pitch, quality, and timing as a means of controlling monotony and expressing varied shades of meaning and feeling. In discussing these, we cannot make rules. Because these elements are capable of constant change and because they do not function independently of each other, the possibilities of their combined variations are endless. This discussion can only make you more aware of possibilities. Practice procedures for improvement should focus on four objectives: awareness of and the ability to use variety in volume, pitch, quality, and timing.

Variety in Volume

In addition to being loud enough to be heard clearly, the general volume used should correspond with the feeling inherent in the selection. The type of material and the ideas being expressed call for an appropriate degree of volume. Some ideas suggest self-assurance, strength, or roughness which may best be expressed by the use of heavy volume or energy; conversational or straight expository material usually calls for a moderate degree of volume; whimsical and personal material may be best projected with a light degree of volume.

Within each paragraph and each sentence there is need for variety in the use of volume. Certain words and phrases must be emphasized and this, in American speech, is done most frequently by adding force or stress to the word or phrase. This clarifies meanings and, in some cases, distinguishes words (the meaning of words as con'-duct and con-duct' is determined only by the syllable stress). But at the same time that we recognize the importance of stress as a means of emphasis, we must recognize its potential dangers. As was pointed out in our discussion of emphasis, it is easy to empha-size a word by making it louder, and so the tendency is to overuse this means. The result is a monotonous stress pattern. Nothing is more disagree-able than too much punching of words with stress.

One of the best ways to use volume variation is to apply loudness and soft-ness to point contrasts. Become conscious of degrees and levels of loudness and softness. A sudden change from loudness to softness or from softness to loudness, at an appropriate time, can enhance meaning and emotion and focus attention. Of course, all changes must be motivated by the context. But, in spite of the demands of the material, readers hesitate to use this kind of vocal variety. The exercises should be done with exaggeration, with extreme contrasts in the use of loudness and softness.

EXERCISES FOR VARIETY OF VOLUME

1 Take breathing exercises 1, 2, and 3 on page 85.

2 Count, maintaining your natural pitch level; start softly and gradually increase the volume (keep abdominal muscles in control of breathing) until you are speaking as loudly as you can without straining the throat. Your purpose here is to increase loudness while keeping the same pitch level. Reverse the count from loud to soft.

3 Concentrating on correct breathing and front placement of the tone in the mouth, speak the following softly but with such sharp articulation that the words can be heard clearly in the back of the room:

In the silence of the night
How we shiver with affright
At the melancholy menace of their tone!
(Poe, "The Bells")

The ferns and fondling grass said "Stay,"
The dewberry dipped for to work delay,
And the little reeds sighed "Abide, abide."
(Sidney Lanier, "Song of the Chattahoochee")

4 Consciously vary the loudness and softness as indicated:

(soft) I hate you! (louder) You're lying!
(soft) I don't believe a word you say!
(louder) You're a liar and a cheat!
(soft) I've been honest with you, while you. . . .
(loud) I hate you! (louder) I wish I'd never seen you!
(soft) I'm going away.
(loud) I never want to see you again—never—never!
(soft) And this time I mean it!

(loud, addressing an army)
Once more unto the breach, dear friends, once more,
Or close the wall up with our English dead,
(softer) In peace, there's nothing so becomes a man
As modest stillness and humility; (build to very loud)
But when the blast of war blows in our ears,
Then imitate the action of the tiger; ...
                    (Shakespeare, *Henry V*, Act III, sc. 1)

Variety in Pitch

Intonation, used in a general sense, refers to the overall pattern of pitch. Some intonation pattern is inherent in almost all spoken languages. The Chinese use pitch to distinguish different meanings for the same word. Though pitch changes are not such an intrinsic part of the English language, they are important to give emphasis and significance to words. When correlated with variations in thought and feeling, pitch changes can suggest the most subtle shades of meaning and emotion.

When a person has pitch monotony the difficulty may be lack of range or lack of the ability to hear pitch variations. Training in hearing differences is essential for any aspect of voice improvement, but nowhere is it more necessary than in working with pitch. Pitch monotony may be due to a pattern—the repetition of inflection or some other recurring sameness. These faults must be heard before they can be corrected. To avoid monotony, you should be aware of three ways pitch variety can be used: (1) using different general levels from high to low, (2) using *steps* which are changes from one pitch to another, and (3) using *slides* which are inflections or movements of the voice up or down or up *and* down (rising, falling, and circumflex) within one phonation. We have already noted the role pitch plays in emphasis and in conveying the right meaning in inflectional endings. Exercises to extend the range above and below the optimum pitch and exercises using exaggerated steps and slides can help to eliminate pitch monotony and increase vocal flexibility and expressiveness.

EXERCISES FOR PITCH VARIETY

1   Practice the exercises for extending pitch range (Ex. 6, pp. 88–89).

2   In the following sentences speak the first clause on your highest pitch and the second on your lowest; reverse from low to high:

Glory be! I got a date!
Don't come near me, or you'll be sorry!
Get out of my way; you are crazy!
How nice she is, but I distrust her.
It's a beautiful day; let's go.

3   Practice for lively conversational steps and slides:

> I said I had the tree. It wasn't true.
> The opposite was true. The tree had me.
> The minute it was left with me alone
> It caught me up as if I were the fish
> And it the fishpole. So I was translated
> To loud cries from my brother of "Let go!
> Don't you know anything, you girl? Let go!"
>   (Robert Frost, "Wild Grapes")[1]

ORLANDO: Did you ever cure any so?

ROSALIND: Yes, one, and in this manner. He was to imagine me his love, his mistress, and I set him every day to woo me. At which time would I, being but a moonish youth, grieve, be effeminate, changeable, longing and liking, proud, fantastical, apish, shallow, inconstant, full of tears, full of smiles; for every passion something and for no passion truly anything. . . . And thus I cured him; and this way will I take upon me to wash your liver as clean as a sound sheep's heart, that there shall not be one spot of love in't.

                   (Shakespeare, *As You Like It,* Act III, sc. 2)

If you appear learned to an ignorant wench, or jocund to a sad, or witty to a foolish, why, she presently begins to mistrust herself. You must approach them in their own height, their own line; . . .

If she love wit, give verses, though you borrow them of a friend, or buy them, to have good. If valour, talk of your sword, and be frequent in the mention of quarrels, though you be staunch in fighting. . . . If she love good clothes or dressing, have your learned council about you every morning, your French tailor, barber, linener, etc. Let your powder, your glass, and your comb be your dearest acquaintance. Take more care for the ornament of your head, than the safety; and wish the commonwealth rather troubled, than a hair about you. That will take her. Then if she be covetous and craving, do you promise anything, and perform sparingly; so shall you keep her appetite still. Seem as you would give, but be like a barren field that yields little; . . . Let your gifts be slight and dainty, rather than precious. Let cunning be above cost.

                   (Ben Jonson, *The Silent Woman*)

4   Suggest characters by pitch levels and inflections:

> "You are old, Father William," the young man said,
>   "And your hair has become very white,
> And yet you incessantly stand on your head—
>   Do you think, at your age, it is right?"

[1] From *Complete Poems of Robert Frost.* Copyright 1923, 1928 by Holt, Rinehart and Winston, Inc. Copyright 1942, 1951, © 1956 by Robert Frost. Reprinted by permission of Holt, Rinehart and Winston, Inc.

"In my youth," Father William replied to his son,
   "I feared it might injure the brain;
And now that I'm perfectly sure that I have none,
   Why, I do it again and again."
                              (Lewis Carroll, *Alice in Wonderland*)

THE COUNTESS: Oh, I wish she hadn't brought up the Alps, Lucy. It always reminds me of that nasty moment I had the day Gustav made me climb to the top of one of them. . . . Anyhow, there we were. And suddenly it struck me that Gustav had pushed me. I slid halfway down the mountain before I realized that Gustav didn't love me any more. But love takes care of its own, Lucy. I slid right into the arms of my fourth husband, the Count.
                              (Clare Boothe Luce, *The Women*)[2]

. . . Lovely ladies, kind gentlemen:
Please to introduce myself.
Sakini by name.
Interpreter by profession.
Education by ancient dictionary.
Okinawan by whim of gods.
History of Okinawa reveal distinguished record of conquerors.
We have honor to be subjugated in fourteenth century by Chinese pirates.
In sixteenth century by English missionaries.
In eighteenth century by Japanese war lords.
And in twentieth century by American Marines.
Okinawa very fortunate.
Culture brought to us. . . . Not have to leave home for it.
Learn many things.
Most important that rest of world not like Okinawa.
World filled with delightful variation.
Illustration.
In Okinawa . . . no locks on doors.
Bad manners not to trust neighbors.
In America . . . lock and key big industry.
Conclusion?
Bad manners good business.
In Okinawa . . . wash self in public bath with nude lady quite proper.
Picture of nude lady in private home . . . quite improper.
In America . . . statue of nude lady in park win prize.
But nude lady in flesh in park win penalty.
Conclusion?
Pornography question of geography.
But Okinawans most eager to be educated by conquerors.

2 From *The Women,* by Clare Boothe Luce, Copyright 1937 and renewed 1964 by Clare Boothe Luce. Reprinted by permission of Random House, Inc.

Deep desire to improve friction.
Not easy to learn.
Sometimes painful.
But pain makes man think.
Thought makes man wise.
Wisdom makes life endurable.
So . . .
We tell little story to demonstrate splendid example of benevolent assimilation
of democracy of Okinawa.   (John Patrick, *Teahouse of the August Moon*)[3]

Variety in Quality

Since quality of tone is most closely associated with mood and feeling, it is
a subjective voice element that is difficult to teach directly. If an interpreter's voice is normal and his feelings are not overly restrained, he usually
uses appropriate quality change naturally and spontaneously.

Variety in quality is heard when different quality tones are used to suggest emotional states, character and age, and when a word is "touched" with
the quality to suggest its emotional meaning. By the quality of tone used,
you can make a word say just what you want it to say. If you touch a word
with a soft mellow tone, it will mean one thing—a harsh tone will make it
mean something else. Your ability to use variety in quality is dependent
upon your sensitivity to the feelings evident in an author's general tone
and specific words, and your control of resonance which can produce the
appropriate feeling tone at the right time.

EXERCISES FOR VARIETY IN QUALITY OF TONE

1   Color these contrasting words and phrases with the tone quality to sug-
    gest their meanings:

sour–sweet   hard–soft   evil–good   murder–love
cold–warm   war–peace   sad–happy   revenge–forgive

2   Use a variety of qualities to suggest characters:

The pompous old time politician (too much mouth and throat resonance):
    My friends, I come to you today to speak on a subject dear to the heart of
    every man, woman and child in this great land.

The sickly, nagging woman (nasal whiney quality):
    I said to him, I says, Will, I'm a sick woman and one of these days you're
    going to be sorry.

3 Reprinted by permission of G. P. Putnam's Sons. From *Teahouse of the August Moon*
by John Patrick. Copyright © 1952 by John Patrick.

The giant calling (guttural harsh quality):
Who's that tramping over my bridge?

A ghost (hollow quality):
I am the Ghost of Christmas Past. Rise and walk with me!

Bible narrator (rich full quality):
And the earth was without form, and void; and darkness was upon the face of the deep.

3   Use varying qualities of tone to suggest feelings:

CYRANO DE BERGERAC:
Ah, no young man, that is not enough! You might have said, dear me, there are a thousand things . . . varying the tone . . . For instance . . . here you are:—

AGGRESSIVE: "I, monsieur, if I had such a nose, nothing would serve but I must cut it off!" . . .

INQUISITIVE: "What may the office be of that oblong receptacle? Is it an inkhorn or a scissor-case?"

MINCING: "Do you so dote on birds, you have, fond as a father, been at pains to fit the little darlings with a roost?"

BLUNT: "Tell me, monsieur, you, when you smoke, is it possible you blow the vapor through your nose without a neighbor crying 'the chimney is afire?' " . . .

TENDER: "Have a little sun-shade made for it! It might get freckled!" . . .

DRAMATIC: "It is the Red Sea when it bleeds!" . . .

RUSTIC: "Hi, boys! Call that a nose? Ye don't gull me! It's either a prize carrot or else a stunted gourd!"

MILITARY: "Level against the cavalry!" . . .

And finally in parody of weeping Pyramus: "Behold, behold the nose that traitorously destroyed the beauty of its master! and is blushing for the same!"— That, my dear sir, or something not unlike it, is what you would have said to me, had you the smallest leaven of letters or of wit. . . .

(Edmond Rostand, *Cyrano de Bergerac*)[4]

Variety in Timing

Timing involves two elements, duration and pause. The way these two elements are combined and varied to form rhythm patterns and to convey subtle meanings is one of the surest ways to keep the meaning of the whole selection alive and interesting.

Duration of tones (also known as quantity) refers to the length of time individual speech sounds are held or prolonged. Prolongation of sounds

---

[4] From *Cyrano de Bergerac* by Edmond Rostand, Mrs. Gertrude Hall Brownell, trans.; Doubleday & Company, Inc., publisher. By permission of the publishers.

within words and syllables is an effective way to emphasize and to bring out the lyrical qualities of the language. Prolonging the sounds along with "quality touch" may also aid in suggesting emotional states. Variety can be obtained by short duration, cutting a word off short, giving it a staccato effect; but too much long *or* short duration is monotonous.

The use of pause in grouping and as a means of emphasis has already been pointed. The interpreter should remember that if too many words are emphasized with pause, this becomes an obvious device. There are other means of emphasizing; various means should be used, pause among them. But, certainly, pause can be one of the most effective ways to point emotional meanings—dramatic and comic. Listen to a comedian and notice how he uses silences. A sudden pause may catch attention, highlight the humor, add suspense or dramatic intensity; but, the pause should be motivated by the idea or emotion and never call attention as a device.

The general rate or tempo is dependent upon control of duration and pause. If a person reads too rapidly, he can correct this by the conscious use of lengthening the duration of words and by pause. If he reads too slowly, he can become aware of shortening the pauses and duration and avoiding meaningless hesitation in his speech.

The interpreter should be sensitive to the general rate most appropriate for a character's utterance or for the dominant mood of a selection. The personality of the character he is interpreting or the nature of the selection being read is a determining influence on general rate. A slow rate is associated with a heavy or melancholy mood; a rapid rate is generally more appropriate for a light or happy mood. But general rate must be varied. Changes of mood within a selection call for changes in rate. To meet these demands you should develop the ability to read at a variety of speeds. One of the most important controls is developing the ability to read rapidly with clear articulation.

EXERCISES FOR VARIETY IN TIMING

1   Read aloud comparing the appropriate general rate for each of the following:

Character lines (politician, nagging woman, and so forth, p. 111)
King Henry's speech (p. 108)
Sakini's speech (p. 110)
Cyrano's speech (p. 112)

2   Notice how, in the following two stanzas, the author controls timing, Read the first stanza to suggest the brook's rapid movement downhill; in the second stanza suggest the slowing of the water as it reaches the meadow:

> Out of the hills of Habersham,
> Down the valleys of Hall,
> I hurry amain to reach the plain,
> Run the rapid and leap the fall, . . .
>
> The rushes cried "Abide, abide,"
> The willful waterweeds held me thrall,
> The loving laurel turned my tide,
> The fern and fondling grass said "Stay,"
> The dewberry dipped for to work delay,
> And the little reeds sighed "Abide, abide," . . .
>
> (Sidney Lanier, "Song of the Chattahoochee")

3   Practice material for the pause:

Pause to reflect, varying the "thinking" pauses as indicated:

> Let me see now, // she was in my class. // I can remember her roommate // and where they lived. // Yes. // I can see their room. /// But what was her name? ///

Pause for suspense:

> I was a low, / dull, / quick sound. /// I scarcely breathed. ///

Pause to point humor:

> By the time you swear you're his /
> Shivering and // sighing /
> And he vows his passion is
> Infinite // undying //
> Lady, / make a note of this ///
> One of you is lying.
>
> (Dorothy Parker, "Unfortunate Coincidence")[5]

Pause for transitions:

> She was silent, but she knew the end had come.
>
> * * * * *
>
> A week or so later . . .

4   Practice material for duration:

Read words in sentences with prolonged or staccato duration:

> The sea is sad and calm; the stars are tarnished silver.
> Get out of here and don't ever come back!
> You're a different people—a whole different kind of people.
> Excited? Who's excited?

[5] From *The Portable Dorothy Parker* by Dorothy Parker. Copyright 1926, 1954 by Dorothy Parker. Reprinted by permission of The Viking Press, Inc.

7 TECHNIQUES FOR
BODY CONTROL

Aesthetic principles of good taste and appropriateness of "style" are of particular importance in regard to the use of the body in oral interpretation. Though the modern interpreter is strongly influenced by the "natural" use of the body, which is the mode of our times, he finds that his oral style is also affected by the literary style of the material at hand—and rightly so.

For a general philosophy regarding oral style (voice and body) we must bow to the culturally accepted mode of the times. The accepted mode of communication in our modern times is realism: be natural, conversational, and underplay the emotion. When the modern writer adheres to this same philosophy, his literary text seems to call for a "natural" mode of oral communication. And though we may regret the modern actor's vocal mumblings and bodily distortions, we must admit that there is a sense of rightness between the modern playwright's mode of writing and this expression of it. In any oral communication the body should aid in expressing the style and tone of the writing. To realize the extremes in the tone of literary texts, we need only to contrast the bigger-than-life characters in a Greek tragedy with the weak, disillusioned characters we find in the modern realistic play. Obviously, a communication of such varied literary tones would find expression in the body stance and body rhythms of either the actor who is playing the roles or an oral interpreter who is suggesting the roles. The actor creating a role and the oral interpreter recreating the roles must see the literary text in its historical environment and give appropriate expression to the inherent cultural attitudes through his body expression.

Other aesthetic principles to serve the oral reader in regard to the control of body expression may be summarized in this statement:

Body techniques should not be obvious; posture, movements, and gestures should seem effortless, as though they resulted only from a spontaneous response to the meaning of the material.

A close relationship exists between body response, vocal response, and the mind: what one sees has a direct influence on what one hears, and both reflect the reader's inner state of mind. If a reader is self-conscious, his body may reflect his self-consciousness in nervous physical mannerisms or in a lifeless slump while his voice trembles or lacks carrying power and variety. If he is confident in attitude, both his voice and body are likely to be under control and alive with energy. To bring about a response where the mind, voice, and body work in harmony, the interpreter must overcome his feeling of insecurity and train his body, as he trains his voice, to be capable of responding effectively to the attitudes expressed in literature. Specific possibilities for improving body expression can be stated, but such statements should be regarded only as guides.

The oral interpreter should give attention to three aspects of his physical response: (1) the rapport he establishes with his audience by means of general poise, (2) his use of audience contact, and (3) his physical reaction to his material evident in overt and covert action.

POISE

Poise is a synthesis of many things; it is acquired through good mental attitude, physical balance, and the right degree of muscle tone in the body.

Mental Attitude

Before he speaks a word, an oral reader's appearance and attitude of mind influence an audience. A good first impression may be gained by very simple means. First, the reader should give attention to neatness and good taste in dress. This will not only make a favorable impression on the audience, but it will make him feel more at ease. Appearance can affect one's mental attitude. Second, the reader should consider his attitude toward the audience. What is he thinking as he faces an audience? A sincere interest in them, a pleasant expression, and an attitude of "Let's enjoy this together" can control his fears and convey a good impression.

Nothing contributes more to inner calm than good preparation. In most cases careful preparation will eliminate concerns of self and enable the interpreter to keep his mind focused on the ideas and feelings within the material as he reads. Sometimes experience is all that is needed for gaining confidence. If a student reader resists the impulse to express dissatisfactions with a performance in the form of facial distortions or apologetic comments, he will gradually gain confidence in his own ability. He will find, too, that the familiar "nothing succeeds like success" works; one successful performance before an audience and he is off with new confidence.

Psychophysical exercises can sharpen an awareness of the interplay between the mind and body. Michael Chekhov in his book *To The Actor* offers concrete help to the actor for using his body to express creative ideas. Some of the exercises are applicable for the oral interpreter. As a reader faces an audience the idea of receiving from them, of drawing them to him through an inner power of mind, can be helpful in establishing good rapport with an audience. Exercises for freeing the body and for sensing a "radiating center" can be helpful in gaining poise and "presence."[1]

Physical Balance

Good posture with correct physical balance may be sufficiently controlled by the right mental attitude, but this is not always the case. Poor posture habits and personal mannerisms sometimes persist and have to be brought under control by direct means. A bad habit must first be recognized and then gradually eliminated through conscious attention in practice periods.

Good posture is when the body is in a state of balance, each part (head, shoulders, torso, legs, and feet) in alignment and balanced one over the other. There are no set rules; the best posture is one that does not draw attention and that allows the body to respond easily to the thought. The body should appear relaxed, but there should be enough muscle tension to give a feel and a look of aliveness. Here are a few statements that are generally helpful in establishing posture habits:

> Stand tall, to full height, with head up (not forward or back) and easily balanced. Do not pull the shoulders back; this causes the head to come forward and the body to be tense. Feel that the shoulders are balanced easily on top of the spine and that the spine is straight.
>
> The weight of the body may be balanced on both feet with the weight centered on the balls (weight on the heels gives the impression of withdrawal); or the weight may be chiefly on the ball of a forward foot with the other foot helping to maintain a good balance. Find the position that is most comfortable for you and, at the same time, is neither careless nor too rigidly set. You should feel that the feet give secure support for the body weight.
>
> The reading stand invites a leaning posture; avoid this. Use the stand "lightly." If you stand too close to it, you give the impression of inse-

---

[1] Michael Chekhov, *To The Actor* (New York: Harper & Brothers, 1953). The exercises suggested can be found on pp. 6–8 in Chekhov's book.

curity; if you stand too far away from it with your hands behind your back, you give an audience the uncomfortable feeling that you may lose your place. When the hands rest lightly on the stand and the body is in a free balanced position that permits change, you and your audience will be much more comfortable. A reading stand is never a barrier if you use it easily.

Muscle Tone

The body "talks" by slight changes in muscle tone: we can sense a person's anger or fear by the degree of tension in his body; we can sense when a person is in a quiet, peaceful frame of mind by the degree of relaxation in his body. Without visible movement, one's body takes on a quality that suggests the emotional state. There is no overt movement, but the change that takes place in the muscles is felt, and the feeling is projected to others.

An oral reader's general poise will be bad if his muscle tone is deficient or excessive: if deficient, his body will suggest laziness or dullness; if excessive, it will suggest fear and self-consciousness. A vital, interested attitude of mind is the best means to bring about a spontaneous degree of muscle tension that carries the meaning of aliveness and poise.

EXERCISES FOR GAINING POISE

1   This exercise is for body relaxation and body alignment. Standing, gradually tense the larger muscles of the body, and then, beginning with the head, relax each part of the body completely until you feel limp, with the upper part of the body hanging. Gradually come to an upright position. Beginning at the base of the spine, try to feel that the spine straightens, and as the body lifts, feel the shoulders resting easily on top of the spine and the head balancing easily on top of the shoulders.

2   This "psychophysical" exercise should help you sense good balance and a degree of muscle tonus to suggest aliveness and "presence."

Imagine vitality coming up from the earth into the *feet*. Feel the energy centering in the balls of the feet. Let this energy make you feel confident and in command. Now imagine these "balls" of energy traveling up the body vitalizing the legs and uniting in the chest. Feel an expansion in the torso and feel that this ball of energy controls the body.

AUDIENCE CONTACT

The oral reader has a special eye problem. He must look at a script and still maintain eye contact with an audience. The solution to this is to be familiar with the material and to learn to read extended phrases at a glance, looking at the script for the next phrase while talking instead of during a pause. In some cases a reader may find it advantageous to have parts of the material memorized. However, if this is done, he should not lose complete contact with the script.

Clues in the material help determine an appropriate degree of eye contact with the audience. Generally speaking, when straight expository prose is read to an audience eye contact should be direct. The eyes do more than any other single feature to establish communication with listeners. When a selection calls for direct contact, the reader should look at individuals. Of course, this does not mean that he attempts to look at each individual in the group. Looking at a few individuals in different areas gives the impression that he is sharing the ideas with each listener. When the oral interpreter visualizes the details of descriptive passages, his eyes move naturally to an area in front of him. When reading reflective or personal material, both the reader and his listeners feel more comfortable if his eye contact is less direct. When a character or characters speak, the reader withdraws from the audience even more. The amount of direct involvement of the audience in the material should be the interpreter's guide, and this is decided when the selection is analyzed.

PHYSICAL REACTION TO MATERIAL

Overt Action

As has been indicated, the amount of visible, overt action (movement and gesture) to use while reading aloud is a matter of taste. No manner of physical action is best for every occasion, for every audience, for every reader every time. There are occasions when the use of movement and gestures is more appropriate than at others; one reader may use broad gestures and somehow stay within the bounds of good taste while another reader, using the same gestures, appears ridiculous. One person may use overt action and be effective; another may use no visible action and be equally effective. Our modern trend away from any display is good; but the fear of overdoing or of moving into the acting area tends to discourage any physical movement or gesture on the interpreter's part, and this is not good. Since oral interpretation is a suggestive art, we agree that it is better to use too little than too much overt action, but this does not mean that appropriate movement and gestures are not to be encouraged. Physical response is a must for the interpreter, and it can be used with as much subtlety and variety as vocal response. But how does one use overt action and stay within the restrictions of modern taste and the restrictions of the suggestive realm?

First, the reading situation itself imposes certain restrictions on the amount of overt movement the interpreter can use; a reading stand and a script are limiting factors. Staying within the suggestive realm also imposes limitations. Physical responses in oral interpretation differ from those used in acting. An actor lets us see an action in full; an interpreter only suggests an action by appropriate small movements or gestures. Suppose a character in a play performs the actions of drinking a toast at a dinner party. In the play, the actor would perform the full action with an actual glass. An interpreter, in the reading situation, would not have a glass, nor would he pantomime the full action of lifting the glass, drinking, and lowering the glass. How would he suggest the action? As he *imagines* the glass and the action of lifting it, he might raise one hand slightly, perhaps no more than two inches off the reading stand. With the hand in this position, he would read the toast; then with another slight upward movement of the hand, he would pause, imagining the actual drinking action, and then lower the hand to the stand. With these small movements and facial response, the audience would join the interpreter in envisioning the full action.

The language of the body is as wide as that of speech; every visible part of the body is a means of gesture. For the interpreter, the face and eyes are, perhaps, most important; but the hands, fingers, shoulders, feet—each part, in countless ways and combinations, is capable of expressing the most subtle and varied meanings. Though the oral interpreter is limited in the use of large overt movement and gesture, he has countless ways of using small overt actions to help convey the meanings and feelings within a piece of literature. Then he has covert action.

Covert Action

Covert action is simply a change in the muscle tone of the body. We said earlier that the well-poised body should have the right degree of muscle tension to convey an impression of alertness and poise. In reading literature aloud, the interpreter finds that the material motivates changes in his muscle tension. Changes in attitude and emotions, within a selection, call for a change in the body tensions; anger calls for a tightening of the muscles; love calls for a relaxing of the muscles. This is of special value to the interpreter because it is an effective means of suggesting. In the example of the reader suggesting the actions of drinking a toast at a dinner party, specific small overt actions were described as a means of indicating the full action. But these small gestures would naturally be accompanied by appropriate changes in body tone, covert actions.

EXERCISES FOR OVERT AND COVERT ACTIONS

1   In this exercise recall an emotional experience and let your body muscles respond completely. Be sure that the mental response comes first, motivating the change in muscle tone. In each recall concentrate on remembering the details and the atmosphere created by your experience.

    Recall an experience that made you feel very angry, afraid, happy and elated, determined, sympathetic, and so forth.

2   In this exercise you are to try to sense the difference in performing a specific action and in suggesting it.

a   As you say the action words (italicized) perform the action:

I am *turning around and around.*
I am *pulling you up from your seat.*
I am *trying to lift this table.*
I am *lifting this book.*

b   Repeat the sentences using only small gestures and covert action to suggest the actions.

3   Read the following passages aloud responding to the imagery and emotions with varying degrees of covert and overt action.

a   Respond to the vital exuberance of a young man who has suddenly discovered the meaning of life—his life.

His heart trembled; his breath came faster and a wild spirit passed over his limbs as though he were soaring sunward. His heart trembled in an ecstasy of fear and his soul was in flight. . . .
. . . His throat ached with a desire to cry aloud, the cry of a hawk or eagle on high, to cry piercingly of his deliverance to the winds.

                  (James Joyce, *A Portrait of the Artist as a Young Man*)[2]

b   Respond to the varied images of "Circus at Dawn."

. . . The great iron-grey horses, four and six to a team, would be plodding along the road of thick white dust to a rattling of chains and traces and the harsh cries of their drivers. The men would drive the animals to the river which flowed by beyond the tracks, and water them; and as first light came one could see the elephants wallowing in the familiar river and the big horses going slowly and carefully down to drink.

    Then, on the circus ground, the tents were going up already with the magic

[2] From *A Portrait of the Artist as a Young Man* by James Joyce. Copyright 1916 by B. W. Huebsch, Inc., 1944 by Nora Joyce. Reprinted by permission of The Viking Press, Inc.

speed of dreams. All over the place (which was near the tracks and the only space of flat land in the town that was big enough to hold a circus) there would be this fierce, savagely hurried, and yet orderly confusion. Great flares of gaseous circus light would blaze down on the seared and battered faces of the circus toughs as, with the rhythmic precision of a single animal—a human riveting machine—they swung their sledges at the stakes, driving a stake into the earth with the incredible instancy of accelerated figures in a motion picture. And everywhere, as light came, and the sun appeared, there would be a scene of magic, order, and of violence.   (Thomas Wolfe, "Circus at Dawn")[3]

4 Read one of the following passages aloud giving attention to appropriate overt gestures:

a "The Nose Speech" from *Cyrano de Bergerac* on p. 112.

b In this passage from *The Merchant of Venice* (Act I, sc. 3), Portia and her waiting-woman, Nerissa, speak. Portia is describing her suitors and how she feels toward each of them.

NERISSA: First there is the Neapolitan prince.
PORTIA: Ay, that's a colt indeed, for he doth nothing but talk of his horse; and he makes it a great appropriation to his own good parts, that he can shoe him himself. I am afeard my lady his mother played false with a smith.
NERISSA: Then is there the County Palatine.
PORTIA: He doth nothing but frown, as who should say, 'If you will not have me, choose.' He hears merry tales and smiles not: I fear he will prove the weeping philosopher when he grows old, being so full of unmannerly sadness in his youth. I had rather be married to a death's-head with a bone in his mouth than to either of these. God defend me from these two! . . .
NERISSA: What say you, then, to Falconbridge, the young baron of England?
PORTIA: . . . He is a proper man's picture, but, alas, who can converse with a dumbshow? How oddly he is suited! I think he bought his doublet in Italy, his round hose in France, his bonnet in Germany, and his behaviour everywhere.

5 Reveal the full actions described in these passages with covert and overt action appropriate in reading aloud.

a Juliet, in Act IV, sc. 2, of *Romeo and Juliet,* picks up a vial and a dagger:

> . . . My dismal scene I needs must act alone.
> Come vial,
> What if this mixture do not work at all?
> Shall I be married then to-morrow morning?—
> No, no; this shall forbid it. Lie thou there.

---

[3] Reprinted with the permission of Charles Scribner's Sons from *From Death To Morning* (Copyright 1935 Charles Scribner's Sons; renewal copyright © 1963 Paul Gitlin).

b   Othello takes Iago by the throat (*Othello,* Act III, sc. 3):

> Villain, be sure thou prove my love a whore,
>   (taking him by the throat)
> Or, by the worth of mine eternal soul,
> Thou hadst been better have been born a dog
> Than answer my wak'd wrath!

c   Read from the play *The Glass Menagerie* (p. 182) Jim's speech beginning: "You think I'm making this up because I'm invited to dinner. . . ." through "Would you care for a mint?" Suggest the gentleman caller's actions through vocal pause, muscle-tone change, and small gestures.

6   Select two of the following passages and suggest each character by appropriate posture, movement, and gesture. Use a reading stand.

a   In John Steinbeck's novel *Sweet Thursday* a middle-aged woman gives advice to a younger girl:

If I was your age with your face and shape and what I know, there wouldn't be no man in the world could get away! I got the know-how—but that's all I got. Oh well! I'm going to tell you a few thousand things, Suzy, that if you would listen you'd get anything you want. But hell, you won't listen! Nobody listens, and when they learn the hard way it's too late. . . . just remember a lot of things: first, you got to remember you're Suzy and you ain't nobody else but Suzy. Then you got to remember that Suzy is a good thing—a real valuable thing—and there ain't nothing like it in the world. It don't do no harm just to say that to yourself. Then, when you got that, remember that there's one hell of a lot Suzy don't know. Only way she can find out is if she sees it, or reads it, or asks it. Most people don't look at nothing but themselves, and that's a rat race.[4]

b   Katharine in *Taming of the Shrew* (Act III, sc. 2) storms at Petruchio:

> Nay, then,
> Do what thou canst, I will not go to-day;
> No, nor tomorrow, nor till I please myself.
> The door is open, sir; there lies your way.

c   In Thomas Wolfe's novel *Of Time and the River* Uncle Bascom gives his view of woman's never changing character:

He paused, stared deliberately across his hands, and in a moment repeated, slowly and distinctly: "The woman gave me of the tree and I did eat. Ah! that's it! There my boy, you have it! There, in a nutshell, you have the work for which they are best fitted." And he turned upon his nephew suddenly with a blaze of passion, his voice husky and tremulous from the stress of emotion. "The

---

[4] From *Sweet Thursday* by John Steinbeck. Copyright 1954 by John Steinbeck. Reprinted by permission of The Viking Press, Inc.

Tempter! The Bringer of Forbidden Fruit! The devil's ambassador! Since the beginning of time that has been their office—to madden the brain, to turn man's spirit from its highest purposes, to corrupt, to seduce, and to destroy! To creep and crawl, to intrude into the lonely places of man's heart and brain, to wind herself into the core of his most secret life as a worm eats its way into a healthy fruit—to do all this with the guile of a serpent, the cunning of a fox—that, my boy, is what she's here for . . . . and she'll never change!" and, lowering his voice to an ominous and foreboding whisper, he said mysteriously, "Beware! Beware! Do not be deceived!"[5]

d   In Dostoyevsky's *Notes from Underground* a man of early middle age, a former civil servant, has gone underground. From his hole he speaks a monologue of self-loathing to an imaginary audience:

I am a sick man. I am a spiteful man. I am an unattractive man: I believe my liver is diseased. However, I know nothing at all about my disease and do not know for certain what ails me. I don't consult a doctor for it, and never have, though I have a respect for medicine and doctors. Besides, I am extremely superstitious, sufficiently so to respect medicine, at any rate (I am well-educated enough not to be superstitious, even though I am). No, I refuse to consult a doctor out of spite. That is something you probably will not understand. Well, I do. Of course, I can't explain whom precisely I am mortifying in this case by my spite: I am perfectly aware that I cannot "get even" with the doctors by not consulting them; I know better than anyone that by all this I am only injuring myself and no one else. But still, if I don't consult a doctor it is out of spite. My liver is bad, well—let it get worse![6]

e   In Eugene O'Neill's play *Long Day's Journey into Night,* Mary Tyrone, the wife and mother, is a dope addict. In this scene she has been playing the piano; she examines her hands as she wanders in.

I play so badly now. I'm all out of practice. Sister Theresa will give me a dreadful scolding. She'll tell me it isn't fair to my father when he spends so much money for extra lessons. She's quite right, it isn't fair, when he's so good and generous, and so proud of me. I'll practice every day from now on. But something horrible has happened to my hands. The fingers have gotten so stiff. The knuckles are all swollen. They're so ugly. . . . Let me see. What did I come here to find? . . . I'm always dreaming and forgetting.[7]

---

[5] Reprinted with the permission of Charles Scribner's Sons from *Of Time and the River* (Copyright 1935 Charles Scribner's Sons; renewal copyright © 1963 Paul Gitlin) by Thomas Wolfe.

[6] From *A Treasury of Russian Literature* edited by Bernard G. Guerney. Copyright, 1943 by Vanguard Press, Inc. Reprinted by permission of Vanguard Press, Inc.

[7] Reprinted by permission of Carlotta Monterey O'Neill and Yale University Press from *Long Day's Journey into Night,* by Eugene O'Neill. Copyright 1955 by Carlotta Monterey O'Neill.

8 TECHNIQUES FOR PSYCHOLOGICAL CONTROL

The basis of the psychological approach to oral interpretation is that a person's own psychology—his thinking, affected by his own actual and vicarious experience—can be used to both understand and to recreate another's experience in literature. In analyzing material for oral reading the interpreter may use his own experience to become more personally involved in the author's experience; when reading the material aloud, he may use his "inner resources" to stimulate emotional expressiveness and effective vocal and body responses.

This approach was discussed in relation to analyzing material, and it was put to use in the exercises for body control. This chapter will be concerned with further clarification through a discussion of three specific recreative aids: imagination, identification, and concentration. These are skills that can be developed through understanding and application. We will explain how these creative faculties relate to each other and how they may be used in oral interpretation.

IMAGINATION AND IDENTIFICATION

In oral interpretation the use of imagination involves the act of forming a mental image of something not present to the senses. We see things in our "mind's eye"; we hear sounds in our "mind's ear"; we imagine smell, taste, touch, and movement through sense thinking or sensory recall.

People vary in their ability to use imagination. As children we start off with a good amount, but it is usually dulled along the way. Watch a child at play; he is in dead earnest; he believes he is a policeman and a certain tree the culprit. For a moment he creates a magic spell, and at the same time he knows that this is only "play-like." Both the actor and the oral interpreter create illusions. If a reader can use his imagination by calling up images as he reads, he has one of the most usable and valuable reading techniques; if he cannot do this successfully, the ability can be cultivated.

Identification is the means by which we use our own experiences to relate to the experiences the author has written about. For example, have you ever entered a small-town bus station at a late hour when only a few sleepy travelers, tired waitresses, and idle noise seekers remained and suddenly become aware of the sounds and of the visual details of this American scene? If so, the remembered experience could be useful in relating to the following passage:

> "You can do ennythang, but keep offa mah blue suede shoes!" shouts the man in the jukebox. "You can burn down mah house, you can steal mah cah, you can drink mah lickah fum a ole fruit jah!"
>
> It is a song: he shouts it from a tight, excited throat against the frantic drumming of the rural guitars. The hidden record spinning in the bloated, winking jukebox blasts the walls of the bus station cafe, walls and ceiling shiny with old white enamel and the congealed grease given off by a million hamburgers; the sound bursts along the counters and booms and rattles in the glass cases of dead pie slices, crusted cake segments and soggy, oily sweet rolls.[1]

When recalling such a scene from your experience, you should not try to remember how you felt at the time; instead, you should activate your memory by asking questions regarding the details: Who was with me? Was it a cold night? How many people were there? What were they doing? In this way it is possible to bring the past experience back into your consciousness and to arouse an attitude toward the scene comparable to the attitude the author expresses in the selection.

CONCENTRATION

The dictionary defines concentration as "the act or process of directing attention on a single object." Concentration is a powerful force and discipline. We sense this power in a period of concentrated study, in a speaker when he forgets himself and is intent on an idea, in an actor when he concentrates on the thoughts of the character, and in a reader when he is able to concentrate on the thoughts of an author, narrator, or character. Concentration brings a kind of selflessness; it makes the genius.

---

[1] From *My Escape from the C. I. A.* by Hughes Rudd (New York: E. P. Dutton & Co. Inc., 1966). Reprinted by permission of the publisher.

The ability to concentrate comes partly through an innate talent and partly through developing the skill. To develop the skill a person should first of all learn to relax. Lee Strasberg, the renowned teacher and director of Actor's Studio, asks his students to relax physically and then to concentrate on relaxing three specific areas for *mental* relaxation. Through experience, Mr. Strasberg has discovered that these three areas are "indicators of mental tensions":

> After he is physically relaxed, he then goes through these three areas. He tries to relax the temple area. Then he tries to relax the eyes. Finally he tries to relax the whole mouth area so that the tension is as much as possible reduced.[2]

How does one concentrate? First try a simple exercise of concentration not involving the emotions. Pick out a definite object in the room and concentrate on this. Suppose you take a classroom chair. To force your mind to stay focused on this concrete object, ask questions and find answers to your questions. Try something like this, orally and silently:

> How many wooden parts does this chair have? Well . . . there is the seat, and there is the back, and the arm—three. What about the height? I'd say the seat is about 18 inches from the floor and the back another 18 inches. What about the legs? . . . and so on.

This exercise points two fundamental guides for concentration:

1 Find concrete objects on which to concentrate.

2 Focus on details that concern the object to keep the concentration going.

When we read literature aloud, where do we concentrate?

Concentration on Physical Objects

At times you must "suggest" the presence of physical objects. For example, in reading Juliet's lines in the vial scene, you should, on one level, concentrate on the vial of poison. To make this possible, concentrate for a time on the object by asking questions and finding answers:

> How large is this vial? What could I compare it to? How heavy is it? How much liquid does it hold? What color is the liquid? . . .

So you become more aware of the object, and when you read the line, "Come vial," you can imagine the actual object—the feel of it in your hand.

---

2 From *Strasberg at the Actor's Studio* by Lee Strasberg and Robert H. Hethmon. Copyright © 1965 by Lee Strasberg and Robert H. Hethmon. Reprinted by permission of The Viking Press, Inc.

Concentration on an Author's Idea

When you read factual material or interruptions of factual information within a narrative, your concentration is chiefly on the idea. Let's take a specific example to illustrate. This paragraph is from Mark Twain's "Six-fingered Pete and Other Killers."[3]

> In Nevada, for a time, the lawyer, the doctor, the banker, the chief desperado, the chief gambler, the saloon-keeper, occupied the same level in society, and it was the highest. The cheapest and easiest way to become an influential man and to be looked up to by the community at large, was to stand behind a bar, wear a clustered diamond pin, and sell whiskey. I am not sure but that the saloon-keeper held a shade higher rank than any other member of society.

Here there is no physical object on which to concentrate. What can you find that is concrete? The *idea*, which is what you want to focus, is formed by the author's use of words; words form a design to make the idea complete. Try concentrating on how Mark Twain uses words to form the thought. Ask, as Mark Twain's spokesman, "What do I do with the words to convey this idea?" You might answer: "First, I make a statement of comparison, and then I state specific benefits and picture the saloon keeper. Finally I make a restatement." As a result of concentration on the design of an idea you may more successfully convey the idea.

Concentration on Reflective Thoughts

In reading lyric poetry or inner monologues within selections of prose and poetry, you concentrate on the speaker's reflective thoughts. Concentration on the design of the words would not help here; it is the emotional response to the thoughts that is important. Here your ability to use your imagination and to identify a personal experience with the author's would serve you well.

The speaker's emotional response in the lyric "A Deep-Sworn Vow" results from reflective thoughts concerning a past love affair. Perhaps you have had no such experience, but you have had an emotional reaction of some kind resulting from a relationship with another person which could serve. Asking questions in order to recall the details of your experience would help to arouse the emotion that you felt in the past. After this relating you should be more successful in projecting the author's emotional response.

---

3 From *Roughing It* by Mark Twain.

Concentration on Imagery

In reading a descriptive passage such as Thomas Wolfe's "Circus at Dawn" (p. 121), your concentration would be on the imagery, the sensory experience. Here, too, you should try to find an experience which you can relate to the scene described. You may not have witnessed the movement of a circus train, but at some time, in all probability, you have viewed a scene with a sense of wonder and excitement. It is the attitude toward the scene that is important to recapture through relating.

Concentration on the Desire of a Character

Similar emotional desires from your own life experience can be found to relate to a character's desire. If you were reading "The Laboratory," you might think your experiences far removed from this character's desire to murder her rival. In his book, *Acting: The First Six Lessons,* Richard Boleslavsky gives the classic example to illustrate how seemingly unrelated experiences may be related through imaginative thinking. (The creature is the pupil; the "I" is the teacher.)

> CREATURE: All right suppose I have to play a murderer. I have never murdered anybody. How shall I find it?
>
> "I": Oh, why do actors always ask me about murder? The younger they are the more intense they want to act. All right, you have never murdered anybody. Have you ever camped?
>
> CREATURE: Yes.
>
> "I": Were there any mosquitoes around?
>
> CREATURE: It was in New Jersey.
>
> "I": Did they annoy you? Did you follow one among them with your eyes and ears and hate until the beast landed on your forearm? And did you slap your forearm cruelly without thinking of the hurt to yourself—with only the wish to . . .
>
> CREATURE: To kill the beast.
>
> "I": There you are. A good sensitive artist doesn't need any more than that to play Othello in Desdemona's final scene. The rest is the work of magnification, imagination and belief.[4]

Notice here that the teacher does not ask the pupil to remember the hate she felt; instead, he asks her to remember how she followed the mosquito with her eyes until it landed and how she slapped it. In remembering what she *did* when she had a desire to kill the mosquito, she arouses an emotion of hate which she can use to relate to a character's desire to murder.

4 *Acting: The First Six Lessons:* Copyright 1949 by Norma Boleslavsky. Reprinted by permission of Theatre Arts Books.

Concentration on Multiple Levels

In the sleepwalking scene Lady Macbeth's concentration is on her hands and on her desire to be free of her guilt. Juliet's concentration in the vial scene shifts from her desire to escape an arranged marriage to her fearful thoughts of the tomb to two physical objects, the vial and the dagger. In the mother's lines from *Long Day's Journey into Night* (p. 124), Mary Tyrone's concentration is vague and shifting. In her drugged state her mind shifts quickly between her hands, the desires of her youth, and her desire to remember why she came into the room.

EXERCISES FOR CONCENTRATION, IMAGINATION, AND IDENTIFICATION

1   Take an exercise to become physically relaxed and then, with the body in a relaxed position, concentrate on relaxing (1) the temples, (2) the nose bridge and eyes, (3) the mouth area.

2   The purpose here is to develop your power to concentrate in the presence of distractions.

    a   Using expository material, test your power to concentrate on the ideas you are reading while members of the class interrupt and deliberately try to distract you. Stop when the instructor signals and explain what you have been reading.

    b   Sing or speak the words of a song you know well, concentrating on gaining the attention of individuals in the audience. Do not let the boos and laughs disturb you.

3   Practice and test your concentration on concrete objects and ideas:

    a   Pick out a concrete object in the room and concentrate on this by asking and answering questions in regard to the details of the object.

    b   Concentrate on the idea of the author by finding what you do with the words to form the idea:

Mass hysteria is a terrible force, yet New Yorkers seem always to escape it by some tiny margin: they sit in stalled subways without claustrophobia, they extricate themselves from frantic situations by some lucky wisecrack, they meet confusion and congestion with patience and grit—a sort of perpetual muddling through. Every facility is inadequate—the hospitals and schools and playgrounds are overcrowded, the express highways are feverish, the unimproved highways and bridges are bottlenecks; there is not enough air and not enough light, and there is usually too much heat or too little. But the city makes up for its hazards and its deficiencies by supplying its citizens with massive doses of a supplementary vitamin—the sense of belonging to something unique, cosmopolitan, mighty, and unparalleled.[5]

4 In this exercise check on your power to summon up images.

   a Open a book and let a word suggest an image. Concentrate on seeing the details. If you use sensory recall, bring the experience to mind by asking questions.

   b Try to hear in your mind's ear the sound of a train whistle, a jazz band, a symphony orchestra, a strange sound outside the house at night.

   c Recall the taste of a lemon, of tooth paste, of pumpkin pie.

   d Recall the smell of coffee, of burning leaves, of a fish market.

   e Recall the feel of fur, of a hand touching yours, of snow, of cool grass under your feet, of hot sand under your feet.

5 In this exercise, try to remember the details of certain actions you have performed in the past; act them out without words.

   a Pour a cup of coffee and drink it as you do in the morning.

   b Wash your hands or take a shower; feel the soap and the hot and cold water.

   c Feel a sharp pain in your body.

6 Read aloud the following selections of prose and poetry. Use your imagination to conjure up images.

   a See the pictures:

SEVEN AGES OF MAN

All the world's a stage,
And all the men and women merely players:
They have their exits and their entrances
And one man in his time plays many parts
His acts being seven ages. At first the infant,
Mewling and puking in the nurse's arms.
And then the whining schoolboy, with his satchel,
And shining morning face, creeping like snail
Unwillingly to school. And then the lover,
Sighing like furnace, with a woeful ballad
Made to his mistress eyebrow. Then a soldier,
Full of strange oaths, and bearded like the pard,
Jealous in honour, sudden and quick in quarrel,

5 From *Here Is New York* by E. B. White (Harper & Row, 1949). Reprinted by permission of the publishers.

Seeking the bubble reputation
Even in the cannon's mouth. And then the justice,
In fair round belly with good capon lin'd,
With eyes severe, and beard of normal cut
Full of wise saws and modern instances;
And so he plays his part. The sixth age shifts
Into the lean and slipper'd pantaloon,
With spectacles on nose and pouch on side,
His youthful hose well saved, a world too wide
For his shrunk shank; and his big manly voice,
Turning again towards childish treble, pipes
And whistles in his sounds. Last scene of all,
That ends this strange eventful history,
Is second childishness and mere oblivion,
Sans teeth, sans eyes, sans taste, sans everything.
(Shakespeare, *As You Like It,* Act II, sc. 7)

b   Sense taste and smell:

THE AMERICAN ICEBOX[6]

Thomas Wolfe

I think—now let me see—h'm, now!—well, perhaps I'll have a slice or two of
that pink Austrian ham that smells so sweet and pungent and looks so pretty
and so delicate there in the crisp garlands of the parsley leaf!—and yes, perhaps,
I'll have a slice of this roast beef, as well—h'm now! yes, I think that's what I'm
going to do—say a slice of red rare meat there at the center—ah-h! there you are!
yes, that's the stuff, that does quite nicely, thank you—with just a trifle of that
crisp brown crackling there to oil the lips and make its passage easy, and a little
of that plump chicken—some white meat, thank you, at the breast—ah, there it
is! how sweetly doth the noble fowl submit to the swift and keen persuasion of
the knife—and now, perhaps, just for our diet's healthy balance, a spoonfull of
those lima beans, as gay as April and as sweet as butter, a tomato slice or two,
a speared forkful of those thin-sliced cucumbers—ah! What a delicate and tooth-
some pickle they do make—what sorcerer invented them? a little corn perhaps,
a bottle of this milk, a pound of butter and that crusty loaf of bread—and even
this moon-haunted wilderness were paradise enow—with just a snack—a snack—
a snack. . . .

c   Hear the sounds:

Turn to page 37 and use the passages from Thoreau's *Walden* and
Matthew Arnold's "Dover Beach."

---

[6] Reprinted with the permission of Charles Scribner's Sons from *Of Time and the
River* (Copyright 1935 Charles Scribner's Sons; renewal copyright © 1963 Paul Gitlin)
by Thomas Wolfe.

7 Read aloud one of the following poems. Try to identify the emotional experience with a personal experience in order to project the speaker's attitude toward his experience.

WAR SONG[7]

Dorothy Parker

Soldier, in a curious land
 All across a swaying sea,
Take her smile and lift her hand—
 Have no guilt of me.

Soldier, when were soldiers true?
 If she's kind and sweet and gay,
Use the wish I send to you—
 Lie not lone till day!

Only, for the nights that were,
 Soldier, and the dawns that came,
When in sleep you turn to her
 Call her by my name.

from CYNARA

Ernest Dowson

Last night, ah, yesternight, betwixt her lips and mine
There fell thy shadow, Cynara! thy breath was shed
Upon my soul between the kisses and the wine;
And I was desolate and sick of an old passion,
 Yea, I was desolate and bowed my head:
I have been faithful to thee, Cynara! in my fashion.

All night upon mine heart I felt her warm heart beat,
Night-long within mine arms in love and sleep she lay;
Surely the kisses of her bought red mouth were sweet;
But I was desolate and sick of an old passion,
 When I awoke and found the dawn was gray:
I have been faithful to thee, Cynara! in my fashion.

---

[7] From *The Portable Dorothy Parker* by Dorothy Parker. Copyright 1944 by Dorothy Parker. Reprinted by permission of The Viking Press, Inc.

Part Four

LITERARY FORMS
FOR INTERPRETATION

9 ORAL INTERPRETATION OF PROSE

A discussion of prose writings appropriate for oral interpretation might include, in addition to the narrative forms, speeches, letters, diaries, descriptions, and various types of essays. Since some of these forms may be considered as implicit elements in the narrative, we will limit our discussion to (1) a brief consideration of the type of essay appropriate for interpretation, (2) the interpretation and projection of narrative prose, and (3) the detailed study of a short story.

THE ESSAY

The writer of the essay speaks for himself; he may use factual information, personal reflections, experience, light satire, or exaggerated humor to support his ideas. His writing may serve to persuade, to arouse, to instruct, to examine, to amuse, or to entertain his reading audience.

Choice

The essay is not always an intellectual hazard for the oral interpreter. There is, of course, a store of reflective essays written in compressed formal styles on subjects of profound depth. These are too complex both in thought and expression to appeal to an average audience, even if an oral reader were able to communicate the meaning. There is available, also, an abundance of modern essay material which should, perhaps, be rejected for other reasons. Every week magazines publish hundreds of essays in the form of autobiographical sketches, editorials, humorous articles, short satirical pieces. These have a certain appeal because they are written on subjects of the day in informal conversational styles, but a closer look may reveal subject matter of little consequence and a style lacking originality or refinement. The oral interpreter should hold to high literary standards; his search for the right essay to share with an audience requires more than a quick perusal of a popular magazine.

There are essay writings from the past and present that retain a natural, relaxed style which appeals to the listening ear and that treat themes of universal appeal with clarity, good taste, and originality. It is these that the interpreter should find and share with others. There is the humor of Mark Twain and James Thurber that seldom fails to delight an audience; there is the poetic language of such writers as E. B. White that is appealing to the ear and the imagination; there are essayists who dramatize a common situation or who reflect on a personal experience in a casual way while implying deeper meanings. These may gain the attention and interest of a particular audience. An audience of students might like this one:

VARIATIONS FROM A THEME[1]

Irwin Edman

The seventeen-year-old boy had come to me partly at his own instigation and partly on that of his father, a house painter. I had not looked forward too much to the interview for, as I understood it, it was something about entering college and something, also, about a poor high school record. I did not anticipate with pleasure the prospect of having to tell the young man it was hard enough to get into a good college—or any college—with a poor high school record at any time, but especially so these days.

The youth came in, looking shy and troubled and rather winning in a not too brilliant way.

"Ah, he knows," I said to myself, "that he is asking help in a rather difficult matter."

He was asking aid, but not about what I expected. "Could you help me," he said earnestly, soon after we began talking, "to persuade my parents that I *oughtn't* to go to college?"

The habits of a lifetime made me, almost automatically, start to remind him of the values of a liberal education, about how important the great books were, about what a resource it was in time of trouble and unhappiness to have the arts and science and philosophy as a refuge. I glanced at him and checked myself. It was a safe bet he had already had some experience in the great books, had already been bored to death by Hamlet and Macbeth and Homer, had had a chance over WQXR to feed his soul on Beethoven and Mozart—and had already rejected these golden opportunities. Who was I to urge him to have some more stuffed down his throat? It turned out in the course of further conversation that

---

1 From *Under Whatever Sky* by Irwin Edman. Copyright 1951 by Irwin Edman. Reprinted by permission of The Viking Press, Inc.

what the boy wanted desperately to be was a dental technician, and that the thought of college was nothing less than revolting to him. His parents, I gathered, felt very strongly that he should have the blessings of higher education, even though he found them a curse.

The situation put a college teacher in an embarrassing spot. "In the confidence of this room" I felt like saying, "don't go to college. Stick by your guns. Be a pure and unsullied dental technician. Don't let them force a higher life upon you. But don't tell anybody I said so." Instead, I was academically fair-minded. In the best tradition of the noncommittal, I pointed out the advantages of both sides, knowing the colleges' admission offices would probably settle the boy's problem for him.

One never knows what ripples one's falling pebble will cause. A few days later I met the boy's father. "My son wants to come see you again," he said. "He says you made college sound very nice."

And, of course, there is the sophisticated humor and the eloquent prose of Adlai Stevenson. Here is a tribute he paid to Eleanor Roosevelt at the time of her death.

She has passed beyond these voices, but our memory and her meaning have not —Eleanor Roosevelt. She was a lady—a lady for all seasons. And, like her husband, she left 'a name to shine on the entablatures of truth—forever.' There is, I believe, a legend in the Talmud which tells us that in any period of man's history the heavens themselves are held in place by the virtue, love, and shining integrity of twelve just men. They are completely unaware of this function. They go about their daily work, their humble chores—doctors, teachers, workers, farmers (never, alas, lawyers, so I understand), just ordinary, devoted citizens— and meanwhile the rooftree of creation is supported by them alone. There are times when nations or movements or great political parties are similarly sustained in their purposes and being by the pervasive, unconscious influence of a few great men and women. Can we doubt that Eleanor Roosevelt had in some measure the keeping of the Party's conscience in her special care? . . . She thought of herself as an ugly duckling, but she walked in beauty in the ghettos of the world, bringing with her the reminder of her beloved St. Francis, 'It is in the giving that we receive.' And wherever she walked beauty was forever there.

In your search for the well-written essay to interest an audience, start with a few models and make comparisons. Consult the list of suggestions on pages 236–37.

Analysis

Of special significance in interpreting the essay is the element of tone: How does the author feel toward his subject and his audience? Because the essay deals with factual materials, with ideas, the student may not give enough attention to the emotional meanings. The emotional tone of an essay is revealed through a careful study of the particular facts and details the writer has chosen to include and the way he has used words in context. Mr. Edman uses direct quotes and the idiom of the day to reveal a light, reflective mood and an easy, personal tone. Mr. Stevenson, on the other hand, uses a legend from the Talmud and polished poetic phrases: "a lady—a lady of all seasons," "walked in beauty in the ghettos of the world," and the like, to establish a reflective mood of dignity and warmth, and a scholarly, yet personal, tone.

Oral Reading

The visible and audible projection of the author's mood and tone may present some difficulties for the student. It is the author's attitude toward the subject that must be projected, not the reader's personal feelings toward the subject. It is wise for the interpreter to select an essay that projects an attitude with which he agrees or is in sympathy, for, then, he is naturally motivated to influence his listeners to feel or believe as the author intended.

An introduction may serve to prepare an audience for the essay, either to explain certain difficult elements, or simply to get the listeners in the right frame of mind for listening. The appropriateness of such opening remarks is dependent upon the particular selection and the audience. In introducing the short sketch by Irwin Edman to a class, the reader might arouse their interest and set a light mood by relating the subject of the essay to them, as students.

To communicate the thought clearly or to project emotional meanings in the essay, the reader may find it necessary to slow the rate by adding duration and pauses and to give special attention to subordination in the flow of speech. Generally, audience contact remains constantly direct, though there may be times when indirect reflections or narrative elements call for a degree of change in directness. It is not necessary to assume the personality of the author; the interpreter remains himself, projecting the author's thoughts and attitudes with appropriate restraint.

NARRATIVE PROSE

Choice

General criteria for guiding the student's choice of narrative material are discussed in Chapter 2. Here we will only add a few particulars in regard to literary standards pertinent to this form of writing. What are some of the criteria for judging the literary worth of a story or novel?

Only after story elements as character, plot, setting, and tone have been employed in a particular story can we really judge their rightness, for we should judge according to how the various elements have been used to achieve the author's purpose. We can only generalize as we point out the most effective use of such elements in narrative prose. These questions are aimed specifically toward helping you, the interpreter, choose material of literary worth:

Are the characters believable?

Is the dialogue according to what we might reasonably expect such persons to use?

Is the situation in the story close enough to familiar experience to permit communication?

Does the story move in logical sequence, at least to the point that the time elements can be clearly defined?

Does the situation arouse genuine natural emotion, or does the story demand an emotional response greater than what is justified by the situation presented? In other words, is it sentimental writing which artificially arouses feelings?

Does the whole story have unity, or are there parts or elements that seem irrelevant?

Does the author leave something for the reader to imagine?

Is the use of language intelligible and fresh or ornate and excessive?

Is the rhythm of the language appealing to the ear or stilted and unnatural?

Adaptation

In large oral interpretation classes teachers find it necessary to set strict time limits on individual readings. If a student has had no experience in adapting or cutting narrative fiction, the guides which follow may be of some assistance.

You may literally "lift out" a section or scene from a story or novel. You select one chapter from a novel or the climactic portion of a short story that has special appeal for you (and your audience) and a structural completeness (beginning, middle, end). You may wish to introduce your reading with a summary of what preceded your scene, but often a scene will stand alone without reference to the whole story.

It is possible to use more than one section from a novel or story and to tie these parts together with appropriate transitional narration. Each adaptation has its own unique problems, and you must find the most effective solutions.

You should be thoroughly familiar with the whole of a longer work before attempting to select a part or to cut it. Your cutting should never distort the author's basic theme or purpose.

You may find material that can be used in its complete form with only minor cuts, or your lifted portion may need minor cuts to meet time limits or to improve the reading. In either case you must consider ways of making minor cuts:

> Cut directive tags: "she said," "he said angrily," "they spoke rapidly" (and the like). Cut these when you can identify the character and his response with voice and body suggestions.
>
> Cut descriptions that do not directly affect the basic idea of the story. This is sometimes painful but necessary.
>
> Cut sub-plots or inserted incidents from the past.
>
> Minor characters may be cut, but it is sometimes possible to retain certain lines and to assign them to another character.

At the end of this chapter, an example of a novel cutting is included to illustrate these matters.

Analysis and Projection of Character

As we have indicated in the chapter on literary analysis, it is important for the oral interpreter to understand how an author handles point of view in a narrative and to decide the proper degree of characterization to use for the storyteller (refer to Chapter 3). To disclose the narrative situation, authors usually alternate between the use of a narrator's descriptions and summaries and his character "scenes." In these scenes, characters engage in dialogue and in inner monologue to reveal themselves, their relationship with other characters, and the movement of the situation. In preparing to share a narrative (or dramatic poetry or drama) with an audience, the interpreter must give close attention to characterization. The oral interpreter should have an intimate knowledge of the central characters in a story, and he should have the skills to suggest them in individual action and in interplay.

Authors use characters for different purposes: minor characters may be stereotypes used to assist in developing the central character(s); a character may be used as a symbol to represent meanings beyond the narrative itself; a central realistic character is used to motivate actions and reactions (involving him) and to solicit a reader's empathic response. Though there may be overlappings of these purposes, the interpreter may find that these identifications are helpful guides for characterization.

A minor character is "flat" or static. He is usually a character typical of a certain social class or work group, and he is not developed as an individual. In preparing to suggest such a character the interpreter would need to consider the dress, the speech, and the body mannerisms that characterize the particular group which the character typifies. When his lines are read, the reader's stance, gestures, and vocal intonations should satisfy and deepen the listener's awareness of the group the character represents.

A character identified as fully symbolic usually appears in the allegory as a personification of an abstract quality. Allegorical characters, as Odysseus or Beowulf, exemplify superhuman qualities, and as such, they are accepted by the reader as bigger-than-life heroes. Often in the allegory animals are used as fictional characters to personify human qualities. The bear's actions in Thurber's fable "The Bear Who Let It Alone" stand for man's intemperate actions. In Orwell's *Animal Farm* pigs behave like human beings; the author provides the animals with a symbolic meaning which enables him to satirize the moral and political philosophies of the totalitarian state. The symbolic character, however, is not confined to the allegory; he is much in evidence in modern literature. A character becomes a symbol when he overtly exemplifies another thing. The reader is allowed to use his imagination beyond the literal and to see a character as standing for some larger aspect of humanity.

How does the oral interpreter suggest such figures? He might suggest the allegorical character by a degree of exaggeration in vocal and bodily tones. Techniques to suggest the symbolic meaning of a character who is appearing in a (more or less) realistic scene are less easy to define. Perhaps a reader can best project a character's symbolic meaning through a sense of removal from the literal scene. The symbolic character (allegorical or fictional), as Brecht's Epic Theatre characters (see p. 209), requires special consideration of aesthetic distance.

A central character may be realistic, lifelike, one with whom the reader and the members of an audience can relate. Such a character may be engaged in a conflict with another character or with an opposing force of some kind, or the opposing force may be within his own personality. He is a complex individual with an outer and inner personality. He usually undergoes some kind of change during the story due to the circumstances in which he is placed. Though the narrator may "tell" some things about the character and other characters may give clues, an interpreter's discovery of a character's outer and inner personality should come chiefly through a study of what the character does, says, and thinks. Such a study should reveal a dominant motivation which is the desire that stimulates the character's actions throughout the story; each "want" and each relationship is controlled by his basic desire. For instance, the motivating force of the character in the dramatic monologue "The Laboratory" is revenge; her immediate want is the poison, and this controls her relationship with the old man: she is willing to "stoop" and offer a kiss and to part with her jewels to obtain her immediate objective—the poison—which is the means by which she will satisfy her basic desire—revenge.

The oral interpreter's characterization of a central character should be controlled through his knowledge of the outer and inner personality. For a time he may be concerned with the voice and body techniques that may best represent the character's personality. He may find it helpful to use a few direct means such as the "play-acting" exercise to help him get the feel of a character's stance and movement, and he may give time to a consideration of the speech (diction and rhythm) most appropriate for the character. But as he proceeds, these mechanical devices should be forgotten. The interpreter's control of characterization should be realized through his concentration on the character's desires or wants while reading the lines. This kind of thinking discloses the inner motivations and gives undertone to each line the character speaks.

In reading the narrative aloud special problems may arise which are related to the need to convey the situation and its movement clearly and to suggest the interplay of characters effectively.

Projection of the Situation and Its Movement

Transitions. Transitions need special attention when reading the story aloud. Shifts in time and place can be clarified by emphasizing transitional words and phrases in the script; but when the transition is indicated only by a paragraph break, the reader must indicate the change with an extended pause and appropriate visible and audible responses. During a transitional silence, he should drop the thought and emotions just completed and take on the attitude of the next paragraph, remembering that the larger the transition, the longer the bridge of silence.

Climax. To handle a climax effectively, the oral interpreter must have a clear understanding of the way the author has built the intellectual and emotional intensity, and he must have good control of his voice and body in order to project this. The intensity may be built with an increase in vocal force, by a faster rate, by raising the pitch, or by a combination of these. An intense build may be projected by muscle-tone change and controlled vocal intensity alone. There are countless ways. The interpreter should take care not to build too soon or too quickly, or to use too much rise in pitch (strain), and he should remember that pause is useful before or after, or before *and* after, a climax.

Problems in Handling Dialogue

Differentiation. In reading story dialogue the interpreter is often required to switch from one character to another—quickly (descriptive tags are usually cut). The student reader needs to perfect his skill of projecting characters through *suggestion.* One technical means that can be used to assist in differentiation is the physical placement of characters. This results in a change of eye focus for each character. When used to any extent, the audience becomes conscious of this mechanical device and the reader feels restricted by its use. Placement of characters—if the eye focus changes within a narrow angle and if not continued too long—can aid the audience in identifying the characters. Once the placement is suggested, however, it does not have to be continued. Characters can be suggested sufficiently by slight vocal and physical changes motivated by understanding and maintained through concentration.

Interplay. The interplay between characters in a scene is sometimes broken because of the reader's tendency to refer to the script between speeches. This causes a slight pause between each speech in the dialogue; this should not be. For instance, when the dialogue is between two characters, the reader should finish the first character's speech and immediately let the audience see the visible response of the second character; then, if necessary, he can look down (in character) and get the next words. An interpreter's contact with the script should be *during* speeches or during a response—not between.

Application

FIRST CONFESSION[2]

Frank O'Connor

It was a Saturday afternoon in early spring. A small boy whose face looked as though it had been but newly scrubbed was being led by the hand by his sister through a crowded street. The little boy showed a marked reluctance to proceed; he affected to be very interested in the shop-windows. Equally, his sister seemed to pay no attention to them. She tried to hurry him; he resisted. When she dragged him he began to bawl. The hatred with which she viewed him was almost diabolical, but when she spoke her words and tone were full of passionate sympathy.

"Ah, sha, God help us!" she intoned into his ear in a whine of commiseration.

"Leave me go!" he said, digging his heels into the pavement. "I don't want to go. I want to go home."

"But, sure, you can't go home, Jackie. You'll have to go. The parish priest will be up to the house with a stick."

"I don't care. I won't go."

"Oh, Sacred Heart, isn't it a terrible pity you weren't a good boy? Oh, Jackie, me heart bleeds for you! I don't know what they'll do to you at all, Jackie, me poor child. And all the trouble you caused your poor old nanny, and the way you wouldn't eat in the same room with her, and the time you kicked her on the shins, and the time you went for me with the bread knife under the table. I don't know will he ever listen to you at all, Jackie. I think meself he might sind you to the bishop. Oh, Jackie, how will you think of all your sins?"

Half stupefied with terror, Jackie allowed himself to be led through the sunny streets to the very gates of the church. It was an old one with two grim iron gates and a long, low, shapeless stone front. At the gates he stuck, but it was already too late. She dragged him behind her across the yard, and the commiserating whine with which she had tried to madden him gave place to a yelp of triumph.

"Now you're caught! Now, you're caught. And I hope he'll give you the pinitintial psalms! That'll cure you, you suppurating little caffler!"

Jackie gave himself up for lost. Within the old church there was no stained glass; it was cold and dark and desolate, and in the silence, the trees in the yard knocked hollowly at the tall windows. He allowed himself to be led through the vaulted silence, the intense and magical silence which seemed to have frozen within the ancient walls, buttressing them and shouldering the high wooden roof. In the street outside, yet seeming a million miles away, a ballad singer was drawling a ballad.

Nora sat in front of him beside the confession box. There were a few old women before her, and later a thin, sad-looking man with long hair came and sat beside Jackie. In the intense silence of the church that seemed to grow deeper from the plaintive moaning of the ballad singer, he could hear the buzz-buzz-buzz of a woman's voice in the box, and then the husky ba-ba-ba of the priest's. Lastly the soft thud of something that signalled the end of the confession, and out came the woman, head lowered, hands joined, looking neither to right nor left, and tip-toed up to the altar to say her penance.

It seemed only a matter of seconds till Nora rose and with a whispered injunction disappeared from his sight. He was all alone. Alone and next to be heard and the fear of damnation in his soul. He looked at the sad-faced man. He was gazing at the roof, his hands joined in prayer. A woman in a red blouse and black shawl had taken her place below him. She uncovered her head, fluffed her hair out roughly with her hand, brushed it sharply back, then, bowing, caught it in a knot and pinned it on her neck. Nora emerged. Jackie rose and looked at her with a hatred which was inappropriate to the occasion and the place. Her hands were joined on her stomach, her eyes modestly lowered, and her face had an expression of the most rapt and tender recollection. With death in his heart he crept into the compartment she left open and drew the door shut behind him.

He was in pitch darkness. He could see no priest nor anything else. And anything he had heard of confession got all muddled up in his mind. He knelt to the right-hand wall and said: "Bless me, father, for I have sinned. This is my first confession." Nothing happened. He repeated it louder. Still it gave no answer. He turned to the opposite wall, genuflected first, then again went on his knees and repeated the charm. This time he was certain he would receive a reply, but none came. He repeated the process with the remaining wall without effect. He had the feeling of someone with an unfamiliar machine, of pressing buttons at random. And finally the thought struck him that God knew. God knew about the bad confession he intended to make and had made him deaf and blind so that he could neither hear nor see the priest.

Then as his eyes grew accustomed to the blackness, he perceived something he had not noticed previously: a sort of shelf at about the height of his head. The purpose of this eluded him for a moment. Then he understood. It was for kneeling on.

He had always prided himself upon his powers of climbing, but this took it out of him. There was no foothold. He slipped twice before he succeeded in getting his knee on it, and the strain of drawing the rest of his body up was almost more than he was capable of. However, he did at last get his two knees on it, there was just room for those, but his legs hung down uncomfortably and the edge of the shelf bruised his shins. He joined his hands and pressed the last remaining button. "Bless me, father, for I have sinned. This is my first confession."

At the same moment the slide was pushed back and a dim light streamed into the little box. There was an uncomfortable silence, and then an alarmed voice asked, "Who's there?" Jackie found it almost impossible to speak into the grille which was on a level with his knees, but he got a firm grip on the molding above it, bent his head down and sideways, and as though he were hanging by his feet like a monkey found himself looking almost upside down at the priest. But the priest was looking sideways at him, and Jackie, whose knees were being tortured by this new position, felt it was a queer way to hear confessions.

"'Tis me, father," he piped, and then, running all his words together in excitement, he rattled off, "Bless me, father, for I have sinned. This is my first confession."

"What?" exclaimed a deep and angry voice, and the sombre soutaned figure stood bolt upright, disappearing almost entirely from Jackie's view. "What does this mean? What are you doing there? Who are you?"

And with the shock Jackie felt his hands lose their grip and his legs their balance. He discovered himself tumbling into space, and, falling, he knocked his head against the door, which shot open and permitted him to thump right into the center of the aisle. Straight on this came a small dark-haired priest with a biretta well forward on his head. At the same time Nora came skeltering madly down the church.

"Lord God!" she cried. "The snivelling little caffler! I knew he'd do it! I knew he'd disgrace me!"

Jackie received a clout over the ear which reminded him that for some strange reason he had not yet begun to cry and that people might possibly think he wasn't hurt at all. Nora slapped him again.

"What's this? What's this?" cried the priest. "Don't attempt to beat the child, you little vixen!"

"I can't do me pinance with him," cried Nora shrilly, cocking a shocked eye on the priest. "He have me driven mad. Stop your crying, you dirty scut! Stop it now or I'll make you cry at the other side of your ugly puss!"

"Run away out of this, you little jade!" growled the priest. He suddenly began to laugh, took out a pocket handkerchief, and wiped Jackie's nose. "You're not hurt, sure you're not. Show us the ould head. . . . Ah, 'tis nothing. 'Twill be better before you're twice married. . . . So you were coming to confession?"

"I was, father."

"A big fellow like you should have terrible sins. Is it your first?"

" 'Tis, father."

"Oh, my, worse and worse! Here, sit down there and wait till I get rid of these ould ones and we'll have a long chat. Never mind that sister of yours."

With a feeling of importance that glowed through his tears Jackie waited. Nora stuck out her tongue at him, but he didn't even bother to reply. A great feeling of relief was welling up in him. The sense of oppression that had been weighing him down for a week, the knowledge that he was about to make a bad confession, disappeared. Bad confession, indeed! He had made friends, made friends with the priest, and the priest expected, even demanded terrible sins. Oh, women! Women! It was all women and girls and their silly talk. They had no real knowledge of the world!

And when the time came for him to make his confession he did not beat about the bush. He may have clenched his hands and lowered his eyes, but wouldn't anyone?

"Father," he said huskily, "I made it up to kill me grandmother."

There was a moment's pause. Jackie did not dare to look up, but he could feel the priest's eyes on him. The priest's voice also seemed a trifle husky.

"Your grandmother?" he asked, but he didn't after all sound very angry.

"Yes, father."

"Does she live with you?"

"She do, father."

"And why did you want to kill her?"

"Oh, God, father, she's a horrible woman!"

"Is she now?" . . . "What way is she horrible?"

Jackie paused to think. It was hard to explain.

"She takes snuff, father."

"Oh, my!"

"And she goes round in her bare feet, father."

"Tut-tut-tut!"

"She's a horrible woman, father." said Jackie with sudden earnestness. "She takes porter. And she ates the potatoes off the table with her hands. And me mother do be out working most days, and since that one came 'tis she gives us our dinner and I can't ate the dinner." He found himself sniffling. "And she gives pinnies to Nora and she doesn't give no pinnies to me because she knows I can't stand her. And me father sides with her, father, and he bates me, and me heart is broken and wan night in bed I made it up the way I'd kill her."

Jackie began to sob again, rubbing his nose with his sleeve, as he remembered his wrongs.

"And what way were you going to kill her?" asked the priest smoothly.

"With a hatchet, father."

"When she was in bed?"

"No, father."

"How, so?"

"When she ates the potatoes and drinks the porter she falls asleep, father."

"And you'd hit her then?"

"Yes, father."

"Wouldn't a knife be better?"

" 'Twould, father, only I'd be afraid of the blood."

"Oh, of course. I never thought of the blood."

"I'd be afraid of that, father. I was near hitting Nora with the bread knife one time she came after me under the table, only I was afraid."

"You're a terrible child," said the priest with awe.

"I am, father," said Jackie noncommittally, sniffling back his tears.

"And what would you do with the body?"

"How, father?"

"Wouldn't someone see her and tell?"

"I was going to cut her up with a knife and take away the pieces and bury them. I could get an orange box for three-pence and make a cart to take them away."

"My, my," said the priest. "You had it all well planned."

"Ah, I tried that," said Jackie with mounting confidence. "I borrowed a cart and practiced it meself one night after dark."

"And weren't you afraid?"

"Ah, no," said Jackie half-heartedly. "Only a bit."

"You have terrible courage," said the priest. "There's a lot of people I want to get rid of, but I'm not like you. I'd never have the courage. And hanging is an awful death."

"Is it?" asked Jackie, responding to the brightness of a new theme.

"Oh, an awful blooming death!"

"Did you ever see a fellow hanged?"

"Dozens of them, and they all died roaring."

"Jay!" said Jackie.

"They do be swinging out of them for hours and the poor fellows leaping and roaring, like bells in a belfry, and then they put lime on them to burn them up. Of course, they pretend they're dead but sure, they don't be dead at all."

"Jay!" said Jackie again.

"So if I were you I'd take my time and think about it. In my opinion 'tisn't worth it, not even to get rid of a grandmother. I asked dozens of fellows like you that killed their grandmothers about it, and they all said, no, 'twasn't worth it. . . ."

Nora was waiting in the yard. The sunlight struck down on her across the high wall and its brightness made his eyes dazzle. "Well," she asked. "What did he give you?"

"Three Hail Marys."

"You mustn't have told him anything."

"I told him everything," said Jackie confidently.

"What did you tell him?"

"Things you don't know."

"Bah! He gave you three Hail Marys because you were a cry baby!"

Jackie didn't mind. He felt the world was very good. He began to whistle as well as the hindrance in his jaw permitted.

"What are you sucking?"

"Bull's eyes."

"Was it he gave them to you?"

" 'Twas."

"Almighty God!" said Nora. "Some people have all the luck. I might as well be a sinner like you. There's no use in being good."

Analysis: the situation and its movement (who, where, how, when, and why). The story is told in the past tense by a third person narrator, but there are times when we almost lose sight of the narrator. The "confession" is a dramatic episode with very few narrative interruptions. Jackie's thoughts sometimes break into the narration, and descriptions of scenes and actions seem, at times, to be more from Jackie's point of view than from an outside observer's. This limiting of the narrator's view increases the illusion of actuality and our sense of immediate involvement in the action.

The three characters in the story are realistic; we see and know them swiftly and vividly. The outward conflict between the two children is established in the first paragraph. Jackie, "newly scrubbed," is being "led," "hurried," and "dragged" by Nora; he "resists," "bawls," and she views him with "a hatred almost diabolical."

Nora appears to be a little hypocrite. Throughout the story she works hard on an outward show of goodness to cover the fact that inside she is a little vixen. She is alternately sweet and sour, soft and shrill. From what we see of her, we might say that her dominant motivation is to impress others with her goodness.

Jackie is an angry little boy, but we like him from the beginning. He is honest. He hates his sister most when he sees her come from the confessional with "her hands joined on her stomach, her eyes modestly lowered, and on her face an expression of the most rapt and tender recollection." His inward fears of damnation as he waits in the church, the "death in his heart" as he enters the confessional, and his feeling of panic inside are terribly and humorously clear. When Jackie confesses his terrible sin we understand what has been going on inside this little boy. Jackie's dominant motivation is to find love and understanding. Lack of love and attention has led him to want to rid himself of the family intruder—his grandmother, and, to bolster his deflated ego, he has made "courageous" plans for doing away with the body. The priest, recognizing his very human need, gives him the respect and understanding that restores his confidence. We see Jackie change. At the church he expects only punishment and God's wrath, so he wants only to escape; when he finds that the priest offers a sympathetic ear, he wants to unburden his troubled heart. At the end he wants to impress Nora, but the hate is gone; he has something of his own.

The priest is a wonderful human being. We like him immediately because he is perceptive, because he is kind and compassionate, and because he laughs. He does not talk down to Jackie but shows respect for his courage, establishes a common ground and relieves the little boy of his terrible burden. He is not a soft, sentimental person. His voice is angry and authoritative at times. He seems able to view his own life and work with a sense of humor (he speaks lightly of the old ones he must get rid of . . .). Perhaps his dominant motivation is simply to view the human condition—to condemn and to comfort as the need arises.

The setting is Ireland, and we are led to believe that it is a city, possibly Dublin. The journey to the church and the scene inside is created swiftly and clearly. Jackie's first impression of the church establishes an atmosphere in close relation to his inner conflicts: "cold, dark and desolate . . . ," "grim iron gates," "intense and magical silence frozen within the ancient walls . . . ."

The story may be divided into three parts or "acts." The beginning or introduction includes the action before Jackie and Nora enter the church. The author provides exposition of place, time, and characters with economy and conciseness. The conflict between the boy and girl catches our attention at once. The girl's "Now you are caught" is the high point of the introduction.

The body of the story includes the action in the church. In the first scene, the tempo of the story is slowed and the atmosphere inside the church is created. In the next scene, the author introduces an obstacle—the confessional box. Jackie's trials within the box mount slowly and reach a high point when he tumbles into the church aisle. The sister, another obstacle, is introduced and taken care of by the priest. Exposition and indirect discourse clarify Jackie's changed state of mind: the priest is no longer a threat but a friend. This realization is the high point: "He had made friends, made friends with the priest, and the priest expected, even demanded, terrible sins." The final scene in this part is the confession. Here we learn at last Jackie's terrible sin: "made it up to kill me grandmother." The general mood is quiet intensity with only light rises as Jackie tells his story. Quietly the priest achieves his goal. His concluding speech: "I asked dozens of fellows like you that killed their grandmothers about it, and they all said, no 'twasn't worth it. . . ." is the master stroke of applied psychology. The highest point in this part is the confession.

The conclusion of the story is the last paragraph. The mood has changed: Jackie's eyes shine; he is a whistling, confident boy as he faces Nora. The confession, beginning with "I made it up to kill me grandmother" and extending through the priest's last speech, may be considered as the climax. Jackie's "Jays" change as he answers the priest, and we know, without being told, that the priest's last speech has made a believer out of him. The climax seems attuned to the quiet atmosphere of the church. The author is more concerned with character than with rising peaks of action.

Analysis: tone. The dominant tone is humor—the kind of humor that Professor George Pierce Baker defined as high comedy: "High comedy consists of people with some depth of character who are funny in a subtle intellectual way." Within the dominant humorous attitude, the author expresses his characters' varying moods through their dialogue, thoughts, and actions. The author's tone and mood combine to *point* the type of humor that is subtle and intellectual. By his tone the author draws us sympathetically toward Jackie, "the sinner," and to the priest who understands the sinner.

The use of simple words, the Irish flavor, and understatement make "First Confession" a very warm and human story: The humor is subtly pointed through understatement. We expect the priest to be outraged by Jackie's confession; instead, he quietly asks how he meant to kill his grandmother and get rid of the body. When Jackie replies, specifically, how he planned to cut up her body into pieces and make a cart to haul them away, the priest replies simply: "My, my, you had it all well planned."

An outstanding characteristic of this story is its economy of language. There is no wasted rhetoric or detail; the style is natural, economical, and satisfying. Figurative language and imagery build atmosphere in the descriptive passages. Sound imagery is especially evident: "trees knocked hollowly at the tall window," "vaulted silence," "ballad singer drawling a ballad. . . ," and sounds of the buzz-buzz-buzz of the woman's voice in the confessional box are answered by the husky ba-ba-ba of the priest's voice.

Analysis: theme. The theme of the story is revealed through the dialogue. If there is a moral to be extracted, it is shadowed by subtle humor. Jackie's inward struggles with rejection, anger, revenge, and guilt might be any man's, but this is so much for one small boy! His immediate and terrible guilt is that he is about to lie to the priest and hence to God. The story's conflict is within Jackie.

The author is simply giving us an observation of life, showing us how an intelligent priest gives a little boy new confidence. For some, the story might further "suggest" that one intelligent human being can relieve the burdens of another or that a sense of humor is a saving grace!

Analysis: aesthetic appreciation of the whole. The rhythm of content furnishes variety. Three short episodes of conflict (Jackie's resistance to Nora, the confessional, and the confession) are followed by changes in mood and tempo. The three characters and those quickly seen waiting in the church (the sad-faced man and the woman in the red shawl) offer interesting contrasts in detail. The mood changes are helpful in holding attention. Jackie undergoes a complete change in attitude.

The structural balance is good; we are held in suspense until the confession and its culmination, and only one paragraph follows. The language, setting, and time are all unifying factors.

Oral Reading

The point of view of this story presents a question in regard to characterization: How much of the story may be presented from the little boy's point of view? Since the narrator, in this case, describes many of the scenes and actions from Jackie's view, it seems appropriate for Jackie to take over as storyteller in some places. By changing a few words (as, "he looked at the sad-faced man . . ." to "there was a sad-faced man . . .") many descriptions might be told from Jackie's view. The description of the action in the confessional box might be more effective (when read aloud) if told by Jackie.

When there are places in the story where direct discourse (the narrator's reporting), indirect discourse (Jackie's thoughts), and dialogue are all used, the reader should practice until he can make the shifts with ease. Here, for instance, the narrator might say directly to the audience: ". . . the knowledge that he was making a bad confession disappeared . . ." and Jackie's thoughts would follow immediately: "Bad confession indeed! He had made friends, made friends with the priest, and the priest expected. . . ." It is important to recognize such changes in focus and to handle them with ease so the audience will not be confused.

There should be no difficulty in suggesting the three characters in this story, for they can be easily differentiated by facial expression, body tone, and vocal characteristics suited to their ages. Nora's personality might be projected by a feeling of energy in the body accompanied by a soft, overly sweet quality of tone and excessive steps and slides in pitch. Later when alone with Jackie her voice and body tone would change in quality. One way to project the confusion and fear that Jackie is experiencing inside the confessional box might be to feel a tensing of muscles and to use a breathy voice quality with fast rate. But the interpreter may have no need for mechanical "plans" if he can control the characterization through concentration. With the dominant motivation of each character in mind, he can find a specific motivation for any speech or action. In the confession scene, the priest's speeches are motivated by his desire to understand and to relieve Jackie's feelings; Jackie's lines are motivated by his desire to unburden guilt. And how would the interpreter use past observations and experiences to help him re-experience the emotion Jackie feels inside the confessional? He may remember from his own childhood a "terrible sin" and his dread of confessing this to someone. Perhaps he can recall some closed-in feeling or the memory of the fear of a great height which would help. Finding related experiences would help the reader believe the situations in the story. But even when using this approach, there may be times when technical "plans" are needed. For instance, the reader should be careful with Nora's speech that ends the story. This should not be too abrupt. The characterization

should be held a moment with appropriate thoughts directed toward
Jackie. This might give the final artistic touch to the interpretation.

Adaptation of a Novel

The following selection is included to illustrate ways of adapting and cutting material to meet necessary time limits. The novel from which this is
taken is episodic in character. Here, the adaptor cuts and combines two episodes to make a five-minute reading. To serve *her* need the adaptor also
changes the point of view from the Father's to the Mother's voice. In this
particular case, this change does not distort the basic purpose of the writing.
The episodes will be given in full in order to show one possible way to cut
and combine.

MY LITTLE BOY[3]

Carl Ewald

My little boy is beginning to live.

Carefully, stumbling now and then on his little knock-kneed legs, he makes
his way over the paving-stone, looks at everything that there is to look at and
bites at every apple, both those which are his due and those which are forbidden him.

~~He is not a pretty child and is the more likely to grow into a fine lad. But he
is charming.~~

~~His face can light up suddenly and become radiant; and he can look at you
with quite cold eyes. He has a strong intuition and he is incorruptible. He has
never yet bartered a kiss for barley sugar. There are people whom he likes and
people whom he dislikes. There is one who has long courted his favour inde-
fatigably and in vain; and, the other day, he formed a close friendship with
another who had not so much as said "Good day" to him before he had crept
into her lap and nestled there with glowing resolution.~~

He has a habit which I love.

When we are walking together and there is anything that impresses him, he
lets go my hand for a moment. Then, when he has investigated the phenomenon
and arrived at a result, I feel his little fist in mine again.

He has bad habits too.

He is apt, for instance, suddenly and without the slightest reason, to go up
to people whom he meets in the street and hit them with his little stick. What
is in his mind, when he does so, I do not know; ~~and, so long as he does not hit
me, it remains a matter between himself and the people concerned.~~

He has an odd trick of seizing big words in grown-up conversation, storing
                                                                    Mother
them up for a while and then asking me for an explanation: "~~Father,~~" he says,
"what is life?"

I give him a tap in his little stomach, roll him over on the carpet and conceal

---

3 From Carl Ewald, *My Little Boy* (New York, Charles Scribner's Sons, 1912).

my emotion under a mighty romp. Then when we sit breathless and tired, I answer, gravely: "Life is delightful, my little boy. Don't be afraid of it!"

Added:

[Today my little boy has learned his first lesson in tolerance.]

There is a battle royal and a great hullabaloo among the children in the court-yard.

I hear them shouting "Jew!" and I go to the window and see my little boy in the front rank of the bandits, screaming, fighting with clenched fists and screaming and without his cap.

I sit down quietly to my work again, certain that he will appear before long and ease his heart.

And he comes directly after.

He stands still, as is his way, by my side and says nothing. I steal a glance at him: he is greatly excited and proud and glad, like one who has fearlessly done his duty.

"What fun you've been having down there!"

"Oh," ~~he says modestly,~~ "it was only a Jew boy whom we were licking."

I jump up so quickly that I upset my chair: "A Jew boy? Were you licking him? What had he done?"

"Nothing. . . ."

His voice is not very certain, for I look so queer.

And that is only the beginning. For now I ~~snatch my hat and~~ run out of the door as fast as I can and shout: "Come . . . come . . . we must find him and beg his pardon!"

My little boy hurries after me. He does not understand a word of it, but he is terribly in earnest. We look in the courtyard, we shout and call. We rush into the street and round the corner, so eager are we to come up with him. Breathlessly, we ask three passers-by if they have not seen a poor, ill-used Jew boy.

All in vain: the Jew boy and all his persecutors are blown away into space.

So we go and sit up in my room again, the laboratory where our soul is crystallized out of the big events of our little life. My forehead is wrinkled and I drum disconsolately with my fingers on the table. The boy has both his hands in his pockets and does not take his eyes from my face.

"Well," ~~I say decidedly,~~ "there is nothing more to be done. I hope you will meet that Jew boy one day, so that you can give him your hand and ask him to forgive you. You must tell him that you did that only because you were stupid. But if, another time, anyone does him any harm, I hope you will help him and lick the other one as long as you can stir a limb."

I can see by my little boy's face that he is ready to do what I wish. ~~For he is still a mercenary, who does not ask under which flag, so long as there is a battle and booty to follow. It is my duty to train him to be a brave recruit, who will defend his fair mother-land~~, and so I continue: "Let me tell you, the Jews are by way of being quite a wonderful people. You remember David, ~~about whom Dirty reads at school~~: he was a Jew boy. And the Child Jesus, whom everybody worships and loves, although He died two thousand years ago; He was a little Jew also."

My little boy stands with his arms on my knee and I go on with my story.

The old Hebrews rise before our eyes in all their splendour and power, ~~quite different from Dirty's Salslev.~~ They rise on their camels in coats of many colours and with long beards: Moses and Joseph and his brethren and Samson and David and Saul. We hear wonderful stories. ~~The walls of Jericho fall at the sound of the trumpet.~~

~~"And what next?" says my little boy, using the expression which he employed when he was much smaller and which still comes to his lips whenever he is carried away.~~

We hear of the destruction of Jerusalem and how the Jews took their little boys by the hand and wandered from place to place, scoffed at, despised and ill-treated. ~~How they were allowed to own neither house nor land, but could only be merchants, and how the Christian robbers took all the money which they had got together.~~ How, nevertheless, they remained true to their God and kept up their old sacred customs in the midst of the strangers who hated and persecuted them.

The whole day is devoted to the Jews. We look at old books on the shelves which I love best to read and which are written by a Jew with a wonderful name, which a little boy can't remember at all. We learn that the most famous man now living in Denmark is a Jew.

And, when evening comes and ~~Mother~~ ^{I sit} sits down at the piano and ~~sings~~ ^{sing} the song which Father loves above all other songs, it appears that the words were written by one Jew and the melody composed by another.

My little boy is hot and red when he falls to sleep that night. He turns restlessly in bed and talks in his sleep.

"He is a little feverish," says his ~~mother.~~ ^{father.}

And I bend down and kiss his forehead and answer, calmly: "That is not surprising. Today I have vaccinated him against the meanest of all mean and vulgar diseases."

10 ORAL INTERPRETATION OF POETRY

A poem often "says one thing and means something else." It pretends—fools us. Robert Frost said about these lines,

> He will not see me stopping here
> To watch his woods fill up with snow[1]

"That's a poetry way of speaking. The woods are not going to fill up with snow. But if you don't like that way of fooling you won't ever like poetry."[2] This is only one characteristic that makes poetry "different" and, for many people, "difficult."

Though the content of good poetry concerns significant ideas or experiences, emotional meaning is more important than factual meaning; and emotional meaning is evasive. In poetry, thought and feeling are expressed in highly imaginative language with no wasted words, saying much in little; and imagery and symbolism are also evasive elements.

The characteristics of verse bring the form close to that of music. The rhythm of poetry, like that of music, is based on repetition, "a turning from and returning to" basic patterns. Verse may have many kinds of patterns: stanza and line, rhythm, meter, alliteration, and assonance. To discover and to understand these intricacies in a poem can be a complex undertaking.

John Ciardi has said, "The essence of a poem is that one thing in it requires another."[3] We can say, then, that the essence of a poem is the inter-

---

[1] From "Stopping by Woods on a Snowy Evening" by Robert Frost (see p. 173).

[2] From Chester Morrison, "A Visit With Robert Frost," *Look Magazine* (March 31, 1959), p. 76. Reprinted by permission of the editors of *Look Magazine*, copyright 1959.

[3] John Ciardi, "A Poem Talks to Itself," *Saturday Review* (January 24, 1959), p. 12. Reprinted by permission of John Ciardi.

acting of many evasive elements. A reader may try to extract a theme only
to discover that there must remain a something that cannot be caught in a
factual statement. Poetry is evasive and undefinable. But in spite of these
inherent problems, poetry is written to give pleasure, to be enjoyed. In an
oral interpretation class, poetry is not approached as a study; instead, the
emphasis is on learning to enjoy it and on learning how to read it aloud.

In this chapter we will consider only the essential of a complex subject
and attempt to reveal some simple solutions to: (1) choosing poetry to read
aloud, (2) general problems in analyzing and reading poetry aloud, and
(3) problems related to specific types: narrative, lyric, and dramatic poetry.
Last, we will apply the techniques to one specific poem. In an effort to
avoid repetitions, we will, at some points, merely refer to discussions in
other parts of the text.

CHOICE OF POETRY TO READ ALOUD

Though we realize that individuals in an oral interpretation class would
never be in complete agreement regarding a poem's degree of difficulty, we
can make some classifications in an attempt to aid the student in his choice
of poems to read aloud. Poems *suitable* for a college classroom audience
might be divided into three categories: *First,* poems that concern an experience where literal meaning cannot be communicated but where the music
and imagery of the poetry can excite an emotional response in the interpreter and in the listeners. *Second,* poems where literal meanings cannot be
immediately understood, but where the poet's "public meanings" are sufficient to communicate the essence of the poet's experience. *Third,* poems
that concern significant experiences and that express the experiences in
language that can be clearly understood by the listeners.

Most people would agree that many of Edith Sitwell's poems would belong in the first group. In the second group would belong those poems that
are difficult but challenging (Eliot's or Pound's poems, for instance). Being
clearly understood does not imply that poems in the third category would
be less significant. This group would include a wealth of modern poems as
well as those which have stood the test of time.

If such a grouping as this has any significance, it is to point the fact that
a student should not be confined to the poem whose meanings are immediately clear, but he should make sure that a poem he selects to read aloud
communicates *something* to him. A poem may convey an idea or tell a story
that is appealing, but often it is simply a feeling, an emotion, that is communicated. We may be drawn to a particular poem because it makes us re-
discover something we have known and forgotten or recognize something
we have dimly sensed. Again, we may like a poem because its music, its

beat, has a special appeal for us. If a poem is selected for any of these reasons, the reader is sure to enjoy sharing it with others, and that is the important thing.

A critic judges the literary worth of a poem on different levels. He considers both the writing technique and the aesthetic effect. He wants to know the degree of skill and originality employed in the use of language, rhythm, rhyme. To determine this, the critic uses standards that have been set by poets in the past; he recognizes if a poet has stayed within or consciously departed from the established forms and to what degree he has succeeded in either case. He wants to know how successful the poet has been in communicating intellectual and/or emotional meaning. And finally, he must judge how successful the poet has been in combining all the elements to achieve a satisfying aesthetic effect. A student cannot be expected to judge a poem's worth on the same level as the critic for the obvious reason that he lacks the knowledge and experience, but he can develop his own standards by asking similar questions: Is the form pleasing? Is an intellectual and/or emotional meaning communicated? and Are all elements combined in a way to achieve a satisfying total effect? The critic is qualified to make judgments, and the student should respect his evaluations and turn to poetry criticisms to broaden his own understandings. At the same time, he should not forget that critics, like all men, are of varying natures and prejudices. The student should dare to express his own convictions even though his judgments differ from others.

GENERAL PROBLEMS AND SOLUTIONS

Analyzing

Chapters 3 and 4 should be reviewed (as needed) to clarify the analysis of:

THE SITUATION AND ITS MOVEMENT: Chapter 3 (pp. 24–34)
                                 Chapter 4 (pp. 45–47)

TONE: Chapter 3 (pp. 35–41)
       Chapter 4 (p. 47)

THEME: Chapter 3 (p. 41)
        Chapter 4 (pp. 47–48)

AESTHETIC EFFECT: Chapter 4 (p. 48)

Two points should always be kept in mind when analyzing a poem:

The elements of poetry are blended to such a degree that they can never be really separated; we make this separation of the elements simply because everything cannot be considered at once.

Time spent in analyzing should be focused on clarifying those particulars that can be of real help when reading the poem aloud.

The "particulars," of course, vary with each poem and each person, but it is always important to unravel difficult sentence constructions, to look up the pronunciation and meaning of unfamiliar words, to clarify the situation (what is happening to whom, where, when, and why), and to understand the emotional tone and what the author is saying in the selection. Some consideration of the poet's subtleties of language is necessary in order to understand these matters. These literary elements are discussed and illustrated in Chapter 3, and procedures for analysis are suggested in Chapter 4. Here something more needs to be said in regard to poetry's disciplines of pattern and order.

Pattern in poetry. Factors that make poetry distinct from prose have to do with its music, its inherent rhythm, its repetitive sound patterns. These factors are not visible on the printed page (with the exception of the poetry line); it is only in hearing a poem read aloud that the elements of a poet's rhythm and sound effects can be really appreciated. This is why we say that poetry should be heard to be fully enjoyed.

Our chief concern is with *patterned verse* which contains both meter and rhyme. Free verse may use some repetitive sound patterns, but it does not conform to any set form. Blank verse has meter pattern within a regular line length, but it does not have rhyme. Distinctions between blank verse and patterned verse will be pointed out as we proceed. Our purpose, now, is to clarify the large and small elements that contribute to the music of poetry. First, these elements must be recognized.

In all forms of poetry (as well as in poetic prose) we hear *repetitions of sound and language structure:*

We hear identical or similar consonant sounds repeated:

And the *s*ilken, *s*ad, un*c*ertain, ru*s*tling. . . .

We hear repeated vowel and diphthong sounds in words:

How the cry of a b*i*rd can st*i*r us.

We hear the repetition of word order and sentence construction:

Praise him for his mighty acts,
Praise him with the sound of trumpet,
Praise him with the timbrel and dance,
Praise him upon the loud cymbals.
(Psalm 150)

In all poetry forms we hear rhythm which is an overall flow of recurring elements. Rhythm is present in varying degrees in prose as well as in poetry, but in poetry it is more evident. This is especially true in patterned verse because the repetitions occur at more regular intervals in the line, in the meter, and in the rhyme.

In *patterned verse* we hear repetitions at approximately equal intervals. In some patterned verse we hear a *pause* that indicates the end of one *stanza* and the beginning of another. Often a transitional pause between stanzas is needed to suggest a degree of thought termination. This is similar to the pause we hear between paragraphs when prose is read. When verse stanzas are of equal length, the repetition of this pause, at these regular intervals, sets up an overall sound pattern. But this pattern may or may not exist. This depends upon the way the poet has chosen to regulate his lines into stanzas. Modern poets take great freedom with stanza forms. They may vary the length of their stanzas and extend the thought from one stanza to another so that a pause is uncalled for. In blank verse this sound pattern is not heard because there is no regularity in the length of the stanzas. In patterned verse we also hear a *pause* that makes a *line* evident. Of course, this is not true when poetry is read like prose. But the poetry line is intended as a unit of speech flow that calls for some degree of sound pause.

We hear a recurrence of similar *stresses* or emphases within the line at approximately equal intervals. This is known as *meter*. We hear four general types of meter or beats (′ represents a stress; ◡ unstress):

1 dă D̄Á̄/ dă D̄Á̄/ dă D̄Á̄/ dă D̄Á̄/
  Ĭ wán/dĕred lóne/lў ăs/ă clóud/

2 D̄Á̄ dă/ D̄Á̄ dă/ D̄Á̄ dă/ D̄Á̄ dă/
  Jénnў/ kiss'd mĕ/ whĕn wĕ/ mét –/

3 dă dă D̄Á̄ / dă dă D̄Á̄ / dă dă D̄Á̄ / dă D̄Á̄ /
  Ĭt wăs mán/ў ănd mán/ў ă yéar/ă gó/

4 D̄Á̄ dă dă/ D̄Á̄ dă dă/ D̄Á̄ dă dă/
  This ĭs thĕ/ fór ĕst prĭ/ mé văl thĕ/

To speak about these matters we do need "terms." Each interval, marked with a slash (/) and containing a stress, is called a foot. The meters demonstrated above are: (1) iambic, (2) dactylic, (3) anapestic, and (4) trochaic.

In patterned verse we hear a turning from, but returning to, one of these basic beats (or a related one). Poets depart from a regular meter to prevent monotony, to draw attention, or to change a mood. Notice how, in our familiar poem "A Deep-Sworn Vow," Yeats, in the first two lines, turns from his basic pattern of dă D̄Á̄/ dă D̄Á̄/ dă D̄Á̄/ dă D̄Á̄/ to draw attention to the words "others" and "deep-sworn vow."

OTH ĕrs/ bĕ CAÚSE/ yŏu DÍD/ nŏt KEÉP/
thăt DEÉP/ SWÓRN-VÓW/ hăve bĕen FRIÉNDS/ ŏf MÍNE/

If a student is sufficiently familiar with the four basic meters above—if he
can *hear* them—then he can usually recognize one of them in a line of
poetry. If the beat is not immediately evident, certain clues can be of aid.

Usually words of more than one syllable give a clue. But, in the lines
above, there are only two, and they have different stresses: "OTH ĕrs" and
"bĕ CÁUSE,": DÁ dă and dă DÁ. Which of these stresses does the poet use
more often? The next clue is given by reading the line aloud, as if talking.
In this case, we hear the natural stress of "dă DÁ" more often. This, then,
is the basic meter beat from which the poet deviates for emphasis and variety purposes. For reading a poem aloud, this is all we really need to know
about meter.

We hear *rhymed syllables* in a regular order at the end of lines:

> The Curfew tolls the knell of parting *day,*
> The lowing herd wind slowly o'er the *lea,*
> The plowman homeward plods his weary *way,*
> And leaves the world to darkness and to *me.*
> Thomas Gray, "Elegy Written in a Country Churchyard"

This is true only in patterned verse, not in blank verse. Of course, there
are many varieties and uses of rhyme, but this need not concern us here. It is
obvious that the rhymed syllables at the end of the line make the *line* more
evident when read aloud.

Reading Poetry Aloud

Certainly, one of the major problems in reading poetry aloud concerns the
control of the elements just pointed. It is obvious that reading difficulties
increase when stanza, line, meter, and rhyme regularities appear in a
single poem.

We respond to rhythms; this is a fact of human nature. And there is a
certain pleasure we all derive from hearing rhythmic rhymes; they cast a
kind of magic spell, and our expectations are built up to have the repetitions continue. This fact is humorously illustrated in the following limerick:

> There was a young bard of Japan
> Whose verses nobody could scan.
>   He said, "I admit
>   That the meter won't fit,
> But I always try to make the last line just as long as I possibly can."

The repetitions of rhythm can please the reader as well as the listener.
They can please him so much, in fact, that he reads along at a steady beat,
giving stress to all sound patterns with never a variation. The listener,
slightly hypnotized by the repetitive sounds, is lulled to sleep; or else he

gives up trying to get some meaning from under the beat and stress, and stops listening. Patterns in poetry can be emphasized to a point where all meaning is lost. On the other hand, patterns can be avoided to the point where there is no indication of the poetry form, and the reading sounds like prose. Two questions naturally arise: Should I read the poem more like prose to get away from the singsong rhythm? Or, Should I stress the recurring patterns of sound and meter to bring out the musical qualities and to make it sound less like prose? Where and how do we compromise between these extremes?

Part of the answer lies in a sensitivity to the poet's purpose. It is evident that some poems call for an exaggeration of meter and sound effects. Vachel Lindsey's "Congo" comes to our minds immediately. In many humorous poems the whole effect depends upon an exaggeration of the beat and rhyme. In this verse from W. S. Gilbert's *Mikado,* for instance, the humorous effect desired by the poet demands the stressing of meter and sound effects:

> To sit in solemn silence in a dull, dark dock,
> In a pestilential prison with a life-long lock,
> Awaiting the sensation of a short, sharp shock
> From a cheap and chippy chopper on a big black block!

The abstract poems that Edith Sitwell recorded[4] may convey no "meaning" to us as we listen, but she does arouse a response in us by the way she makes her chants run and skip and soar! By emphasizing the music—freely —she arouses a kind of emotional excitement in her listeners. We are sure this is what Miss Sitwell intended to have happen. But unless there is an evident reason for using exaggerated effects, we had best find a way to "move away from" or to subordinate the meter and rhyme. The distance of such a move is important. To what degree does one subordinate meter and rhyme and how?

Martin Cobin[5] offers a systematic approach to this matter by identifying and illustrating two patterns: (1) a *structural pattern* which conforms to the metrical pattern used by a poet and (2) a *speech pattern* which seeks to lessen the monotony of the metrical pattern by employing the natural time elements that we use in conversational speech. In which direction and to what degree a poem should move, he says, should be determined by the mood or purpose of the poem, and he adds:

> You must make your decision on the basis of your own sensitivities. You can be helped by an awareness of the responses of other people to sensitivity; you can

4 Recording: *Facade,* Columbia, ML 5241.
5 Refer to Cobin: Chapter 12 (pp. 196–202).

be guided by the extent to which the functions or advantages of pattern are exploited by the poet in the particular poem.[6]

When we read a poem naturally as in lively conversation, metrical stress tends to take care of itself. Stresses inherent in the rhythm fall in where they belong because we use time elements when we read this way. We can say, then, that to move away from meter and all regular patterns, we simply let the time elements of pause and duration play *over* the pattern. A person may do this instinctively: without giving any though to metrics, he reads the sense phrases as in lively talk—pausing, giving some sounds more, some less, time. In such reading the poem's inherent rhythm is generally maintained, but it remains a kind of under-flow with *meaning* on top. Let us consider ways of handling the specific verse elements that give the most trouble.

First, there is the poetry line. A reader may pause at the end of every line; but when the sense of the line overflows into the next line, the pause sacrifices the sense meaning. Instead of ignoring the line ending and sacrificing the line pulse, the reader should let the element of timing play a part. In most cases the last word in a "run-on" line contains a long vowel sound that can be prolonged. The reader may, in a sense, substitute duration for the line-ending pause and thus preserve both the sense and the metrical line pause or its equivalent in time.

> On either side of the river l*ie* →
> Long fields of barley and of rye.

Here, the long *i* in "l*ie*" is extended by drawing it out longer; an upward inflection is maintained and the long *i* sound flows into the word "long."

Next, how do we control meter in reading? We may turn away from the structural meter by adding internal pause in the line, by substituting duration (or length) for the metrical stress (or strength), and by reading short syllables and words faster to have the longer syllables stand out. Let us consider a specific poem. The metrical stress in Blake's "The Tiger"

> Tí gĕr/ Tí gĕr/ búrn ĭng/ bright/
>
> Ín thĕ/ fór ĕsts/ óf thĕ/ níght/

might be read with only two primary metrical stresses:

> Tí ger Tiger burning bright
>
> In the fór ests of the night

---

[6] From *Theory and Technique of Interpretation* by Martin Cobin, © 1959. Reprinted by permission of Prentice-Hall, Inc.

This does not imply that no other syllables or words are stressed; it means that others are stressed in a different way. Duration would be used instead of metrical stress. Advantage would be taken of the poet's use of long sounds by lengthening the long *i* in the second "tiger," the *er* sound in "burn," the long *i* in "bright" and "night." The reader would also add internal pauses in the line, and he would hurry over the small words "in the" and "of the." To represent this reading the lines would be marked: (lines *under* indicate duration stress; "/" indicates time pause)

Tiger/ Tiger/ burning bright/

In the forests/ of the night/

The strict line-end rhyme pattern in verse can be controlled in much the same way. The reader simply avoids emphasizing the end-line rhyme. He may use duration instead of volume stress to give the word less prominence; he may divert attention to other words and phrases within the line by using various vocal means (pitch inflection especially) to make the rhyme less noticeable. In the two lines from "The Tiger," the rhyme of "bright" and "night" would be less evident with duration than with metrical stress.

When internal sound patterns occur in the form of alliteration or assonance, the interpreter emphasizes the recurring sounds to heighten the emotional aspects, according to the poet's intention; but he should remember that if sound patterns are too strong and too regular, they become mere effects—not a means of heightening the emotion and the beauty in a poem.

Other vocal elements play a large part in making the reading of verse effective. Clear articulation and pleasing vowel sounds, quality touch on words (see p. 111), and pitch variation are important. When listening to Edith Sitwell's recordings, we are aware that it is pitch flexibility that makes her lines "run and skip and soar!" Verse is meaningless when volume stress falls on each metric beat; but, if, in addition, we hear a voice drone with never a slide or key change, the result is deadly.

John Ciardi, in reviewing recent albums of poets reading their own works, has something to say about the state of reading in our time. His comments are properly directed toward poetry reading:

> There is a more or less standard way of reading in our time. That style may fairly be called "reticent," or "modest," or "hushed," or "choked back," or even —perhaps most accurately—"English department." Its premise seems to be that it is bad form to allow any voice coloration into the reading for fear that one may appear guilty of trying to persuade the reader to like the poem. It seems to be good form, on the other hand, to stand aloof from the poem, giving it the least possible *saying* at the same time that one's voice emerges in a reverent hush of dry precision. Such reading is more or less singsong, it tends to leave line-ends hanging in achingly understated suspension, it ticks along at an un-

deviating dead pace, and it is exactly calculated to make monotony the entire human condition. . . . The reticence of such readings may pass as honorable if one is ready to subscribe to the ideal of Puritan restraint, but let me argue that it is time to call down a damnation upon all such self-rapt primness. Gusto, too, is an honorable creed of life.[7]

An oral interpretation class might do well to take as its motto: "Gusto is an honorable creed of life!"

Further problems and solutions of reading poetry aloud can best be considered in relation to three specific types of poetry: lyric, narrative, and dramatic. This divisioning does not mean to imply that there is no overlapping of lyrical, narrative, and dramatic qualities in poetry. Even the most subjective lyric may imply a narrative story and a dramatic situation, or a narrative or dramatic poem may have lyrical qualities. This divisioning is helpful because it emphasizes the point of view from which poetic experiences are told. Each type relates an experience from a more or less particular point of view: the lyric relates a poetic experience from the poet's view; the narrative relates a story from the view of a semiobjective narrator (either the poet or his narrator); the dramatic relates an experience from the point of view of a character who is distinct from the poet and who is immediately involved in the experience. Our concern now is to find solutions for the special problems that each of these types may present.

Lyric Poetry

The lyric expresses a poet's most subjective emotional reactions to experience, and this is expressed by the poet in a musical form. Emotion and song are at the heart of the lyric. Here are five short lyrics by poets of past and recent times. Notice how their emotional responses to the large and small realities of life make us respond and know the realities a little better.

CHANSONS INNOCENTES[8]

I

e. e. cummings

in Just-
spring   when the world is mud-
luscious the little
lame balloonman

whistles   far   and wee

---

7 John Ciardi, "Reading, Dronings, etc.," *Saturday Review,* January 15, 1966, p. 48. Reprinted by permission of John Ciardi.

8 "in-Just" Copyright 1923, 1951, by E. E. Cummings. Reprinted from his volume, *Poems 1923–1954,* by permission of Harcourt, Brace & World, Inc.

and eddieandbill come
running from marbles and
piracies and it's
spring

when the world is puddle-wonderful

the queer
old balloonman whistles
far   and   wee
and bettyandisbel come dancing

from hop-scotch and jump-rope and

it's
spring
and
      the

          goat-footed

balloonMan   whistles
far
and
wee

THE LONELY STREET[9]

William Carlos Williams

School is over. It is too hot
to walk at ease. At ease
in light frocks they walk the streets
to while the time away.
They have grown tall. They hold
pink flames in their right hands.
In white from head to foot,
with sidelong, idle look—
in yellow, floating stuff,
black sach and stockings—
touching their avid mouths
with pink sugar on a stick—
like a carnation each holds in her hand—
they mount the lonely street.

LI-FU-JEN[10]

Emperor Wu-ti

The sound of her silk skirt has stopped.
On the marble pavement dust grows.
Her empty room is cold and still.
Fallen leaves are piled against the doors.
    Longing for that lovely lady
How can I bring my aching heart to rest?

THE SILKEN TENT[11]

Robert Frost

She is as in a field a silken tent
At midday when a sunny summer breeze
Has dried the dew and all its ropes relent,
So that in guys it gently sways at ease,
And its supporting central cedar pole,
That is its pinnacle to heavenward
And signifies the sureness of the soul,
Seems to owe naught to any single cord,
But strictly held by none, is loosely bound
By countless silken ties of love and thought
To everything on earth the compass round,
And only by one's going slightly taut
In the capriciousness of summer air
Is of the slightest bondage made aware.

DELIGHT IN DISORDER

Robert Herrick

A sweet disorder in the dress
Kindles in clothes a wantonness;
A lawn about the shoulders thrown
Into a fine distraction,
And erring lace, which here and there

[10] From *Translations From The Chinese,* by Arthur Waley, trans. Copyright 1919 by Alfred A. Knopf, Inc. and renewed 1947 by Arthur Waley. Reprinted by permission of Alfred A. Knopf, Inc.

[11] From *Complete Poems of Robert Frost.* Copyright 1923, 1928 by Holt, Rinehart and Winston, Inc. Copyright 1942, 1951, © 1956 by Robert Frost. Reprinted by permission of Holt, Rinehart and Winston, Inc.

Enthralls the crimson stomacher,
A cuff neglectful, and thereby
Ribands to flow confusedly,
A winning wave, deserving note,
In the tempestuous petticoat,
A careless shoe-string, in whose tie
I see a wild civility,
Do more bewitch me than when art
Is too precise in every part.

The reflected thoughts and emotions in the lyric represent the thoughts and emotions of the poet. The experience is told from his point of view. The poet does not address his reflections to any one in particular; instead, he thinks out loud. In the short lyrics above, we overhear poets reflecting on the sounds of spring, personal griefs, and simple observations. It seems obvious that the reader, when interpreting these reflections, would not address the audience as directly as he would if he were reading expository material. The private and personal nature of a poet's reflections demands a degree of aesthetic distance. The reader does not suggest the poet in any physical sense. His identification is only in attitude.

In some lyrics, the poet, obviously, puts his thoughts and reflections into the mouths of "characters." T. S. Eliot does this in "The Love Song of J. Alfred Prufrock," and it may be that Marvell was doing this in "To His Coy Mistress." Wouldn't these poems be classified as dramatic since each poet has used a character outside his personality to speak his thoughts? We would say that they are lyrics *approaching the dramatic*. In both of these poems the reflections seem to belong more to the poets than to distinct characters. Marvell's character is more concerned with imagined impressions and responses than with an immediate experience, and the immediacy of Prufrock's experience is veiled by the nature of his reflections. But what possible difference can it make if we call such poems dramatic, dramatic lyrics, or lyrics approaching the dramatic? It matters only because these classification "handles" suggest, not only the appropriate degree of audience contact for the reader to use, but also the appropriate degree of character identification. "Dramatic" suggests a degree of identification with the character that is not called for. The reader, when interpreting character reflections, simply uses his sense of good taste to determine the proper degree of characterization to use.

Communicating the emotional impact of the lyric involves a directive that has appeared many times in this text: relate another's experience to your own personal experience. Only in this way can we really understand another's emotion, and only in this way can we become enough involved to forget self and fears when before an audience. An interpreter may carefully note every metaphor and simile, identify every image, and recognize every shading of tone, but unless these matters affect him personally in some way, they mean little. Have you ever observed a small occurrence that made you aware of the loneliness in American life? Such a recall would help you project the undercurrent of feeling in "The Lonely Street" (p. 167). Have you ever compared the physical properties of an object to the spiritual qualities of a human relationship? Such an experience would help you understand and communicate the tribute Robert Frost pays to his wife in "The Silken Tent" (p. 168). Concentration on the poet's reflections in the lyric can be maintained when the reader finds a way to become personally involved in those reflections.

Ways of recognizing and controlling a poet's recurrent sound patterns have been discussed in this chapter, but two points regarding this should be stressed. First, when a lyric has a regular metrical scheme, the reader should give careful attention to the poet's mood and purpose in order to judge the appropriate degree of pattern subordination. Then, the beauty and excitement in a lyric can best be communicated by a voice that is pleasant and rich in tone quality (with no flat vowel sounds!) and that is flexible and expressive in volume and pitch variations.

Narrative Poetry

Usually in narrative poetry the chief interest is in the story, but interest is sustained by emotional and dramatic elements which are also present. When emotional reflections are of some importance in the story's telling, the narrative approaches the lyric; when characterization is of some evident concern, the narrative approaches the dramatic. But in any case, the conflict and its outcome—the story—remain in clear focus.

The interpreter's analysis and oral reading of the narrative should emphasize the movement of the story, its build to high points, and the climax of the whole. Character and character relationships are also important to understand and to project through suggestion. In fact, all the problems inherent in narrative fiction are found to some extent in narrative poetry.

As we have said, the narrative poem is told from the point of view of a semiobjective narrator who may be either the poet or his appointed narrator. If the story is told in the third-person past tense, the interpreter does not give the narrator any specific individuality; he merely represents an unidentified storyteller. He looks at his audience directly, bringing them "in" to share the enjoyment of the moving scene. If the narrator speaks in the first person and participates in the story to some degree, the interpreter must use his good taste to judge the appropriate degree of characterization the eye-focus variation.

There are long narrative poems which tell stories comparable to short stories or even novels. Here, characterization plays an important role. In

most cases, it is the narrator who "suggests" the characters engaged in dialogue, but in some instances, as in Frost's familiar "Death of the Hired
Man," the third-person narrator almost fades from view. As sometimes
happens in narrative fiction, a character may, to some degree, take over the
point of view. Blank verse is a popular metrical form for the long narrative
poem. Since the iambic meter seems to encourage a natural conversational
speech flow, the student-interpreter usually handles these forms with less
difficulty than the rhythm and rhyme of "patterned" verse.

The folk ballad is a narrative with a strong story line (often implying a
plot) which moves swiftly to a climax. A definite meter and rhyme pattern,
repetitious refrains, and direct dialogue are characteristics of the form. The
narrator of the folk ballad speaks from a more impersonal point of view
than he does in any other form of poetry. He is purely objective, reporting
a swiftly moving action story without frills. In reading the old ballads
aloud, the interpreter should keep them objective, simple, and vivid. He
should let the refrains and all aspects of the rhythm heighten the emotional
meanings without distorting sense meaning. A mere suggestion of the dialogue is better than a close approximation; a close approximation often
distorts sense meaning.

Poets have imitated the folk ballad in varying degrees. Their imitations
(sometimes referred to as literary ballads) are often close to the old forms
in structure and purpose, but the poets use more descriptions and more
details, and they develop the plot (the why) more fully. Many poets have
told and continue to tell their poem stories in ballad form. We think at
once of Coleridge's "Rime of the Ancient Mariner" and, perhaps, of Millay's haunting "The Ballad of the Harp Weaver."

Here is a stark little ballad by some unknown storyteller of the past.
Notice the objectivity of the narrator, the dramatic quality of the conversation between the ravens, the emotional response the murder scene arouses,
and the story it relates of betrayal and murder—complete in five short
stanzas.

THE TWA CORBIES

Anonymous

As I was walking all alane,
I heard twa corbies° making a mane;°   *ravens, moan*
The tane° unto the t'other say,   *one*
"Where sall we gang and dine today?"

"In behint yon auld fail dyke,°   *old turf wall*
I wot there lies a new-slain knight;
And naebody kens that he lies there,
But his hawk, his hound, and lady fair."

"His hound is to the hunting gane,
His hawk to fetch the wild-fowl hame,
His lady's ta'en another mate,
So we may mak our dinner sweet."

"Ye'll sit on his white hause-bane°   *neck-bone*
And I'll pike out his bonny blue een,
Wi'ae lock o' his gowden hair
We'll theek° our nest when it grows bare."   *thatch*

"Mony a one for him make mane,
But nane sall ken where he is gane;
O'er his white banes when they are bare,
The wind sall blaw for evermair."

Dramatic Poetry

It is the immediacy of happenings and revelations that place them in the dramatic mode. Because of this, the oral interpreter may recognize as "dramatic" only those poems where characters are immediately engaged in an action or revelation. Such a character (or characters) is distinct from the poet, and he is, at the moment, participating in an action which concerns him. This, of course, limits our choice of dramatic poetry to the verse play, the monologue, and the soliloquy. But it should be remembered that plays written in verse furnish abundant and interesting selections and that single character speeches can take on the characteristics of the monologue or the soliloquy and make excellent dramatic poetry readings.

In the dramatic monologue, a character addresses another character (or characters) imagined to be present. An action is taking place in the present; the character speaking and the imaginary "audience" are closely involved in this. Robert Browning's "The Laboratory," which we have referred to many times, is an example of this type of dramatic poetry. "My Last Duchess" is another familiar one. In all dramatic monologues characterization receives major focus.

In reading a dramatic monologue for an audience, the interpreter assumes a character role much like the actor in a play. Character suggestion may move closer to the actor's character representation. In the monologue and in the play reading, he is allowed more freedom to use physical evidence of the character than in other types of oral reading. But he should take care that all physical manifestations (voice and body) are well motivated and that they do not call attention to him—as a performer. It is sometimes suggested that the dramatic monologue be memorized and that it be given without a reading stand. There is no real necessity for this; using the stand (with a script) makes the reading less of a performance, and the interpreter wants to avoid a reading "performance" at all costs.

The soliloquy differs from the monologue by the fact that no imagined characters are present. The character speaking is alone; he is ostensibly speaking only to himself.

In reading the soliloquy, the interpreter's eye contact is indirect; he looks out at the audience without seeing them as individuals. His interpretation is like that he would use in the reflective lyric. The difference lies in the fact that this is a "character" speaking in the present; his reflections are the result of an immediate situation in which he is involved. Since the cause of the character's reverie is usually due to some emotional conflict, it is important for the reader to understand the background that has helped to form the character's outer and inner personality and the present conflict. The familiar poem "Patterns," by Amy Lowell, is an example of the dramatic soliloquy. A young woman who has just received news of her lover's death is speaking. Alone, she recalls this relationship, its pleasant as well as its tragic moments. In Robert Browning's "Soliloquy of the Spanish Cloister," a monk is observing a brother working in his rose garden; this arouses him to express his inner feelings. There are examples of monologues and soliloquies to be found in verse plays listed on page 243.

APPLICATION OF TECHNIQUES

STOPPING BY WOODS ON A SNOWY EVENING[12]

Robert Frost

Whose woods these are I think I know.
His house is in the village though;
He will not see me stopping here
To watch his woods fill up with snow.

My little horse must think it queer
To stop without a farmhouse near
Between the woods and frozen lake
The darkest evening of the year.

He gives his harness bells a shake
To ask if there is some mistake.
The only other sound's the sweep
Of easy wind and downy flake.

The woods are lovely, dark and deep,
But I have promises to keep,
And miles to go before I sleep
And miles to go before I sleep.

12 From *Complete Poems of Robert Frost.* Copyright 1923, 1928 by Holt, Rinehart and Winston, Inc. Copyright 1942, 1951, © 1956 by Robert Frost. Reprinted by permission of Holt, Rinehart and Winston, Inc.

Analysis

The situation and its movement. The whole poem concerns a single incident as told by a man who is driving through the countryside on a dark December evening. It is snowing. As he passes a patch of woods, he stops his horse to watch the snow falling into the deep, dark woods. He stays here for a time, reflecting on the scene, the owner of the woods, and his horse's reaction to the delay. Then he comes to a decision: he must be on his way.

The first stanza may be considered as the introduction, or scene one. Here the man's relationship with the scene is established, but much is left unsaid. We are not told where the man has been or where he is going on this winter night. We may wonder about the owner of these woods. The body of the poem (or scene two) includes the next two stanzas. Here a conflict arises: the horse shakes his bells to urge the man to get along, but it is evident that the man would like to stay. In the final scene, the last stanza, the man makes his decision. The poem is quiet, low in tension. Both the structural and emotional climaxes come at the end with the decision.

Tone and symbolic meaning. The tone of the poem is largely due to its understatement. It pretends to be about a simple incident, but something more is implied, and what is left unsaid is important.

The owner of the woods is associated with the village. Perhaps it is implied that he is more interested in village matters and in "owning" the woods than in viewing his property on a snowy evening. This leads us to believe that the owner and the village symbolize society's materialistic forces. The man in the poem appears to have a different attitude; viewing the simple beauty of this scene has significance for him. But certain forces seem to be pulling him away from the scene. We might recognize one force as the materialistic world represented by the owner of the woods and the village. The horse visibly urges him on. Could Frost be suggesting that the horse stands for the force that drives us on in life? And where has the man been and where is he going? Traditionally, any journey or "path" in poetry symbolizes "life." If we can see these meanings in the poem, then we can understand the man's "promises." They are clearly his duties and obligations in the practical world of the village from which he has separated himself briefly.

But what about the repetition of the line "And miles to go before I sleep?" Perhaps he means what he says—a distance to go before he sleeps. But why does the poet repeat it? Does the repeated line imply a larger meaning? If we think of the man's journey as *life,* we can say that "sleep" symbolizes death, the end of life; his life is not yet over; there is some distance yet to travel before the end of his life and final rest.

The dominant mood is quiet and reflective. There are, perhaps, shadings of this mood when the conflict is felt by the man and when he makes his decision. The tone is never bitter or heavy. The visual images set a pleasing tone: woods filling up with snow and the dark, deep woods. We are aware of the silence and the sound of "easy wind and downy flake" and of the sound of the harness bells breaking into this quiet. The repetition of sounds aids in conveying the quiet mood: the long *o* sound (know, snow, go), the *au* and long *e* sounds (out, house, sound, town, see, sleep, easy, sweep, keep) as in "sound's the sweep of easy wind and downy flake." The sounds make delicate music. There is an easy conversational flow to the lines in spite of the fact that the poet adheres strictly to patterns. Frost does not vary the regular four-stress iambic line, and except for the repeated last line in the poem, the rhyme pattern is regular.

The speaker's, and likewise the poet's, attitude seems to be one that accepts life's obligations without bitterness. There is (for this reader) a touch of humor hovering over the whole of his attitude. The poet's attitude toward death (if we believe this is implied) is not morbid: "sleep," the end of life, means restful sleep, and that is good.

Theme. Now, perhaps, we can venture a statement of what the poet is saying; but because the language is highly suggestive and deceiving in its simplicity, this poem will always have different meanings for different people and new meanings for each of us as our experiences change.

Frost is not saying that the world is an ugly place from which to escape, nor is he preaching to us to remember our "promises." He is, perhaps, showing us through a simple incident that life offers opportunities to find a relationship with beauty by briefly separating ourselves from mankind. But, he seems to say, our duties and obligations remind us that we cannot remain apart from mankind; the practical world exists, and it will continue to make its demands until we come to the end of life and final rest.

Aesthetic effect. The poem moves from specific, simple, and vivid details to the larger implied meaning at the end. The details balance the intensity of the ending. How could a poem be better unified? All the elements of structure—stanza form, meter, and rhyme—unify. The simple incident and the simple words that flow as human speech belong together. Even the larger implication at the end seems to have come about naturally—without plan.

Problems and Solutions in Reading Aloud

First, let us consider the problem of handling the sound pattern. There is nothing in the mood or purpose of Frost's poem to demand a strong regularity of rhythm. So in this case, the oral reader would move away from the meter and rhyme pattern to a conversational flow, preserving at the same time the beauty of the images and sounds. The poet makes this easy to do. In the marked lines which follow, the markings *above* the words represent the metrical beats. If the poem were read according to these markings, we would hear beats instead of sense. The "/" mark indicates the pause between thought groups; the italics indicate the words emphasized either by a degree of volume stress or time duration. The words not italicized are subordinated, hurried along.

> Whose *woods* these are/ I *think* I know//
>
> His house/ is in the village though//
>
> He will *not see* me/ *stopping* here
>
> To *watch* his woods/ *fill up* with *snow*///
>
> My little *horse* must think it *queer*
>
> To stop without a *farmhouse* near/
>
> Between the *woods*/ and *frozen lake*/
>
> The *darkest evening*/ of the year///
>
> He *gives* his *harness bells*/ a *shake*
>
> To *ask*/ if there is *some mistake*/
>
> The only *other* sound's/ the *sweep*
>
> Of *easy wind*/ and *downy flake*///
>
> The *woods* are *lovely*/ *dark* and *deep*//
>
> But I have *promises*/ to *keep*//
>
> And *miles* to go before I *sleep*//
>
> And *miles* to go/ before I *sleep*///

When the repeated long vowel sounds are given proper duration and pleasant tone, the beauty of the language and the emotional meanings are reinforced.

Though the poem tells a little story, it is predominately a reflective lyric. The reader's contact with his audience would be, to a degree, indirect, and it would not be necessary to give the speaker any individual personality traits. Concentration should be on the speaker's thoughts, and the projection of the man's attitude would be most important. The poet is speaking, and we are fortunate enough to overhear.

11 ORAL INTERPRETATION
OF DRAMA

Action is the essential element in drama. The play is not *about* characters in action; it *is* characters in action. Narrative fiction or narrative poetry may also concern the movement of a plot with characters engaged in dialogue, but these forms rely on exposition to describe characters and actions. Usually (though there are exceptions) a play presents background exposition only through the dialogue and the actions of characters. When a story writer, such as Hemingway, engages his characters in direct dialogue with little narrative exposition or when a poem is written in a form where the story is revealed through the character's speech, we say these forms approach the "dramatic mode."

Since a play represents characters in action to be seen and heard by a live audience, we may wonder how the form can be effectively performed by a single reader. Obviously, the oral interpreter cannot perform the actions of a play or represent characters in action as the actor does; but he can, through activating his own imagination, cause his listeners to re-create the characters, the scene, and the action in their minds as he reads. This is no easy assignment, but it is a challenging and rewarding one.

Because many of the elements important in the narrative are also important in the play, much of our previous discussion of the narrative is applicable to the drama. In analyzing either form, the emphasis is on a clarification of plot and characters. The problems associated with the oral reading of narrative fiction are generally the same for the play, though the play form demands a stronger emphasis on "suggestive" skills. There is no need to repeat these discussions. We will give some emphasis to the suggestive skills here and point out previous discussions in the text for review. The points of concern involve: (1) preparatory steps, (2) analysis, and (3) the techniques for suggesting character. Last, we will analyze and discuss the reading of a particular play cutting.

PREPARATORY STEPS

Choice

In judging a play's suitability for oral reading, the student should keep in mind the following characteristics: a credible plot, good pace and climax, believable and appealing characters, purposeful and original dialogue, symbolic interest, and emotional excitement. These same elements should be evident in the scene or scenes selected from the play.

Seldom, if ever, can a full-length play be used in its entirety. Time limits make cutting a necessity. Unless the oral reader confines his choice to the one-act play (even these need minor cuts), he is not really selecting a play to read for an audience; he is selecting a play that has a scene (or combination of scenes) which makes an effective reading. Usually a scene from the last act is more satisfactory because it concerns the outcome of the conflict. It is also wise to select a scene that is more dependent upon characterization and dialogue than upon physical actions.

Preparation of Script

General problems in relation to major or minor cuts are discussed in Chapter 9 (p. 141). When the student reader lifts a scene or scenes from a full-length play, he should make sure that the cutting has a beginning, middle, and end—that it is, in a sense, a little play within a play. If he wishes to read a scene found in an anthology, eliminating the necessity of making a major cut himself, this is permissible, provided he reads the play from which the scene was taken. But whether he chooses to read a prepared scene or one of his own making, it is important to read the entire play to be able to see the part in relation to the whole. The number of characters, their sex, and other matters that affect the success of a performance should, of course, be taken into consideration. Sometimes characters can be cut or line combinations made without distorting the playwright's intent.

Plays most easily adapted for oral reading are those in which a character (or chorus), serving as narrator, stands outside the action and comments on the action and characters. The stage manager in *Our Town* and the chorus in *Antigone* are examples. Such plays are easily adapted for oral interpretation because narration is a natural part of the total play structure (it is built in). But few plays are so constructed; and since in a play reading the audience must be given information concerning the scene, the cast, and so forth, it becomes necessary to add narration. The interpreter's original words, spoken directly to the audience, play a part in determining the total success of the play reading. He should make every effort to keep such explanation clear, terse, vivid, and in tone with the spirit of the scene.

A good introduction arouses an immediate interest in the play, the scene, and the characters. But everything cannot be done in the introduction. Sometimes it is necessary to break the flow of a scene and to add narration to describe a character or an action, to indicate an entrance, an exit, or a change of scene. These interruptions should be as few as possible, and they should be carefully planned.

Slight additions and changes in the script may be helpful. Adding a character's name now and then may help with differentiation; an added greeting or an exit line may indicate a character's entrance or exit and eliminate an awkward stage direction; added lines of dialogue may replace the explanation of an action involving a prop. For instance, instead of breaking into the scene with: "As Mary watched, with a curious twinkle in her eyes, John walked to the table, picked up the letter, and left the room," John might be given the line: "I'll take this letter with me." If this line is said with accompanying vocal and body suggestions to make the attitudes of the two characters evident, the listener can visualize John's action of picking up the letter and of leaving the room without any explanation. Certainly, such a change is not appropriate in every case. Narrative additions are sometimes necessary, and they can go unnoticed as "interruptions" when the mood of the situation is unbroken.

Analysis

First, the scene must be considered in relation to the complete play. How does it contribute to the meaning of the whole? Does the chosen scene contain the climax or a high point that leads up to the climax of the whole? Is it a scene that focuses on the plot, or is it a scene that concerns a character relationship with little to do with the main plot?

After this it is best to change the focus of the analysis from the whole play to the scene itself. This is what the interpreter is to read, so this is what he must analyze fully. He should recognize the divisions in the cutting, the high points in each division, and the climax. Perhaps the best way to "see" the structure is to divide the cutting into units which represent small segments of scenes of action during which there are no exits or entrances (see p. 190). Since there is no narration in the play cutting once it begins (except necessary stage directions), the interpreter should recognize key speeches that point up the situation, the movement of the plot, and its culmination. Character analysis is, of course, the key to a good play reading. Review Chapter 9 (pp. 142–44). In view of the differences between the analysis of the play and the analysis of the other forms of literature, we suggest this procedure:

1 Relate the scene to the whole play: comment on the position of the scene and how it contributes to the meaning of the whole play.
2 Analyze the movement of the situation: identify unit divisions or parts; comment on high points and climax; locate key speeches; comment on the conflict.
3 Analyze characters: analyze fully the central characters; comment briefly on minor characters.
4 Analyze for emotional meaning: comment on the dominant tone, changing moods and attitudes.
5 Analyze for logical meaning: comment on the theme of the scene.

Oral Practice

Preparation for reading a play cutting for an audience parallels the preparation for an acting role, but since the interpreter must analyze and suggest several characters instead of one, the play reading can be more demanding. The actor, too, has the help of a director and the stimulation that comes in group rehearsals; the oral interpreter must work alone in rehearsals as well as in performance. The play reading is also more demanding than most narrative and poetry readings. The fact that the speed of the interplay between the characters calls for a near memorization of the script and that character suggestion calls for a high degree of technical control makes this true. To be able to handle the character concentration and the interplay with ease, the student should begin his oral practice far in advance of a performance. In practice sessions he may, for a time, work on details, but he should not fail to practice the whole reading—at one time—many times. It is the flow of the scene that is most difficult to perfect.

ORAL READING

Character Suggestion

As we have seen, the line between the suggestive role of the interpreter and the more literal role of the actor is vague. What is important is that identification techniques do not call attention to themselves. When a play is read aloud by an individual, a too literal representation of characters may, and often does, draw attention and interfere with communication. For instance, when a reader attempts to *literally* represent both men's and women's voices in a dialogue, he draws attention, for this sounds false. He is attempting to do the impossible: to "be" many different people at the same time. He should not pretend to be other than what he is, himself, a reader "showing" the play. In most cases good taste and a feeling of truth guide us to the interpreter's suggestive role.

Differentiation and Interplay

Analysis reveals the personality traits of each character in a scene. The next step is to find outward manifestations for each of the personalities. Each character can be thought to live in a general tempo, and the tempo of his speech and body rhythm to "fit" his personality. Even though a character's tempo may change at certain moments in the scene, the change can be within his general tempo. An aggressive character may be given a quick tempo, a timid person a slow hesitant tempo; but when two characters of the same general tempo appear together, the reader must find finer distinctions. For instance, two quick aggressive tempos might be distinguished by a touch of coldness in one and an impulsive warmth in the other. There are varied speech and body characteristics to distinguish characters: slow, quick, loud, soft, warm, cold, quiet, impulsive, light, heavy, sarcastic, friendly, to name only a few. There are countless vocal means to make fine character distinctions: pitch, quality, rate, volume, a dialect, or an accent. Visible body suggestions of character traits can be made evident in facial expression, muscle tone, and small gestures (see Chapter 7, pp. 119–20). As was indicated in an earlier chapter, a degree of physical eye focus can be used to help with identification; and, as we indicated in this chapter, the addition of a character's name in the script can sometimes help. These mechanical aids are helpful in setting the characterization, but they should not be relied on too long. In the end, differentiation should be automatically controlled through concentration on each character's inner motivations. And the only solution to handling the speed of the interplay between the characters is to stay mentally alert and emotionally involved in performance. A reader cannot pause between speeches to find the next character's lines; cues have to be picked up immediately, but cues can be picked up by a slight change in body expression with no sense of rushing.

Special Plays with Special Problems

The modern antitheatre play presents unique problems for the interpreter.

Contemporary playwrights such as Beckett, Genet, Ionesco, and others upset all the usual play conventions by presenting characters engaged in what appears to be nonsense dialogue and automatic behavior. The intent of such plays is to reveal the "emptiness" of modern life. Such plays "say" that the behavior of modern man is nonsensical, that he has no identity, no "self." In *The Maids,* Genet has each character play the role of a character playing a role. This shifting of roles shows the contradictions in life—the contrasts between appearance and reality. In Ionesco's *Bald Soprano,* the Smiths and the Martins babble nonsense that is comic, yet tragic, since it mirrors man's inability to communicate or to think. Man, Ionesco is saying, behaves automatically and without meaning; his life is absurd. He has called his plays "tragical farces."

When these plays with their antiplots, antipersonalities, shifting roles, and repetitious and empty dialogue are used for oral reading, the interpreter, in most instances, would avoid inner motivations for character speeches. A kind of vocal underplay would point the sterile vigorless state of mind. Sharp stylized physical suggestions might also point the dehumanization of the characters.

APPLICATION

THE GLASS MENAGERIE[1]

Tennessee Williams

(From Scene 7)

[Tennessee Williams' play *The Glass Menagerie* is a memory play. Remembered episodes from the past tell the story of four people: the narrator, Tom Wingate; Laura, his crippled sister; Amanda, his mother; and one person outside the family group, a young man of Tom's age, Jim O'Connor.

The action of the play takes place in a St. Louis tenement in America's depression era of the 1930's. The setting is a drab middle-class flat which faces an alley and is entered through a fire escape. We are given a view of two dimly lit rooms: a living room and a dining room. Within this dim setting our attention is caught by a large photograph which hangs on the wall. The handsome young man in a World War I doughboy's cap smiles out at us from his frame. This is the absent husband and father. Our attention is also caught by two pieces of furniture: one is an ancient looking victrola; the other is an old-fashioned what-not which contains tiny transparent glass animals.

These two pieces are loved possessions of Laura, Tom's crippled sister. Laura who is a shy, delicate, young girl escapes her world of reality by talking to her glass animals and by playing old phonograph records that her father left behind when he abandoned her mother.

Amanda, the mother of Tom and Laura, is an aging but "gayish" southern lady who has known better days. She sometimes escapes her present life through her memories of a gay girlhood in the Deep South. But, usually, Amanda is battling life. She is both a tragic and a comic figure as she nags, scolds, and tries to do her best for her children.

Tom, who shows us the play, is "a poet with a job in a warehouse." As his father before him, he wants to escape—escape from his job in the warehouse and escape from his home.

As we look in on this family, they are entertaining a guest. Leading up to this occasion, important things have taken place. Amanda, in an effort to find some secure place in life for Laura, nags Tom to bring home a gentleman caller. The best Tom can do is Jim O'Connor, who works with him in the warehouse. Amanda makes great preparations for what she considers the most important event in their lives. Dresses are made, a new rug and lamp are purchased, her most tempting meal is prepared. All is in readiness, but, meanwhile, Laura has discovered that the expected caller is the same Jim O'Connor she knew in high school days. Jim had been the most popular boy in the school and her only secret romance. Now she cannot face him. When he arrives she is so overcome with shyness that she becomes ill. She has to lie down in the living room while the others eat. But after supper Amanda sees that Laura and Jim are left alone together.

Jim, a very ordinary but nice young man, is sorry for Laura. He gives her brotherly advice about overcoming her shyness and even manages to get her to dance with him. During the dance, he knocks against the what-not, and one of Laura's little glass animals falls and breaks. It is her favorite, the unicorn. Jim says:]

JIM: Aw, aw, aw. Is it broken?
LAURA: Now it is just like all the other horses.
JIM: It's lost its—
LAURA: Horn!
It doesn't matter. Maybe it's a blessing in disguise.
JIM: You'll never forgive me. I bet that was your favorite piece of glass.
LAURA: I don't have favorites much. It's no tragedy, Freckles. Glass breaks so easily. No matter how careful you are. The traffic jars the shelves and things fall off them.
JIM: Still I'm awfully sorry that I was the cause.
LAURA: (Smiling) I'll just imagine he had an operation.
The horn was removed to make him feel less—freakish!
(They both laugh.)
Now he will feel more at home with the other horses, the ones that don't have horns. . . .
JIM: Ha-ha, that's very funny! (Suddenly serious.)
I'm glad to see that you have a sense of humor.
You know—you're—well—very different!
Surprisingly different from anyone else I know!
(His voice becomes soft and hesitant with a genuine feeling.)
Do you mind me telling you that?
(LAURA is abashed beyond speech.)
I mean it in a nice way . . .
(LAURA nods shyly, looking away.)

You make me feel sort of—I don't know how to put it!

I'm usually pretty good at expressing things, but—

This is something that I don't know how to say!

(LAURA touches her throat and clears it—turns the broken unicorn in her hands. Even softer.)

Has anyone ever told you that you were pretty?

(PAUSE: MUSIC. LAURA looks up slowly, with wonder, and shakes her head.)

Well, you are! In a very different way from anyone else.

And all the nicer because of the difference, too.

(His voice becomes low and husky. LAURA turns away, nearly faint with the novelty of her emotions.)

I wish that you were my sister. I'd teach you to have some confidence in yourself. The different people are not like other people, but being different is nothing to be ashamed of. Because other people are not such wonderful people. They're one hundred times one thousand. You're one times one! They walk all over the earth. You just stay here. They're common as—weeds, but—you—well, you're—Blue Roses!

(IMAGE ON SCREEN: BLUE ROSES. MUSIC CHANGES.)

LAURA: But blue is wrong for—roses . . .

JIM: It's right for you!—You're—pretty!

LAURA: In what respect am I pretty?

JIM: In all respects—believe me! Your eyes—your hair—are pretty! (He catches hold of her hand.)

You think I'm making this up because I'm invited to dinner and have to be nice. Oh, I could do that! I could put on an act for you, Laura, and say lots of things without being very sincere. But this time I am. I'm talking to you sincerely. I happened to notice you had this inferiority complex that keeps you from feeling comfortable with people. Somebody needs to build your confidence up and make you proud instead of shy and turning away and—blushing—

Somebody—ought to—

Ought to—kiss you, Laura!

(His hand slips slowly up her arm to her shoulder. MUSIC SWELLS TUMULTUOUSLY. He suddenly turns her about and kisses her on the lips. When he releases her, LAURA sinks on the sofa with a bright, dazed look. JIM backs away and fishes in his pocket for a cigarette. LEGEND ON SCREEN: "SOUVENIR.")

Stumble-john!

(He lights the cigarette, avoiding her look. There is a peal of girlish laughter from AMANDA in the kitchen. LAURA slowly raises and opens her hand. It still contains the little broken glass animal. She looks at it with a tender, bewildered expression.)

Stumble-john!

I shouldn't have done that—That was way off the beam.

You don't smoke, do you?

(She looks up, smiling, not hearing the question. He sits beside her a little gingerly. She looks at him speechlessly—waiting. He coughs decorously and moves a little farther aside as he considers the situation and senses her feelings, dimly, with perturbation. Gently.)

Would you—care for a—mint?

(She doesn't seem to hear him but her look grows brighter even.)

Peppermint—Life-Saver?

My pocket's a regular drug store—wherever I go . . .

(He pops a mint in his mouth. Then gulps and decides to make a clean breast of it. He speaks slowly and gingerly.)

Laura, you know, if I had a sister like you, I'd do the same thing as Tom. I'd bring out fellows and—introduce her to them. The right type of boys of a type to—appreciate her.

Only—well—he made a mistake about me.

Maybe I've got no call to be saying this. That may not have been the idea in having me over. But what if it was?

There's nothing wrong about that. The only trouble is that in my case—I'm not in a situation to—do the right thing.

I can't take down your number and say I'll phone.

I can't call up next week and—ask for a date.

I thought I had better explain the situation in case you—misunderstood it and—hurt your feelings . . .

(Pause. Slowly, very slowly, LAURA's look changes, her eyes returning slowly from his to the ornament in her palm. AMANDA utters another gay laugh in the kitchen.)

LAURA: (Faintly.) You—won't—call again?

JIM: No, Laura, I can't. (He rises from the sofa.)

As I was just explaining, I've—got strings on me.

Laura, I've—been going steady!

I go out all of the time with a girl named Betty. She's a home-girl like you, and Catholic, and Irish, and in a great many ways we—get along fine.

I met her last summer on a moonlight boat trip up the river to Alton, on the *Majestic*.

Well—right away from the start it was—love!

(LEGEND: LOVE! LAURA sways slightly forward and grips the arm of the sofa. He fails to notice, now enrapt in his own comfortable being.)

Being in love has made a new man out of me!

(Leaning stiffly forward, clutching the arm of the sofa, LAURA struggles visibly with her storm. But JIM is oblivious; she is a long way off.)

The power of love is really pretty tremendous!

Love is something that—changes the whole world, Laura!

(The storm abates a little and LAURA leans back. He notices her again.)

It happened that Betty's aunt took sick; she got a wire and had to go to Centralia. So Tom—when he asked me to dinner—I naturally just accepted the invitation, not knowing that you—that he—that I—(He stops awkwardly.)

Huh—I'm a stumble-john!

(He flops back on the sofa. The holy candles in the altar of LAURA's face have been snuffed out. There is a look of almost infinite desolation. JIM glances at her uneasily.)

I wish that you would—say something.

(She bites her lip which was trembling and then bravely smiles. She opens her hand again on the broken glass ornament. Then she gently takes his hand and raises it level with her own. She carefully places the unicorn in the palm of his hand, then pushes his fingers closed upon it.) What are you—doing that for? You want me to have him?—Laura? ~~(She nods.)~~ What for?

LAURA: A—souvenir . . .

(She rises unsteadily and crouches beside the victrola to wind it up. LEGEND ON SCREEN: "THINGS HAVE A WAY OF TURNING OUT SO BADLY!" OR IMAGE: "GENTLEMAN CALLER WAVING GOOD-BYE! GAILY." At this moment AMANDA rushes brightly back in the front room. She bears a pitcher of fruit punch in an old-fashioned cut-glass pitcher and a plate of macaroons. ~~The plate has a gold border and poppies painted on it.~~)

AMANDA: Well, well, well! Isn't the air delightful after the shower? I've made you children a little liquid refresment.

~~(Turns gaily to the gentleman caller.)~~

Jim, do you know that song about lemonade?

"Lemonade, lemonade

Made in the shade and stirred with a spade—

Good enough for an old maid!"

JIM: ~~(Uneasily)~~ Ha-ha! No—I never heard it.

AMANDA: Why, Laura! You look so serious!

JIM: We were having a serious conversation.

AMANDA: Good! Now you're better acquainted!

JIM: ~~(Uncertainly)~~ Ha-ha! Yes.

AMANDA: You modern young people are much more serious-minded than my generation. I was so gay as a girl!

JIM: You haven't changed, Mrs. Wingfield.

AMANDA: Tonight I'm rejuvenated! The gaiety of the occasion, Mr. O'Connor!

~~(She tosses her head with a peal of laughter. Spills lemonade.)~~

Oooo! I'm baptizing myself!

JIM: Here—let me—

AMANDA: ~~(Setting the pitcher down.)~~ There now. I discovered we had some maraschino cherries. I dumped them in, juice and all!

JIM: You shouldn't have gone to that trouble, Mrs. Wingfield.

AMANDA: Trouble, trouble? Why it was loads of fun!

Didn't you hear me cutting up in the kitchen? I bet your ears were burning! I told Tom how outdone with him I was for keeping you to himself so long a time! He should have brought you over much, much sooner! Well, now that you've found your way, I want you to be a very frequent caller! Not just occasional but all the time.

Oh, we're going to have a lot of gay times together! I see them coming!

Mmmm, just breathe that air! So fresh, and the moon's so pretty!

I'll skip back out—I know where my place is when young folks are having a —serious conversation!

JIM: Oh, don't go out, Mrs. Wingfield. The fact of the matter is I've got to be going.

AMANDA: Going, now? You're joking! Why, it's only the shank of the evening, Mr. O'Connor!

JIM: Well, you know how it is.

AMANDA: You mean you're a young workingman and have to keep working-men's hours. We'll let you off early tonight. But only on the condition that next time you stay later.

What's the best night for you, Isn't Saturday night the best night for you workingmen?

JIM: I have a couple of time-clocks to punch, Mrs. Wingfield. One at morning, another one at night!

AMANDA: My but you ARE ambitious! You work at night, too?

JIM: No, Ma'am, not work but—Betty!

(He crosses deliberately to pick up his hat. The band at the Paradise Dance Hall goes into a tender waltz.)

AMANDA: Betty? Betty? Who's—Betty?

(There is an ominous cracking sound in the sky.)

JIM: Oh, just a girl. The girl I go steady with!

AMANDA: (A long drawn exhalation.)

Ohhh . . . Is it a serious romance, Mr. O'Connor?

JIM: We're going to be married the second Sunday in June.

AMANDA: Ohhh—how nice!

Tom didn't mention that you were engaged to be married.

JIM: The cat's not out of the bag at the warehouse yet.

You know how they are. They call you Romeo and stuff like that.

(He stops at the oval mirror to put on his hat. He carefully shapes the brim and the crown to give a discreetly dashing effect.)

It's been a wonderful evening, Mrs. Wingfield. I guess this is what they mean by Southern hospitality.

AMANDA: It really wasn't anything at all.

JIM: I hope it don't seem like I'm rushing off. But I promised Betty I'd pick her up at the Wabash depot, an' by the time I get my jalopy down there her train'll be in. Some women are pretty upset if you keep 'em waiting.

AMANDA: Yes, I know— The tyranny of women! (Extends her hand.)

Good-bye, Mr. O'Connor.

I wish you luck—and happiness—and success! All three of them, and so does Laura!—Don't you, Laura?

LAURA: Yes!

JIM: (Taking her hand.) Good-bye, Laura. I'm certainly going to treasure that souvenir. And don't you forget the good advice I gave you. (Raises his voice to a cheery shout.)

So long, Shakespeare!

Thanks again, ladies— Good night!

(He grins and ducks jauntily out. Still bravely grimacing, AMANDA closes the door on the gentleman caller. Then she turns back to the room with a puzzled expression. She and LAURA don't dare to face each other. LAURA crouches beside the victrola to wind it.)

AMANDA: ~~(Faintly.)~~ Things have a way of turning out so badly.

I don't believe that I would play the victrola.

Well, well—well—

Our gentleman caller was engaged to be married!

Tom!

TOM: ~~(From back.)~~ Yes, Mother?

AMANDA: Come in here a minute. I want to tell you something awfully funny.

TOM: ~~(Enters with macaroon and a glass of the lemonade.)~~ Has the gentleman caller gotten away already?

AMANDA: The gentleman caller has made an early departure.

What a wonderful joke you played on us!

TOM: How do you mean?

AMANDA: You didn't mention that he was engaged to be married.

TOM: Jim? Engaged?

AMANDA: That's what he just informed us.

TOM: I'll be jiggered! I didn't know about that.

AMANDA: That seems very peculiar.

TOMS What's peculiar about it?

AMANDA: Didn't you call him your best friend down at the warehouse?

TOM: He is, but how did I know?

AMANDA: It seems extremely peculiar that you wouldn't know your best friend was going to be married!

TOM: The warehouse is where I work, not where I know things about people!

AMANDA: You don't know things anywhere! You live in a dream; you manufacture illusions! ~~(He crosses to the door.)~~

Where are you going?

TOM: I'm going to the movies.

AMANDA: That's right, now that you've had us make such fools of ourselves. The effort, the preparations, all the expense! The new floor lamp, the rug, the clothes for Laura! All for what? To entertain some other girl's fiancé!

Go to the movies, go! Don't think about us, a mother deserted, an unmarried sister who's crippled and has no job! Don't let anything interfere with your selfish pleasure!

Just go, go, go—to the movies!

TOM: All right, I will! The more you shout about my selfishness to me the quicker I'll go, and I won't go to the movies!

AMANDA: Go, then! Then go to the moon—you selfish dreamer!

(TOM smashes his glass on the floor. He plunges out on the fire-escape, ~~slamming the door. LAURA screams—cut by door. Dance hall music up.~~ TOM goes to the rail and grips it desperately, lifting his face in the chill white moonlight, ~~penetrating the narrow abyss of the alley. LEGEND ON SCREEN: "AND SO GOOD-BYE . . . ." TOM's closing speech is timed with the interior pantomime. The interior scene is played as though viewed through soundproof glass. AMANDA appears to be making a comforting speech to LAURA who is huddled upon the sofa. Now that we cannot hear the mother's speech, her silliness is gone and she has dignity and tragic beauty. LAURA's dark hair~~

(hides her face until at the end of the speech she lifts it to smile at her mother. AMANDA's gestures are slow and graceful, almost dancelike, as she comforts the daughter. At the end of her speech she glances a moment at the father's picture—then withdraws through the portieres. At close of TOM's speech, LAURA blows out the candles, ending the play.)

TOM: I didn't go to the moon, I went much further—for time is the longest distance between two places—

Not long after that I was fired for writing a poem on the lid of a shoe-box.

I left Saint Louis. I descended the steps of this fire-escape for the last time and followed, from then on, in my father's footsteps, attempting to find in motion what was lost in space—

I traveled around a great deal. The cities swept about me like dead leaves, leaves that were brightly colored but torn away from the branches.

I would have stopped, but I was pursued by something.

It always came upon me unawares, taking me altogether by surprise. Perhaps it was a familiar bit of music. Perhaps it was only a piece of transparent glass—

Perhaps I am walking along a street at night, in some strange city, before I have found companions. I pass the lighted window of a shop where perfume is sold. The window is filled with pieces of colored glass, tiny transparent bottles in delicate colors, like bits of a shattered rainbow.

Then all at once my sister touches my shoulder. I turn around and look into her eyes . . .

Oh, Laura, Laura, I tried to leave you behind me, but I am more faithful than I intended to be!

I reach for a cigarette, I cross the street, I run into the movies or a bar, I buy a drink, I speak to the nearest stranger—anything that can blow your candles out! (LAURA bends over the candles.)

—for nowadays the world is lit by lightning! Blow out your candles, Laura— and so good-bye . . . (She blows the candles out.)

THE SCENE DISSOLVES

Analysis: relation of cutting to whole play. The cutting begins in the middle of the last scene of the play. Amanda (mother of Tom and Laura), in her efforts to find security for her crippled daughter, Laura, has finally persuaded Tom to "find" a gentleman caller. When the much prepared for evening arrives, Laura is so overcome with shyness that she becomes ill, but after supper Amanda manages to see that Laura and Jim, the gentleman caller, are left alone. It is during this scene between Laura and Jim that the cutting begins; it continues to the end of the play and involves all four characters. The cutting includes the climax when it is learned that Jim is engaged and the culmination when Tom leaves—and looks back. The scene with Laura and Jim is a long one, so we have chosen to begin near the climax in order to include the culmination.

Analysis: movement of the situation. These units represent small segments of action during which there are no exits or entrances.

Unit 1

Laura and Jim	Jim and Laura speak of the broken unicorn who has lost his horn and his "differentness."
high point	Jim compliments Laura and kisses her.
high point in unit	Jim explains to a dazed Laura why he can't call again.

Unit 2

Laura, Jim, and Amanda	Amanda enters and chats gayly.
	Jim mentions a steady girl and Amanda is immediately tense.
climax of scene and of whole play	Jim explains that he is engaged and Amanda's "sky falls."
	Jim escapes after tense but mannered good-byes.

Unit 3

Amanda and Laura	Amanda and Laura, left alone, dare not look at each other.
	Amanda calls to Tom.

Unit 4

Amanda, Laura, and Tom	Tom is told that the gentleman caller is engaged.
	Amanda's inner tension is given outward voice as she upbraids Tom.
high point in unit	Tom storms back at her and finally plunges out the door—not to return.

Unit 5

Tom	Tom talks directly to the audience, explaining his future in relation to the past we have shared.

Analysis: conflict. Amanda, in her efforts to make her life and the lives of her children more secure, encounters difficulties; her purposes conflict with the circumstances and with the desires of Tom and of Laura. Finally, the conflict centers on the question of whether or not Amanda will succeed in her attempt to marry Laura off to the gentleman caller. Scene 7, from which this cutting is taken, is the crisis of the play. When Amanda learns that the gentleman caller is engaged, she knows that she has failed. From this crisis comes the final resolution of the conflict—Tom's escape.

Analysis: key speeches. Key speeches would include Jim's lines that determine the outcome of the conflict:

"I've—got strings on me, Laura. I've—been going steady!"

"We're going to be married the second Sunday in June."

The lines which illuminate the meaning of this scene, as well as the meaning of the whole play, are Tom's:

"Oh, Laura, Laura, I tried to leave you behind me, but I am more faithful than I intended to be!"

"—for nowadays the world is lit by lightning! Blow out your candles, Laura— and so good-bye . . ."

Analysis: characters. Laura is a shy, delicate, half-out-of-this-world young girl. A childhood illness left her crippled. Perhaps, because of this, she became shy and withdrawn. Her withdrawal from the world of reality increased until now she is "like a piece of her own glass collection, too exquisitely fragile to move from the shelf." Her basic motivation is to escape. Though she is drawn to Jim because he was her high school hero and because he is kind and warm to her, we feel that she can find restoration for the hurt in her world apart.

Amanda can best be described in the playwright's own words: "A little woman of great, but confused, vitality clinging frantically to another time and place. Her characterization must be carefully created, not copied from type. She is not paranoiac, but her life is paranoia. There is much to admire in Amanda, and as much to love and pity as there is to laugh at. Certainly she has endurance and a kind of heroism, and though her foolishness makes her unwittingly cruel at times, there is tenderness in her slight person."[2] Amanda's motivating desire is to find some securities in her insecure world. To assure that her daughter does not become "a little birdlike woman without any nest," she schemes and nags until a gentleman caller is promised. Her preparations for the event and her management of the occasion are the actions of a frustrated and silly woman, but the actions are motivated by love and give evidence of inner strength and courage. When she learns that she has failed, her hopes crash, but we somehow feel that Amanda will go on battling life.

2 *Ibid.*

Jim, the gentleman caller, is an outgoing young man. His personality made him the most popular boy in high school, but, since those days, it has failed to lead him to any success. Now he is trying to pull himself out of the rut of a dull warehouse job and to recover his old self-esteem. His desire to be liked and to find material success seems to be his basic drive.

Tom is a young man of intelligence and imagination who feels trapped by life. He suffocates in a shoe factory, writes poems on the lids of shoe boxes, and goes to movies to daydream of escape. When he does escape his family and job, he finds that he is still trapped by his memories of the past. He will always be haunted by the memory of his crippled sister.

Analysis: tone. There are extreme contrasts and delicate shadings of mood created in this scene. This is done largely through the symbolic meaning that one can easily attach to objects and character. The glass menagerie as a symbol of Laura's escape from a difficult, realistic world is clear. At the beginning of the scene the choicest piece, the unicorn, has been broken. And while Laura is able to make light of this because the unicorn has become "less freakish" and "more at home," we are aware that this unicorn is a symbol of herself and that she too *might have been* less freakish and more at home in the world. So, while the opening mood is light there is an undertone of the deeply serious. Jim as the Gentleman Caller is to Laura (and certainly to Amanda) "that long delayed but always expected something that we live for." Laura, perhaps for a moment, almost believes that Jim is that "something" that can become a part of her life. But Jim's revelation of a fiancée quickly dispels this illusion, and Laura is again lost and desolate. When Amanda enters, she briefly injects a gay mood into the tense scene, but this is short lived. Though Amanda's attitude is suddenly suspicious on the line, "Betty—Betty—Who's Betty?" and her sky falls on the line, "We're going to be married the second Sunday in June," she manages to control her emotion for mannered good-byes. When Jim leaves (without fully realizing how he has contributed to the pathos of their lives) the dream is gone. Laura, seeking escape, turns to wind the victrola (another symbol of her escape), but Amanda seeks a reason for her failure. Amanda's control breaks as she upbraids Tom for not knowing of Jim's engagement. The tension rises to a violent pitch when Tom plunges out of the room on to the fire escape and Amanda hurls her final accusation. The emotion of the scene is further charged because we sense the presence of the desperate and panic-stricken Laura. The final scene, in contrast, is one of quiet reflection.

The author's attitude toward his characters is compassionate and understanding. He is sympathetic as each character yearns and strives for his particular bit of happiness. But in the end his tone seems to imply that this is unattainable, that the reality of life is one of "quiet desperation." And we are emotionally aroused by the pathos of the situation and the tragedy of the individual lives.

Analysis: theme. What Tennessee Williams is saying in the whole play is caught in Tom's final speech. He implies here that the future will always be caught in the past. Tom cannot forget Laura; he cannot separate himself from those painful memories no matter how far he roams. But the playwright is not implying that Tom should have remained trapped by the love and pity he felt for his crippled sister; instead, he seems to be saying that although the past will always return and affect Tom, he must find ways to blow out Laura's candles for "nowadays the world is lit by lightning."

Oral Reading

Transitions, the climax, and abrupt changes in mood need to be handled carefully in this scene. The audience must have a clear idea of the setting, the characters involved, and the situation as it exists when the cutting begins. This can be accomplished by an introduction that "pictures" and brings an audience into the scene. The other difficult transition is between units 4 and 5. Tom's speech "I won't go to the movies," Amanda's last speech, and the narration should all prepare the audience for the transition that follows. The pause between the units should be significant. Control of the tension at the climax in unit 2 and the interplay of unit 4 (Amanda's and Tom's quarrel) are, perhaps, the most difficult parts of the scene. Care should be taken not to build with too much vocal strain—or to build too soon. The climax is one of *controlled* tension.

Contrasting tempos should be used as a means of differentiating the characters. Amanda's confused energy might be evident in a flexible voice, touched with the warm tones of Southern speech, and in a vital body with quick movements. Laura's shyness and out-of-this-world quality should be evident in her quiet, light voice and hesitant speech. Her body tempo would be slow and rather awkward to show her mental insecurity and physical handicap. Jim's general tempo, evident in speech and body rhythm, would be quicker and more vital than Tom's. The male reader might suggest the female characters by using his weaker vocal tones; the female might suggest the males by using her stronger tones, thus avoiding affected pitch changes to suggest the sex of the characters. In either case the rhythms of the separate personalities and the responses to various moods in the scene should help to suggest the sex differences.

There are some troublesome problems in the scene regarding the handling of props and physical contact. There is no need for narration to describe many of the actions such as Jim's drawing articles from his pockets and Amanda's baptizing herself. These can be suggested by body expression and small gestures. As the script indicates, narration should describe the kiss, but care should be taken not to break the mood.

12 LECTURE RECITAL, READER'S THEATRE, AND CHAMBER THEATRE

THE LECTURE RECITAL

A lecture recital is, as the name indicates, part lecture (speaking) and part recital (reading). An arrangement of selected pieces of literature is read aloud and illuminated with running comments, and what is said and what is read are bound together with a specific purpose. The focus may center around one of two purposes: (1) to clarify some aspect of an author's writing, or (2) to develop a theme by using selections from the works of different authors. In either case a specific purpose should lead the arranger to a theme or central idea which gives unity to the program. Everything he selects to read should focus and sharpen his theme, and any selection that does not do this should be discarded no matter how much he wants to include it. Much of the success of a lecture recital depends upon the interpreter's ability to keep everything "on theme" and to keep that theme clearly evident through his transitional remarks. An hour lecture recital is a good length for a club program. Unfortunately, students in an oral interpretation class are usually allowed no more than twenty minutes. This time limit is restrictive, but with careful planning an effective program can be arranged.

A student may find his inspiration for a "theme" lecture recital in a single poem. If, for instance, he likes a particular poem that has something to say about communication (war, love), he might set about finding what other authors have had to say about this subject. During his search he might decide to use a variety of forms—poetry, prose, and drama, or he might decide to build his lecture recital with selections of poetry alone. A student might wish to focus attention on a single writing: a novel, a long poem, or a play about which he wants to say something specific. Another student might prefer to use several examples from an author's works to focus attention on some aspect of the author's content or style. There are countless ways and means as well as numberless subjects to explore. Here are a few suggestions:

An investigation of some aspect of content or style (theme, character, humor, philosophy, structure, language) employed by one of these authors:

Sherwood Anderson	Tennessee Williams
Bertolt Brecht	Edna St. Vincent Millay
Truman Capote	Ogden Nash
e. e. cummings	Eugene O'Neill
Emily Dickinson	Katherine Anne Porter
T. S. Eliot	E. A. Robinson
William Faulkner	Carl Sandburg
Thomas Hardy	J. D. Salinger
Ernest Hemingway	Dylan Thomas
Eugene Ionesco	James Thurber
Henry James	Mark Twain
D. H. Lawrence	Eudora Welty

Frost's Comments on Human Nature
Thomas Wolfe on the Streets of His Time
F. Scott Fitzgerald and the Roaring Twenties
The Fantasy of Oscar Wilde
James Thurber and Children

The following titles may offer suggestions for the theme-lecture recital:

I Wonder As I Wander	Lincoln—The Man
Fathers	Poetry and Music
Roads	Folk Literature
Childhood	Children's Literature
Women in War	The Creation in Literature
Women in Poetry	Man and His Rebellions
The Negro Speaks	Love
Satires of Circumstances	The South

American Thought Revealed in Recent Pulitzer Prize Plays

The proper development of a central idea in a lecture recital assures the unity; but it does not always assure variety, balance, and harmony. In general, these aesthetic principles (as applied to an arrangement of program materials) say:

The most dramatic selection should be used as the climax of the whole program. This should be placed somewhere *near* the end, but not at the end.

The beginning selection should serve to establish a good relationship

between the reader and the audience and to give them time to adjust
to each other.

Although contrasts in mood are good within a program, it is usually
wise to lead away from one mood to another with material that shades
into the next mood.

To make for a smoother flow of the whole, short selections can be
grouped together (the listener forewarned of this).

The ending selection should be neither too short nor too long. It should
be selected to leave a sense of unity and harmony of the whole and
to give a feeling of a satisfying finale.

We can say, too, that a lecture recital subject is never too serious to take
a little humor, and a light subject is never too light to take a little serious-
ness. Too much laughter deadens humor, and too much gloom deadens the
listeners.

In giving the lecture recital, the interpreter's rapport with his listeners is
important. The lecture should not be read; it should be "talked." If the introduction, conclusion, and transitional comments are written out, they
should be said directly to the audience and referred to no more than an
effective speaker would refer to his notes. Although some of the transitions
between the readings may be short, they should furnish a moment of relaxation and direct communication with the audience.

Here are five lecture recital plans which were given by students:

The Ladies

1　Short excerpt from Kipling's poem "The Ladies."

2　Short poem, "Saint Catherine" (The Milton Abbas Rhyme).

3　Group of short poems by Dorothy Parker:
　"The Little Old Lady in Lavender Silk"
　"On Being a Woman"
　"Wisdom"

4　Short poem by Hughes Means, "The Lady with Technique."

5　Two excerpts from *John Brown's* Body by Stephen Vincent Benét:
　Mary Lou Wingate
　Lucy Weatherby

6　Poem by Ogden Nash, "The Seven Spiritual Ages of Mrs. Marmaduke
　Moore."

7　Poem by Shakespeare, "Sigh No More Ladies."

Robert Sherwood's Plays: Mirror to His Times

1　Passage from *Robert E. Sherwood* by Robert Shuman.

2　Passage from the preface to *Reunion in Vienna*.

3　Character speech from *The Petrified Forest*.

4   Character speech from *Idiot's Delight.*

5   Scene cutting from *Abe Lincoln in Illinois.*

6   Character speech from *There Shall Be No Night.*

7   "A Colleague's Eulogy" by Maxwell Anderson (*Time* 66:22, November 28, 1955).

Authors on the Streets of Their Time

1   London: Nineteenth Century
    from *Sketches by Boz* by Charles Dickens.

2   Wales: Twentieth Century
    from *Quite Early One Morning* by Dylan Thomas.

3   America: Twentieth Century
    from *Look Homeward, Angel:* "The Square" and "You Musta Been Away"
    by Thomas Wolfe.

Mothers

1   Poem, "Epilogue to Mother's Day . . ." by Ogden Nash.

2   Poem, "Sonnet to My Mother" by George Barker.

3   Two poem portraits:
    "Nancy Hanks" by Rosemary and Stephen Vincent Benét.
    "Mountain Woman" by DuBose Heyward.

4   Bible Story: I Kings 16–28.

5   Scene cutting from *The Caucasian Chalk Circle* by Bertolt Brecht.

Primitivism in Literature of the 1920's

1   Passage from "Melanchtha" by Gertrude Stein.

2   Passage from "Hands" from *Winesburg, Ohio* by Sherwood Anderson.

3   Passage from *The Great Gatsby* by F. Scott Fitzgerald.

4   Passage from *The Sun Also Rises* by Ernest Hemingway.

5   Passage from *The Sound and the Fury* by William Faulkner.

READER'S THEATRE

Reader's Theatre is a popular form of interpretative reading for group participation. Sometimes it is presented in an informal setting with the performers seated around a table reading assigned parts in a play; sometimes it becomes a formal "production" with the readers arranged on stage with lighting and sound effects used to suggest the dominant and changing mood of the reading. Since Reader's Theatre conforms to no one style, it invites imaginative experimentation.

There are, however, two characteristics that remain constant in any true Reader's Theatre performance. In every case the readers use scripts and the performance remains in the suggestive realm of oral interpretation. The performers suggest characters rather than represent characters; the effects suggest setting and atmosphere rather than represent them literally. The viewer, supplying the literal details of scene and action through his imagination, is able to feel into the dramatic situation.

An oral interpretation class may find Reader's Theatre an exciting and challenging final project. To serve as a guide for such a project we will briefly consider the choice and adaptation of material, the production style, and the performance techniques.

Choice and Adaptation of Material

Although drama is, perhaps, most frequently used for Reader's Theatre, prose and poetry adaptations can be equally successful. It is wise to avoid material where the situation and actions are of chief importance; selections emphasizing ideas, character, and character relationships are most suitable. Here are a few selections of prose, poetry, and drama which have been successfully adapted and performed.

Prose

"A Child's Christmas in Wales"   Dylan Thomas
"Brother to Dragons"   Robert Penn Warren
A Death in the Family   James Agee
Diary of Adam and Eve   Mark Twain
Alice in Wonderland   Lewis Carroll
* *The Ballad of the Sad Cafe* (arranged by Edward Albee)   Carson McCullers
The Little Prince   Antoine de Saint-Exupéry
The Pearl   John Steinbeck
The Thirteen Clocks   James Thurber
* *Thurber Carnival*   James Thurber

Poetry

God's Trombones   James W. Johnson
* *John Brown's Body*   Stephen Vincent Benét
The Bomb That Fell on America   Hermann Hagedorn
* *Spoon River Anthology*   Edgar Lee Masters
* *The World of Carl Sandburg* (arranged by Norman Corwin)   Carl Sandburg
* *An Evening's Frost* (A Portrait of the Poet by Donald Hall)   Robert Frost

Plays

Antigone   Sophocles
* *Don Juan in Hell*   George Bernard Shaw
Murder in the Cathedral   T. S. Eliot

Our Town   Thornton Wilder
The Boy with the Cart   Christopher Fry
The Enemy of the People   Henrik Ibsen
The Green Pastures   Marc Connelly
J. B.   Archibald MacLeish
*Under Milk Wood   Dylan Thomas
Blues for Mister Charlie   James Baldwin

Combined Materials

"I Wonder As I Wander" (Selected prose and poetry to represent the Negro's
voice in America)
"Man and His Rebellions" (Man's voiced rebellion in literature)

*In White America (Material from authentic historic documents dramatizing
the Negro's plight; arranged by Martin Duberman)

The above selections marked with an asterisk were produced professionally
on or off Broadway. Each was an adaptation and each employed techniques
similar to those used in Reader's Theatre; however, in most of these professional productions the lines were memorized and the scenes were created
"on stage" rather than out front in the minds of the audience. This removed the performance from the reader's realm and into the actor's. These
same selections, however, would be suitable for Reader's Theatre. Dylan
Thomas' *Under Milk Wood* has been produced both as a dramatization
and as a reading; it is, perhaps, more successful when it remains, as the
author intended, "a play for voices." Several years ago *John Brown's Body*
and *Don Juan in Hell* were professionally produced as Reader's Theatre.
Audiences responded enthusiastically, and Reader's Theatre as a form of
entertainment rose in popularity.

The director-adaptor of Reader's Theatre should select material that *can*
be arranged to accommodate the participating group and the time limit.
Material such as *Under Milk Wood* can be used as it is written with only
minor cuts. A long poem such as *John Brown's Body* contains different
themes. The arranger might decide to use one of the subordinate themes in
the poem. For instance, if he were limited to a thirty-minute arrangement
he might use the portraits of Lee, Lincoln, and other Civil War heroes and
tie the passages together with appropriate narration. The same process
could be followed in arranging a program featuring the writings of any
one author or the writings of several authors used to focus a theme. *An
Evening's Frost* and *The World of Carl Sandburg* are examples where each
arranger used various selections and appropriate narration to say something about the author's life and work. *In White America* is an example in
which the arranger told the story of the American Negro through recorded
speeches, diaries, and letters, and bound them together with narration.

In adapting narrative fiction the adaptor may use one or two narrators to represent the "central intelligence" of the story, or he may assign this to a chorus of voices. In most cases the character roles in the story are given to separate individuals. The arrangement, in a sense, becomes a dramatization for voices.

A group reading of drama may be handled in a similar way. The character roles may be assigned to individuals, each reader to be responsible for only one character, or three or four individuals may be responsible for all the roles. In some cases a narrator is added to handle the descriptions of the scenes and the explanations of change.

Production Style

The best production style for Reader's Theatre must be determined by the director as he considers the requirements of the material, the number of people to be involved, and the physical setting to be used. While he is making necessary changes in the script to best serve his particular group, he must also make decisions regarding the staging. He may decide that the best effect can be obtained by having the readers seated on stools with individual reading stands, or he may find that the use of platforms with central reading stands would be most effective. Usually, an appropriate degree of uniformity in dress is used. The possible ways of handling the material and the production are too numerous to mention. In each Reader's Theatre production the important criteria is that all elements be unified into an aesthetically pleasing whole.

Performance Techniques

Techniques for the individual performer are the same as those he has learned to use in solo readings of dramatic material. But in Reader's Theatre the individual performances must be synchronized into a group performance. A general clarification of performance techniques can be made through answering certain questions:

What about eye focus? When two characters are talking do they look at each other as they would in the play? When two or more characters are "on scene" talking, they do not address each other directly as in the play, for the scene should not be created on stage but in the minds of the listeners. To create and maintain this kind of illusion the *speaker* should visualize the character he is addressing out front in the realm of the audience. The listening character(s), while responding with facial expression and muscle tone changes which reflect his attitude, may either direct his eye focus on the speaker or out front. This is a subtle matter which must be decided by the director. In any case the interplay should be kept within the suggestive realm of oral interpretation.

What does the reader do when he is visible to the audience and yet off-scene? He should make himself as inconspicuous as possible by maintaining a quiet physical and mental attitude. Directors may have an off-scene reader either face the audience or turn slightly away to suggest his removal from the scene in progress. In either case, the reader should follow the script.

How does a reader enter a scene? For an entrance he may turn and speak, rise and speak, or move to a stand and speak. The reader's timing and mental alertness are very important when entering. His cue must be picked up properly and his first speech should reflect his character's motivation and attitude.

How does he exit from a scene? Generally, he exits in reverse of the way he entered. He may take a slight step back, turn, and return to his original place, or he may sit and/or turn and quickly assume his off-stage attitude. Smooth transitions for entrances and exits and change in scene are important concerns of the director (music and lighting can be effective aids for smooth transitions and change in focus), but each member of the cast should be aware of his responsibility in regard to transitions.

May the interpreter in Reader's Theatre go further in his character suggestions than in solo reading? Generally, he should go no further. As in reading drama alone, the interpreter is not being the character; he is suggesting the physical aspects and the mental attitude of his character in order that each listener can imagine the character and the scene in his mind's eye. We may say, however, that the degree of movement, gesture, and the vocal interpretation must always be considered in relation to the style of the particular production. This, of course, is determined by the director.

When both the arrangement of the literature and the production are handled with imagination, good taste, and skill, audiences respond enthusiastically. The demand that Reader's Theatre makes on the imagination is appealing to modern audiences.

CHAMBER THEATRE

Chamber Theatre, a relatively new method of staging short stories and novels, originated in the School of Speech of Northwestern University under the direction of Dr. Robert S. Breen.[1] To date, little has been written on the technique, but graduates of Northwestern have successfully intro-

[1] *Chamber Theatre* by Robert S. Breen (in preparation for publication).

duced the method into speech and drama departments in various colleges and universities. In this way it has gained attention and acclaim.

This brief discussion is (1) to report a specific experiment with the technique and (2) to offer a few basic guides for the uninitiated experimenter.

A Chamber Theatre Experiment

This report concerns an experiment in Chamber Theatre undertaken by a college oral interpretation class. The group consisted of twenty-six students, ranging from college sophomores to seniors, some with several years experience in dramatics, some with no experience; the majority were English majors who planned to teach on the secondary level. We proceeded in the following manner:

1   An example of a Chamber Theatre adaptation was mimeographed and distributed to the class along with a copy of the story (section) from which the arrangement was made (see "The Marriages," p. 25 and p. 206). The students were asked to study the two scripts.

2   A lecture on the basic principles of Chamber Theatre was given by a former student of Dr. Breen.[2] This was followed by a demonstration, using members of the class in the roles of the adaptation with other members observing. Answers to questions from the group and general discussion of the technique followed.

3   Each student in the class was asked to make a ten- to fifteen-minute arrangement of a scene from a short story or a novel and to submit plans for staging this.

4   From the submitted plans six were selected by the instructor to be given as class exercises, each to be directed by the adaptor with members of the class playing the roles.

Among the plans submitted were arrangements from the following stories and novels:

"The Stolen White Elephant"   Mark Twain
"The Secret Life of Walter Mitty" and "The Last Clock"   James Thurber
"A Detail"   Stephen Crane
Huckleberry Finn   Mark Twain
"Aerial Football: The New Game"   George Bernard Shaw
Ulysses   James Joyce
The Great Gatsby   F. Scott Fitzgerald
The Ballad of the Sad Cafe   Carson McCullers
"The Doll's House"   Katherine Mansfield
"How the Imp Made Amends for the Crust of Bread"   Leo Tolstoy

2 Mr. Kent Gravett, at that time director of Dramatics at Berea College.

The class response to this experiment was good. The members agreed that this experience had been both enjoyable and worthwhile. It had furnished an opportunity for creative work in a new dramatic form and method, an opportunity for directing others, and an opportunity for extending their experience in literature. Future teachers in the class felt, too, that they had been introduced to a valuable technique which could be used effectively in teaching literature on the secondary level.

To undertake an experiment such as the one described, students would need some knowledge of the basic principles of Chamber Theatre, the techniques for directing, staging and acting. We will undertake to clarify the basic principles and techniques.

Principles and Techniques of Chamber Theatre

General principles. Principles of Chamber Theatre are related to the philosophy of Bertolt Brecht and the methods he advanced in Epic Theatre. The epic method is an intellectual approach to drama. The intention is not to arouse an empathic response from an audience, but rather to hold up a narrative situation for an audience's "cool" judgment. This is done through the acting method (the *demonstration* of character) and through the use of screen projections, songs, dance, and so forth. These injected "effects" tend to remove the scene so that it can be viewed and judged in a detached manner without emotional involvement. Brecht's theories, however, cannot be applied fully to any but his own work, and Chamber Theatre has no intention of any such attempt.

Since interruptions, in the form of descriptions and comments, are inherent in narrative fiction, the transference of these to the stage in a Chamber Theatre production creates a degree of Brecht's "alienation" effect. But the use of further interruptions to create unusual effects or to discourage an audience's emotional involvement in the narrative situation and characters is entirely dependent upon the type of story or novel under consideration. An allegory, such as Huxley's *Brave New World* or a Thurber fable, in which the emphasis is less on literal surface meaning than on an implied moralistic-didactic meaning, might appropriately employ additional alienation effects in a Chamber Theatre production; but in a story like Hemingway's "A Clean Well Lighted Place," in which the characters present "a study in empathy," alienation effects would be out of place.

Dr. Breen explains the purpose of Chamber Theatre techniques in this way:

> The techniques of the Chamber Theatre were devised to present the novel, or narrative fiction, on the stage so that the dramatic action would unfold with

full and vivid immediacy, as it does in a play, but at the same time allowing the sensibility of the narrator, or the central intelligence in the form of the narrator or character to so condition our view of the action that we who listen and watch would receive a highly organized and unified impression of it.[3]

In narrative fiction authors *show* us the dramatic situation and its movement through the dialogue and the inner thoughts of characters, but they also interrupt the flow of events to have a narrator *tell* us through summaries and descriptions. In most plays a playwright only shows us the dramatic situation through dialogue and action. Only occasionally does a playwright borrow a narrative device (the use of a narrator) to tell us as well as show us (we find an example in *The Glass Menagerie,* in which Tom is both the narrator and a character involved in the action). Chamber Theatre uses the short story or novel as it is written to show us *and* to tell us; it uses the narrative form while it borrows from the dramatic form.

One theatrical quality borrowed, or transferred by the combining of the two forms, is "simultaneous action." The effect created in a play that many things are happening at the same time, as in life, is rarely found in narrative fiction (though James Joyce attempts this in *Ulysses*); but when the two forms (drama and narrative fiction) are united in Chamber Theatre, the effect of simultaneous action is conveyed. Dr. Breen says in regard to this:

> The Chamber Theatre is dedicated to the proposition that the ideal literary experience is one in which the simultaneity of the drama, representing the illusion of actuality (that is social realism), can be combined with the novel's privilege of examining human motivation at the moment of action.

But now let us be more specific as to how a short story or novel may be transferred to Chamber Theatre. This involves the recognition of a story's dramatic and narrative elements and the dramatization of its point of view.

Recognition and assignment of narrative and dramatic elements. Chamber Theatre handles the dramatic episodes within narrative fiction in much the same way as they are handled in a play. One actor is assigned to play each role; the parts are memorized and the actors play together and—to a degree—identify with their characters (see p. 143). Dramatic elements in the form of dialogue are easily recognized by quotation marks:

"Look! There's a man on the shore!"
"Where?"
"There. See 'im? See 'im?"
"Yes, sure! He's walking along."[4]

In a Chamber Theatre production these lines would be spoken as direct address by the persons acting the roles.

3 From Dr. Robert S. Breen's unpublished manuscript. Used with permission.
4 From "The Open Boat" by Stephen Crane.

Dramatic elements in the form of inner monologues are usually recognized by the author's use of directives such as "He thought that . . . ." "He feared that . . . ." "He remembered . . . ." and the like. There are examples of this in the same story, "The Open Boat." The correspondent, one of the men in the boat, tells us something of his unspoken thoughts in this passage:

> The correspondent, observing the others, knew that they were not afraid, but the full meaning of their glances was shrouded.
>
> *As for himself, he was too tired to grapple fundamentally with the fear. He tried to coerce his mind into thinking of it, but the mind was dominated at this time by the muscles, and the muscles said they did not care. It merely occurred to him that if he should drown it would be a shame.*

In Chamber Theatre the italicized lines would be spoken by the character as reflective thoughts.

Narrative elements in the form of directives and descriptions are easily recognized:

> "They'll have a boat out here for us in less than no time, now that they've seen us."
>
> *A faint yellow tone came into the sky over the low land. The shadows on the sea slowly deepened. The wind bore coldness with it, and the men began to shiver.* "Holy smoke!" *said one, allowing his voice to express his impious mood.* "If we keep on monkeying out here! If we've got to flounder out here all night!"

The italicized lines are, of course, narrative interruptions. In Chamber Theatre these are usually assigned to the narrator or to the character who represents the "central intelligence" of the story. The lines would be addressed to the audience.

As a student arranges a narrative for Chamber Theatre, he may wish to cut some of the narration and dialogue. And there may be legitimate reasons for doing this: time limits or a limited number of actors may make cuts necessary; cutting may make the selection more suitable or further the dramatic action. However, the adaptor should resist the impulse to turn the arrangement into a dramatization by cutting *all* the directive "tags" and other narrative interruptions. He should remember that this is a technique for presenting narrative fiction as it is written.

Dramatization of point of view. An author gives us a certain position from which we view the happenings in a narrative. This position is determined by identifying the author's appointed viewer, through whose eyes we see the action. To dramatize this view is the purpose of Chamber Theatre, and, to accomplish this effectively, the adaptor should have a clear understanding of the point-of-view techniques used by authors,[5] and he should have the knowledge of how to transfer these to Chamber Theatre.

[5] See Chapter 3 (pp. 24–32) for a discussion of point of view.

First, how is the external third-person narrator characterized in Chamber Theatre? He can be thought of as the author's imagined observer. If so, what is he like? How can he be characterized by the person assigned the role of narrator? Dr. Breen says:

> For the Chamber Theatre the first consideration is to look to the style of the narration to evaluate the tone of a particular novel or short story and to discover the character and personality of the narrator. Any relevance to the authorial point of view is purely accidental as far as the aesthetics of Chamber Theatre are concerned.[6]

To illustrate how an external point of view might be dramatized, we will use the quoted scene from "The Marriages" (p. 25). Note in this arrangement that the narrator and Adela are given the responsibility of reporting and focusing on *Adela's view* and that the other characters share the responsibility of describing their own actions and attitudes with the narrator. This is done to emphasize point of view. The characters' shifts from direct address with each other to audience-directed descriptions of themselves allow for varied perspectives of the scene without altering the central focus which is controlled by the narrator and Adela. This, of course, is only *one* way the passage might be arranged:

MRS. CHURCHLEY: *(to other characters)* Won't you stay a little longer?

NARRATOR: *(to audience)* the hostess said, holding the girl's hand and smiling.

MRS. CHURCHLEY: It's too early for everyone to go; it's too absurd. *(to audience)* Mrs. Churchley inclined her head to one side and looked gracious; she held up her face, in a vague, protecting, sheltering way,

NARRATOR: an enormous fan of red feathers.

ADELA: Everything about her, to Adela Chart, was enormous. She had big eyes, big teeth, big shoulders, big hands, big rings and bracelets, big jewels of every sort and many of them.

NARRATOR: The train of her crimson dress was longer than any other; her house was huge; her drawing-room, especially now that the company had left it, looked vast, and it offered to the girl's eyes a collection of the largest sofas and chairs, pictures, mirrors, and clocks that she had ever beheld.

ADELA: Was Mrs. Churchley's fortune also large, to account for so many immensities?

NARRATOR: Of this Adela could know nothing, but she reflected while she smiled sweetly back at their entertainer,

ADELA: that she had better try to find out.

NARRATOR: Mrs. Churchley had at least a high-hung carriage drawn by the tallest horses, and in the Row she was to be seen perched on a mighty hunter. She was high and expansive herself,

MRS. CHURCHLEY: though not exactly fat;

NARRATOR: her bones were big, her limbs were long,

[6] *Ibid.*

ADELA: and she had a loud, hurrying voice like the bell of the steamboat.

MRS. CHURCHLEY: While she spoke to his daughter she had the air of hiding from Colonel Chart, a little shyly, behind the wide ostrich fan.

COLONEL: But Colonel Chart was not a man to be either ignored or eluded. *(to others)* Of course everyone is going on to something else. I believe there are a lot of things to-night.

MRS. CHURCHLEY: And where are you going?

NARRATOR: Mrs. Churchley asked, dropping her fan and turning her bright, hard eyes on the Colonel.

COLONEL: Oh, I don't do that sort of thing!

ADELA: he replied, in a tone of resentment just perceptible to his daughter. She saw in it that he thought Mrs. Churchley might have done him a little more justice. But what made the honest soul think that she was a person to look to for a perception of fine shades?

When the *objective* third-person narrator's view is transferred to Chamber Theatre there is less distortion, for this view is closer to the dramatic mode. Hemingway in his story "A Clean Well Lighted Place" uses a third-person narrator (sparingly) throughout. This story is easy to arrange for Chamber Theatre because it is written in dramatic form. The narrator remains outside the action describing the bare details of setting and directing the shifts in scene; three characters are seen and understood through their terse dialogue and inner thoughts. This limiting of the point of view tends to increase a reader's or an audience's immediate involvement in the action.

When dramatizing either the first-person view, in which a character tells his own story, or the first-person-observer view, in which the narrator is a character in the action, the adaptor's main problem concerns the movement of the character-narrator in and out of the action of the story. In *The Adventures of Huckleberry Finn* the first-person view might be dramatized in Chamber Theatre as it is written with Huck as both narrator and character. He would move in and out of the action as Tom does in the play *The Glass Menagerie*. For instance, in Chapter 23 of *The Adventures of Huckleberry Finn*, Huck, the narrator, would speak directly to the audience when telling of the king's and duke's theatrical adventures, and then he would move into the acting area as he says:

By and by, when they was asleep and snoring, Jim says,

And the scene would continue as in a play:

JIM: Don't it s'prise you de way dem kings carries on, Huck?

HUCK: No, I says, it don't.

JIM: Why don't it Huck?

HUCK: Well it don't, because it's in the breed. I reckon they're all alike.

JIM: But, Huck, dese kings o'ourn is reglar rapscallions; dat's jist what dey is; reglar rapscallions.

HUCK: Well, that's what I'm a-saying; all kings is mostly rapscallions, as fur as I can make out.

JIM: Is dat so?

HUCK: You read about them once—you'll see. Look at Henry the Eight; this'n' 's a Sunday-school Superintendent to *him*. . . . My, you ought to seen old Henry the Eight when he was in bloom. He *was* a blossom. He used to marry a new wife every day, and chop off her head next morning and he would do it just as indifferent as if he was ordering up eggs. 'Fetch up Nell Gwynn,' he says. They fetch her up. Next morning, 'Chop off her head!' And they chop it off. 'Fetch up Jane Shor,' he says; and up she comes. Next morning, 'Chop off her head'— and they chop it off. . . . You don't know kings, Jim, but I know them; and this old rip of ourn is one of the cleanest I've struck in history. Well, Henry he takes a notion he wants to get up some trouble with this country. How does he go at it—give notice?—give the country a show? No. All of a sudden he heaves all the tea in Boston Harbor overboard, and whacks out a declaration of independence, and dares them to come on. That was *his* style—he never give anybody a chance. . . . All I say is, kings is kings, and you got to make allowances. Take them all around, they're a mighty ornery lot. It's the way they're raised.

JIM: But dis one do *smell* so like de nation, Huck.

HUCK: Well, they all do, Jim. *We* can't help the way a king smells; history don't tell no way.

JIM: Now de duke, he's a tolerble likely man in some ways.

HUCK: Yes, a duke's different. But not very different. This one's a middling hard lot for a duke. When he's drunk there ain't no near-sighted man could tell him from a king.

JIM: Well, anyways, I doan' hanker for no mo'un um, Huck. Dese is all I kin stan'.

HUCK: It's the way I feel, too, Jim. But we've got them on our hands, and we got to remember what they are, and make allowances. Sometimes I wish we could hear of a country that's out of kings.

Sometimes, however, the shifts from narrator to character occur too swiftly to be handled in this way. One student, adapting scenes from this novel used two Huck Finns: one to tell his story, another to act out the remembered scenes. This method, with the aid of lighting effects, proved dramatically successful. The subjective "telling" was accompanied by an objective "showing," and, in this case, the showing helped the audience to understand and share Huck's point of view.

Directing and staging. The most troublesome problems in directing Chamber Theatre concern the integration of the performers' actions with the actions of the story and the handling of narrative interruptions. The actor's shifts from a character to a storyteller, from contact with another character to contact with the audience and the narrator's or character's "he said" interruptions are awkward to perform at first.

A director is wise to arrange a number of reading and discussion rehearsals to clarify the "idea" of Chamber Theatre for his cast. A general foreknowledge of the objectives in relation to the particular story or novel makes for harmonious ensemble work.

Early rehearsals must be given to "setting" the form and the movements. A director's prerehearsal plans for line assignments, movements, and so forth may not work in practice; creative ideas develop during rehearsals. The actor should be given the opportunity to improvise, to co-create with the director. The blocking and the memorization of lines should be set early enough in the rehearsal schedule to allow time for polishing, for the "shifts" take time and good ensemble work to perform smoothly. The form gives the director the chance to move his cast freely and to insert stage business and effects. Though the narrator is usually given a designated area from which to move and return, he is not confined; he may move into the acting area as a character—or as a narrator. Sometimes he moves close to the characters as he describes or comments, or, in some instances, he may move into the audience. Repetition of certain movements, dance, or any unusual effect with figures can be used to make an event striking or funny. In a student adaptation of "The Secret Life of Walter Mitty," figures formed the revolving door for Walter Mitty to enter. In an adaptation of another Thurber story, "The Last Clock," characters stood with their backs to the audience until called into the scene; and at other times, they moved together into "set" positions, all turning together to enter the scene at the end. Thurber's stories and fables lend themselves to playful stylized effects.

The staging of Chamber Theatre depends, of course, upon the purpose of the presentation and available resources. One of the values of the form is its flexibility; it lends itself to different purposes. A Chamber Theatre arrangement may be staged fully as an evening's entertainment—a "major production;" or an arrangement may be presented in a living room or classroom to entertain or to "instruct," using only a minimum of suggestive set pieces. In any case, the imaginative director can put his creative ideas to work as he experiments with Chamber Theatre.

Acting. As we have said, a narrator's characterization can be discovered by studying the style and tone of the story or novel from which the arrangement was made. In the same way, an actor, playing a character role, finds evidences of his character's outer appearance and inner motivation by what the character says and does in the story, by what other characters say about him, and by the comments and descriptions in the narration.

The narrator or a character, as has been explained, may change roles. These shifts discourage the actor from a close identification with his character—from "feeling" the part. Some stories may be handled in the more traditional manner (characters creating an empathic response as in a play), but often, the actor's identification is close to "suggestion," as in oral readings or Reader's Theatre. Epic Theatre calls for the "demonstration" of a character, and perhaps this is the term that best describes the degree of character identification appropriate in many cases.

Ensemble playing is important. A character in a Chamber Theatre production does not "remove" himself while still on scene as he does in Reader's Theatre. While on scene, players respond and listen to each other. Their actions and reactions during a narrator's descriptions and comments give the impression that many things are happening at the same time. There is a constant process of giving and taking going on. This communication is between the players and between the players and the audience. As Dr. Breen says:

> The Chamber Theatre recognizes the difference between a novel and a play, but it insists that the two can be brought into functional harmony, not by adapting the novel into a conventional play, but by presenting the novel on stage as written, using such borrowed advantages of the drama as simultaneity.

COMBINED FORMS

Though it is well for students to recognize Reader's Theatre as defined in this chapter, the fact should be stressed that few productions are "true" Reader's Theatre. Directors, experimenting with form, have found the conventional "rules" (mainly, the use of scripts and off-stage focus) confining. Often the techniques of the play form are combined with those of Reader's Theatre. A director may feel that "on-stage" focus is more appropriate for certain segments of an adaptation. For example, in a production of *The Little Prince* by Antoine de Saint-Exupéry, the little Prince moved between the past and the present. When in the present, he used a reading script and stand, and maintained off-stage focus; but when he moved into scenes of the past, there was a shift to on-stage focus: he and the other characters spoke memorized lines directly to each other, as in a play. Sometimes the techniques of Chamber Theatre and Reader's Theatre are combined. For example, in a class production of a compiled script inspired by *In White America,* the major part of the production was presented as Reader's Theatre; but at a certain point, a Chamber Theatre arrangement of Faulkner's "Dry September" was used. In the hands of a sensitive director, such combinations of forms and techniques may serve to enhance the communication of the literature.

APPENDICES

APPENDIX I
BIBLIOGRAPHY

GENERAL

Aggertt, Otis J., and Elbert R. Bowen. *Communicative Reading.* Second Edition. New York: The Macmillan Company, 1963.

Anderson, Virgil A. *Training and Speaking Voice.* Second Edition. New York: Oxford University Press, 1961.

Bacon, Wallace A., and Robert S. Breen. *Literature as Experience.* New York: McGraw-Hill Book Co., Inc., 1959.

Beloof, Robert. *The Performing Voice in Literature.* Boston: Little, Brown and Company, 1966.

Cobin, Martin. *Theory and Technique of Interpretation.* Englewood Cliffs, New Jersey: Prentice-Hall, Inc., 1959.

Fairbanks, Grant. *Practical Voice Practice.* New York: Harper & Row, 1964.

Geiger, Don. *Oral Interpretation and Literary Study.* San Francisco: Peter Van Vloten, 1958.

Geiger, Don. *The Sound, Sense, and Performance of Literature.* Chicago: Scott, Foresman and Company, 1963.

Grimes, Wilma H., and Alethea Smith Mattingly. *Interpretation: Writer-Reader-Audience.* San Francisco: Wadsworth Publishing Company, Inc., 1961.

Heinberg, Paul. *Voice Training—For Speaking and Reading Aloud.* New York: The Ronald Press Co., 1964.

Katz, Robert L. *Empathy: Its Nature and Uses.* New York: The Macmillan Company, 1963.

Lee, Charlotte I. *Oral Interpretation,* Third Edition. Boston: Houghton Mifflin Company, 1965.

Lowrey, Sara, and Gertrude E. Johnson. *Interpretative Reading.* Revised Edition. New York: Appleton-Century-Crofts, Inc., 1953.

Lynch, Gladys E., and Harold C. Crain. *Projects in Oral Interpretation.* New York: Henry Holt, 1959.

Mouat, Lawrence H. *Reading Literature Aloud.* New York: Oxford University Press, 1962.

Parrish, Wayland Maxwell. *Reading Aloud.* Third Edition. New York: The Ronald Press Co., 1953.

Philipson, Morris. *Aesthetics Today.* Meridian Books M112. Cleveland: The World Publishing Company, 1961.

Rahv, Philip. *Image and Idea.* New York: New Directions, 1957.

Roach, Helen. *Spoken Records.* New York: The Scarecrow Press, Inc., 1963.

Smith, Joseph F., and James R. Linn. *Skill in Reading Aloud.* New York: Harper and Brothers, 1960.

Sypher, Wylie. *Loss of Self in Modern Literature and Art.* New York: Vintage Books: a division of Random House, 1964.

Thrall, William F., Addison Hibbard, and C. Hugh Holman. *A Handbook to Literature.* New York: The Odyssey Press, Inc., 1960.

Vivas, Eliseo, and Murray Krieger, eds. *Problems of Aesthetics.* New York: Rinehart & Company, Inc., 1953.

Woolbert, Charles H., and Severina E. Nelson. *The Art of Interpretative Speech: Principles and Practices of Effective Reading.* Fourth Edition. New York: Appleton-Century-Crofts, Inc., 1956.

PROSE

Bloom, Edward A. *The Order of Fiction: An Introduction.* New York: The Odyssey Press, Inc., 1964.

Brooks, Cleanth, and Robert Penn Warren. *Understanding Fiction.* New York: F. S. Crofts and Company, 1943.

Forster, E. M., *Aspects of the Novel.* New York: Harcourt, Brace and Company, Inc., 1947.

James, Henry. *The Art of Fiction.* New York: Oxford University Press, 1948.

Mizener, Arthur. *The Sense of Life in the Modern Novel.* Boston: Houghton Mifflin Co., 1964.

O'Connor, William Van. *Modern Prose: Form and Style.* New York: Thomas Y. Crowell Company, 1954.

Sklare, Arnold B., ed. *The Art of the Novella.* New York: The Macmillan Company, 1965.

Thompson, David W., and Virginia Fredericks. *Oral Interpretation of Fiction: A Dramatic Approach.* Minneapolis: Burgess Publishing Co., 1964.

Walcutt, Charles Child. *An Anatomy of Prose.* New York: The Macmillan Company, 1962.

Wesserstrom, William. *The Modern Short Novel.* New York: Holt, Rinehart and Winston, Inc., 1965.

POETRY

Blackmur, R. P. *Form and Value in Modern Poetry.* New York: Doubleday Anchor Books, 1957.

Bloom, Edward A., Charles H. Philbrick, and Elmer M. Blistein. *The Order of Poetry: An Introduction.* New York: The Odyssey Press, Inc., 1961.

Brooks, Cleanth, and Robert Penn Warren. *Understanding Poetry.* New York: Holt, Rinehart and Winston, Inc., 1950.

Ciardi, John. *How Does a Poem Mean?* Boston: Houghton Mifflin Company, 1959.

Ciardi, John, ed. *Mid-Century American Poets.* New York: Twayne Publishers, 1950.

Dolman, John, Jr. *The Art of Reading Aloud.* New York: Harper & Row, 1956.

Drew, Elizabeth. *Poetry: a Modern Guide to Its Understanding and Enjoyment.* New York: Dell Publishing Company, Inc., 1959.

Drew, Elizabeth, and George Connor. *Discovering Modern Poetry.* New York: Holt, Rinehart and Winston, Inc., 1961.

Eastman, Max. *Enjoyment of Poetry with Anthology for Enjoyment of Poetry.* New York: Charles Scribner's Sons, 1951.

Hillyer, Robert. *In Pursuit of Poetry.* New York: McGraw-Hill Book Co., Inc., 1960.

Wright, George T. *The Poet in the Poem: The Personae of Eliot, Yeats and Pound.* Berkeley and Los Angeles: University of California Press, 1960.

DRAMA

Bentley, Eric. *The Life of the Drama.* New York: Atheneum, 1964.

Boleslavsky, Richard. *Acting: The First Six Lessons.* New York: Theatre Arts Books, 1949.

Brooks, Cleanth, and Robert B. Heilman, eds. *Understanding Drama.* New York: Holt, Rinehart and Winston, Inc., 1945.

Brustein, Robert. *The Theatre of Revolt.* Boston: Little, Brown and Company, 1964.

Chekhov, Michael. *To the Actor.* New York: Harper and Brothers, 1953.

Kerr, Walter. *How Not to Write a Play.* New York: Simon and Schuster, 1955.

McGaw, Charles. *Acting Is Believing: A Basic Method for Beginners.* New York: Holt, Rinehart and Winston, Inc., 1953.

Roby, Robert C., and Barry Ulanov. *Introduction to Drama.* New York: McGraw-Hill Book Co., Inc., 1962.

Wellwarth, George E. *The Theatre of Protest and Paradox: Developments in the Avant-Garde Drama.* New York: New York University Press, 1964.

APPENDIX II
CLASS PROJECTS

The following are oral projects which may be used with this textbook at the discretion of the teacher.

Oral Project I   (refer to pp. 51–68)

The following are oral projects which may be used with this textbook at the discretion of the teacher.

1 Reading the selection aloud for the class.
2 Discussing the problem presented in the exercise.
3 Asking for questions or comments from the group.

The purpose of this oral project is to provide immediate application of the analysis techniques (Chapters 3 and 4) and to stimulate interesting classroom activity.

For each exercise assigned to you, you should prepare carefully to keep the reading and discussion within the required time limit. Form 1 (p. 223) may be used to clarify the individual or group assignments.

Oral Project II   Voice and Diction: Chapter 6

These specific applications of voice and speech techniques are based on the assumption that speech laboratory equipment is available and that practice and conference periods can be scheduled outside of class. The work in the speech laboratory may be divided in the following way (dependent, of course, on available equipment and supervision):

Early in the semester 5 or 6 laboratory periods are scheduled within a two-week period for concentrated work on voice and speech needs.

For the remaining weeks in the semester, one laboratory period is scheduled each week. This weekly laboratory period is for continued work on voice and speech as needed by the individual student and for recording and listening in preparation for class performances.

Your work on voice and diction in both the classroom and the laboratory may include these steps:

1 Meet with group in speech laboratory to receive instructions in operating equipment. Individual tapes will be issued at this time.
2 On your individual tape, record prose, poetry (own choice), sentences, and impromptu reading (Form 2, p. 225). This recording is for your voice and speech evaluation.
3 Read "Voice Production" from Chapter 6 (pp. 84–91). Participate in class discussion and demonstration of exercises: control of breathing, control of phonation, and control of resonance (one class period).
4 Read "Vocal Variety" from Chapter 6 (pp. 106–14). Participate in class discussion and demonstration of exercises: variety of volume, pitch, quality, and timing (one class period).
5 Read "Word Production" from Chapter 6 (pp. 91–106). Participate in class discussion and demonstration of exercises: vowel sounds, diphthongs, consonant sounds, assimilation, and rapid speech flow (one class period).
6 With your teacher's written evaluation of your voice and speech (Form 3, p. 227) in hand, *listen* to your recording to become aware of your particular strengths and weaknesses in voice and diction as pointed out in the evaluation.
7 Meet in conference with your teacher to discuss your voice and speech evaluation. Be prepared to offer suggestions to help set up a laboratory program of most benefit to you.
8 When your semester laboratory program is completed (Form 4, p. 229), study this form to make sure you understand your program and your particular goals.
9 Meet at your scheduled laboratory period. Be prompt. Other people will be there to assist you. Consider the time spent in the laboratory as part of your preparation for class work. Work on one problem at a time:

take the exercise
record sentences or passage to apply technique
listen and *evaluate*
repeat the recording and listening process until you have made some improvement and have begun to set up a new habit
add other exercises as indicated on your evaluation
at each practice period in the laboratory, go back over your first exer-

APPENDICES

cises and reading applications and add a new exercise; proceed in this way until you have completed your program.

10 At the end of each week, hand in an evaluation of your progress in the laboratory work (Form 5, p. 230).

Oral Project III   The Essay

One semester is too short to allow time for all the projects included here. Since something must be omitted, your instructor may decide to omit the essay. Such a decision will be made on the basis of class interests and needs.

General assignment:

Prepare a five- to eight-minute essay reading to be shared with the class.
Read essays by various authors before making your choice.
Hand in an annotated list of this reading.
Hand in a written analysis of your reading *at least* two days before your scheduled reading.

Prepare carefully:

1   Read Chapter 9, "Oral Interpretation of Prose" (pp. 137–40), and participate in class discussion.
2   Select your essay carefully. Read essays that are new to you in order to become acquainted with new writers. As you read, write down your reactions briefly: Why, or why not, would this essay be a good choice for oral reading? In this way, prepare your annotated list.
3   Cut the essay so that it can be read within the time limit.
4   Record and listen in the laboratory:

Mark a copy of your essay to call attention to techniques (voice, diction, phrasing, emphasis, and subordination that you need to consciously apply).
Be conscious of using the techniques as you record.
Listen and evaluate and repeat until you can note improvement.
Let some time pass without such practice; then read from an *unmarked* copy, keeping your focus on the author's thought and attitude. Listen to this recording and evaluate.

5   Practice orally outside the laboratory:

Use the classroom, if possible, and read from the unmarked copy. Imagine an audience present. Do not think about techniques or yourself; keep the focus on sharing the author's thought and attitude.

6 Turn in to your instructor a written analysis of your essay (at least two days before your scheduled reading). Turn in your annotated list of reading for this assignment.

Oral Project IV   Reading of Narrative Fiction

General assignment:

Prepare a ten- to twelve-minute reading of narrative fiction.
   Read stories from various authors before making your choice.
   Hand in an annotated list of this reading.
   Hand in a written analysis of your chosen reading two days before your scheduled class reading.

These steps should precede your class performance:

1 Read in Chapter 9, "Oral Interpretation of Prose," (pp. 140–56), and participate in the class discussion of the problems and solutions of reading the narrative effectively (one class period).
2 Select a short story or a cutting from a novel which *combines narration, description, and dialogue.* Make your selection at least two weeks in advance of your reading date.
3 Cut the story or section of a novel so that it can be read within the time limit. If you wish to introduce the entire story in the alloted time, you may summarize in the introduction and at intervals in the reading.
4 Analyze your reading (note the analysis of "First Confession" at the end of Chapter 9, pp. 150–52). If you choose a climactic episode from a novel, analyze the cutting, not the entire novel; but be sure to relate the cutting to the whole novel.
5 Record and listen in the laboratory:

   Mark a copy of your story to call attention to techniques that you need to consciously apply.
   Listen and evaluate and repeat until you can note improvement.
   Let some time pass without such practice; then read from an unmarked copy, keeping your focus on the author's thought, images, and his characters' desires. Listen and evaluate.

6 Practice orally outside the laboratory:

   For a time, work on character voices and body suggestions. Then, put techniques out of mind and control characterization through concentration.

7   Turn in an annotated list of reading done for this assignment. Note the annotated list of suggestions on p. 238. This reading may disclose appropriate material for the lecture recital and Chamber Theatre needed later in the course.
8   Turn in a written analysis of your narrative selection.
9   Read what other text books have to say about reading narrative material:

Beloof, *The Performing Voice in Literature* (Chapter 10, pp. 329–336).
Lee, *Oral Interpretation*, 3rd edition (Chapter 7, pp. 201–218).
Cobin, *Theory and Techniques of Interpretation* (Chapter 2, pp. 178–187; Chapter 13, pp. 204–217).

10 Listen to prepared tapes of interpretations of narrative prose by professional readers.

Oral Project V   Poetry Reading

General assignment:

Prepare a 10- to 12-minute reading of poetry including a lyric poem, a narrative *or* dramatic poem, and a humorous poem. Read widely before choosing; make a written report of this reading, and analyze your selections as you did for Project IV.

These steps should precede your class performance:

1   Read Chapter 10, "Oral Interpretation of Poetry" (pp. 157–76). Your selections should be made two weeks in advance of your scheduled reading.
2   Consult the list of suggestions for each type of poetry (p. 241).
3   Analyze each poem that you are to read. Note the analysis form used for "Stopping by Woods on a Snowy Evening" at the end of Chapter 10 (pp. 173–75).
4   Record, listen, and evaluate your poetry reading in the laboratory in the same way you did for prose.
5   Practice reading your poems outside the laboratory as you did for prose.
6   Turn in to your instructor the written analysis and your comments on any poetry "discoveries" you might have made.
7   Read what other text books have to say about reading poetry:

Lee, 3rd edition, Chapters 10 and 11.
Cobin, Chapters 12 and 15.
Grimes-Mattingly, *Interpretation*, Chapter 5.
Beloof, "Rhythm," Chapter 12.

8 Listen in the laboratory to tapes of interpretations of poetry by professional readers.

Oral Project VI   Drama Reading

General assignment:

Prepare a fifteen-minute cutting of a play to be read in class.
Analyze your cutting.
Hand in a report or an annotated list of your reading done for this assignment.

These steps should precede your class performance:

1 Read Chapter 11, "Oral Interpretation of Drama," (pp. 177–93), and participate in class discussion (one class period).
2 Consult the list of suggested plays (p. 244) to aid you in your choice.
3 Analyze your cutting (note the form suggested on p. 180).
4 As for other projects: record, listen, and evaluate your drama reading in the laboratory.
5 Practice reading your drama outside the laboratory many times.
6 Hand in your analysis and an annotated list (or comments) of reading done for this assignment.
7 Read what other text books have to say about reading drama:

Lee, Chapters 8 and 9.
Cobin, Chapter 13.
Grimes-Mattingly, Chapter 7.

8 Listen in the speech laboratory to a tape of drama interpretations by professional readers.

Oral Project VII   Lecture Recital

Time limitations may make it necessary for you to choose between a drama reading and a lecture recital.

General assignment:

Arrange and present a twenty-minute program. Your purpose may be:

1 To clarify some aspect of an author's writing by reading from his works.
2 To develop a theme by using selections from the works of different authors.

Either of these purposes would require the following steps:

1 Read Chapter 12 (pp. 194–97) and note subject suggestions.
2 Arrange for a conference with your instructor.
3 Read widely to find the right material and to become acquainted with your author (if this is your approach).
4 Arrange selections in the best order to develop the central idea and to contribute variety and harmony to the whole.
5 Prepare good narration (introduction, transitions, and conclusion) to tie the program together.
6 Hand in a list of your reading for this assignment.

Project VIII   Chamber Theatre

General assignment:

Select and arrange a short story or a part of a novel for Chamber Theatre (not to exceed fifteen minutes).

1 Read Chapter 12 (pp. 201–10) and participate in the discussion and the *demonstration* in class.
2 Submit your adaptation with plans for staging. (If time permits, some of the arrangements may be produced as class exercises.)

Project IX   Reader's Theatre

As a final project your teacher may wish to include a classroom production or a fully staged production of Reader's Theatre. If this is done, it may be necessary to devote the last few weeks of the course to this group activity. Read Chapter 12, "Reader's Theatre" (pp. 197–201).

APPENDIX III
FORMS

FORM 1

ASSIGNMENT FORM

ORAL PROJECT I
Assigned to: .

ANALYSIS EXERCISES

Oral Analysis Exercises (Language)

Exercise 1 (p. 52) **Relationships of Words and Phrases**: selected sentences.
Time Limit: 8 minutes. _____

Exercise 2 (p. 53) **Allusions, Imagery, and Figurative Language**: "The Scoffers" by William Blake.
Time Limit: 8 minutes. _____

Oral Analysis Exercises (Situation)

Exercise 3 (p. 53) **Point of View and Language**: "Since There's No Help" by Michael Drayton.
Time Limit: 8 minutes. _____

Exercise 4 (p. 54) **Situation and Language**: "A Box to Hide In" by James Thurber.
Time Limit: 10 minutes. _____

Exercise 5 (p. 55) **Point of View and Time**: "The Laboratory" by Robert Browning.
Time Limit: 12 minutes. _____

Oral Analysis Exercises (Movement of Situation)

Exercise 6 (p. 57) Structure and Language: "The
River Merchant's Wife: A Letter" by Ezra Pound.
Time Limit: 10 minutes.   _____

Exercise 7 (p. 58) Structure and Language: "The
Harbor" by Carl Sandburg.
Time Limit: 6 minutes.   _____

Exercise 8 (p. 58) Structure and Language:
"The Bombardment" by Amy Lowell.
Time Limit: 15 minutes.   _____

Oral Analysis Exercises (Tone)

Exercise 9 (p. 60) Tone and Language:
"The Auto Wreck" by Karl Shapiro.
Time Limit: 10 minutes.   _____

Exercise 10 (p. 61) Tone and Language:
"next to of course god america i" by e. e. cummings.
Time Limit: 10 minutes.   _____

Exercise 11 (p. 62) Tone and Language:
"Acquainted with the Night" by Robert Frost.
Time Limit: 8 minutes.   _____

Exercise 12 (p. 62) Tone and Language: "The
Bear Who Let It Alone" by James Thurber.
Time Limit: 10 minutes.   _____

Exercise 13 (p. 63) Tone and Situation:
"Porphyria's Lover" by Robert Browning.
Time Limit: 12 minutes.   _____

Exercise 14 (p. 64) Tone and Language:
"To His Coy Mistress" by Andrew Marvell.
Time Limit: 12 minutes.   _____

Oral Analysis Exercise (Theme)

Exercise 15 (p. 66) Importance of Theme:
"I Like to See It Lap the Miles" by Emily Dickinson
and "London" by William Blake.
Time Limit: 12 minutes.   _____

Written Analysis Exercises (Theme)

Exercise 16 (p. 67) Theme: "Sonnet 73"
by Shakespeare.

Exercise 17 (p. 67) Theme and Aesthetic Effect:
"Snake" by D. H. Lawrence.

Exercise 18 (p. 68) Theme and Research: "The
Parsi Woman" by Edna St. Vincent Millay.

FORM 2

RECORDING FORM

VOICE AND SPEECH EVALUATION

I Say:
   This is _____ in my first recording on _____ (date).

II Record prose and poetry of own choice (six minutes).

III Record the following sentences (announce by groups):

Group I
1 Pretty children played with pure white caps.
2 Bobby brought some bumble bees to the baby's crib.
3 She made a proper cup of coffee in a copper coffee pot.
4 When white whales appear, sailors whisper and whine.
5 Wild winds were awake in the woods.
6 The three thousandth apothecary had great wealth.
7 The little brother saw six thick thistle sticks.
8 Large and melodious bells were tolling a funeral knell.
9 Certain sophisticated speakers gave six tests at once.
10 She was singing a song in the English language.

Group 2
1 Eager boys meet in the evenings on the ball fields.
2 Twenty American gentlemen met to get the ten best men.
3 Stand back from the ranks.

4 There is Sara's share of her parents' legacy, impair if you dare!

5 Sometimes the sublime lines of Milton have no rhyme.

6 Voiced sounds should be voiced, not unvoiced.

7 Greyhounds bounded over the ground.

8 Ears were made for hearing, never fear.

Group 3

In a storm at sea a vessel struggles against the elements, quivering and shivering, shrinking and battling like a thinking being. The merciless ranking whirlwinds, like frightful fiends, howl and moan, and send sharp, shrill shrieks through the creaking cordage, snapping the sheets and masts.

This is the
House, and the hound, and the horn, that belonged to the
Farmer, that sowed the corn, that kept the
Cock, that crowed in the morn, that waked the
Priest all shaven and shorn, that married the
Maiden all forlorn, that owned the
Dog that worried the
Cat that killed the
Rat that ate the
Malt that lay in the House that Jack built.

IV A copy of an unprepared reading will be handed to you to record. Say: This is an unprepared reading . . .

V Say: This is the end of my first recording on _____ (date).

VOICE AND SPEECH

Name_____ Date_____

Evaluation Scale   1   never or almost never
2   occasionally
3   frequently
4   always or almost always

Voice Production

Voice Quality   Voice Flexibility

					Poor	*Good*	*Sup.*
BREATHY	_____	METALLIC	_____				
COARSE	_____	MUFFLED	_____	VOLUME			
NASAL	_____	THIN	_____	PITCH			
DENASAL	_____	THROATY	_____	G. RATE			
DULL	_____	WHINING	_____	PAUSE			
GLOOMY	_____	FULL	_____	DURATION			
GRATING	_____	BEAUTIFUL	_____	QUALITY			
HARSH	_____	PLEASANT	_____		*High*	*Medium*	*Low*
HOLLOW	_____	RESONANT	_____	PITCH KEY			
HUSKY	_____	CLEAR	_____				

Use of Vocal Devices to Project Meaning

	Poor	*Fair*	*Good*
GROUPING			
INFLECTIONAL ENDINGS			
EMPHASIS			
SUBORDINATION			

COMMENTS:

Word Production

Vowel and Diphthong Production

	i	ɪ	ɛ	æ	a	ɝ	ə	ʌ	u	ʊ	ɔ	ɑ	ɑɪ	ɑʊ	ɔɪ	ɛɝ	ɪɝ	ETC.
SUBSTITUTIONS																		
NASALIZATION																		
ADDITIONS																		
OMISSIONS																		

Specific words:

Consonant Production

	s	z	θ	ð	ʃ	ʒ	tʃ	dʒ	t	d	m	n	ŋ	OTHERS
OMISSIONS														
FAILURE TO VOICE	X		X		X		X		X					
SHOULD NOT VOICE		X		X		X		X		X	X	X	X	

General Evaluation of Articulation and Pronunciation

STANDARD_____   OVER-PRECISE_____

SUB-STANDARD COLLOQUIAL_____   SELF-CONSCIOUS_____

ACCEPTABLE COLLOQUIAL_____   AFFECTED_____

Flow of Speech

USE OF STRONG FORMS_____

USE OF WEAK FORMS_____

USE OF ASSIMILATION_____

UNEVEN FLOW_____

DISTINCT WITH NATURAL FLOW_____

LABORATORY PROGRAM ASSIGNMENT

Date_____
Program of voice and speech training for_____
Scheduled period _____ Extending from _____ to _____

Voice (needed exercises will be circled)

Breathing Exercises:
1   Relaxation, p. 85   3   Exhalation, p. 85
2   Inhalation, p. 85   4   Control in Reading, p. 86

Control of Phonation
5   Open Throat, p. 88
6   Extending Range of Pitch, p. 88

Control of Resonance
5   Open Throat, p. 88   8   Control of Nasality, p. 90
7   Control of Tone and Vowels, p. 90

Vowel and Diphthong Sounds

Front Vowels
ē (i) p. 92   ĕ (ɛ) p. 93   à (a) p. 93
ĭ (ɪ) p. 92   ă (æ) p. 93

Middle Vowels
û (ɝ) p. 94   ŭ (ʌ) p. 94
(ə) and (ɚ) p. 94

Back Vowels
ōō (u) p. 95   ô (ɔ) p. 95   ä (ɑ) p. 96
ŏŏ (ʊ) p. 95   ŏ (ɒ) p. 95

Diphthongs
ī (ɑɪ) p. 96   oi (ɔɪ) p. 96   (ɪɚ) p. 97
au (aʊ) p. 96   ā (eɪ) p. 97   (ʊɚ) p. 97
                     ō (oʊ) p. 97   (oɚ) p. 98
                     (ɛɚ) p. 97   ū (ju) p. 98

Consonant Sounds

Plosives	1	*t* and *d*, p. 101	2	other plosives, p. 101

Fricatives 3   *f*, *v*, *th*, p. 101   6   (ʃ) and (ʒ), p. 103
            4   *th*, *t*, *d*, p. 101   7   (tʃ) and (dʒ), p. 103
            5   *s* and *z*, p. 101   8   *l* and *r*, p. 103

Nasals   Exercise 8, p. 100

Assimilation and Rapid Speech Flow

Exercises 1, 2, 3, p. 105

Vocal Variety

Volume   Exercise 1, 2, 3, 4, pp. 107–8
Pitch   Exercise 1, 2, 3, 4, pp. 108–11
Quality Exercise 1, 2, 3, pp. 111–12
Timing   Exercise 1, 2, 3, 4, pp. 113–14

Comments:

FORM 5

LABORATORY REPORT

LABORATORY REPORT FORM

Student_____ Date_____
On what project does this report apply?_____

DATE	HOURS	PROJECT	WHAT DID YOU DO?	HELPER SIGN

Total time spent with assistant or class partner_____
Please explain below the progress you may be making and any difficulties
you may be having.

Confer immediately with instructor concerning any difficulties that arise
in which you might need help.

EVALUATION OF ESSAY READING

Student Reader_____ Date_____
Title of Reading_____ Author_____

Evaluation Scale   4   Excellent
                  3   Good
                  2   Fair
                  1   Poor

Comments	Specific Ratings	Score
	CHOICE INTRODUCTION COMMUNICATION OF MEANING COMMUNICATION OF MOOD AND TONE QUALITY OF SHARING	
	VOCAL PROJECTION VOCAL VARIETY FLOW OF SPEECH DICTION USE OF BODY AESTHETIC CONTROL	
	Grade Total	

EVALUATION OF NARRATIVE READING

Student Reader_____ Date_____
Title of Reading_____ Author_____
Evaluation Scale   4   Excellent
                   3   Good
                   2   Fair
                   1   Poor

Comments	Specific Ratings	Score
	CHOICE COMMUNICATION OF MEANING COMMUNICATION OF MOODS COMMUNICATION OF AUTHOR'S TONE QUALITY OF SHARING	
	CHARACTER SUGGESTION CHARACTER INTERPLAY FLOW OF CONTENT AND CLIMAX FLOW OF SPEECH VOCAL PROJECTION VOCAL VARIETY DICTION USE OF BODY AESTHETIC CONTROL	
	Grade Total	

EVALUATION OF POETRY READING

Student Reader_____   Date_____
Title of Reading_____   Author_____
Evaluation Scale   4   Excellent
                   3   Good
                   2   Fair
                   1   Poor
Narrative or Dramatic Selection

Comments	Specific Ratings	Score
	CHOICE COMMUNICATION OF MEANING COMMUNICATION OF MOOD AND TONE SHARING POINT OF VIEW	
	FLOW OF CONTENT AND CLIMAX RHYTHM PATTERNS VOICE USE OF BODY DICTION	
	Grade Total	

Lyric Selection

Comments	Specific Ratings	Score
	CHOICE COMMUNICATION OF MEANING COMMUNICATION OF MOOD AND TONE	
	FLOW OF CONTENT AND CLIMAX RHYTHM PATTERNS VOICE USE OF BODY DICTION	
	Grade Total	

Humorous Selection

	CHOICE COMMUNICATION OF MEANING COMMUNICATION OF MOOD AND TONE	
	FLOW OF CONTENT AND CLIMAX RHYTHM PATTERNS VOICE USE OF BODY DICTION	
	Grade Total	

FORM 9

EVALUATION FORM

ORAL PROJECT V

EVALUATION OF DRAMA READING

Student Reader_____ Date_____

Title of Reading_____ Author_____

Evaluation Scale   4   Excellent
                 3   Good
                 2   Fair
                 1   Poor

Comments	Specific Ratings	Score
	CHOICE INTRODUCTION AND BRIDGES CUTTING COMMUNICATION OF MEANING COMMUNICATION OF MOODS	
	CHARACTER SUGGESTION CHARACTER INTERPLAY FLOW OF CONTENT AND CLIMAX FLOW OF SPEECH VOCAL PROJECTION VOCAL VARIETY DICTION AESTHETIC CONTROL USE OF BODY	
	Grade Total	

EVALUATION OF THE LECTURE RECITAL

Student Reader_____ _____ Date_____
Title of Reading_____ Author_____
Evaluation Scale   4   Excellent
                   3   Good
                   2   Fair
                   1   Poor

Comments	Specific Ratings	Score
	CHOICE OF SUBJECT	
	UNITY OF CONTENT	
	VARIETY OF CONTENT	
	ARRANGEMENT OF CONTENT	
	INTRODUCTION AND BRIDGES	
	COMMUNICATION OF MEANING (WHOLE)	
	COMMUNICATION OF MOODS	
	FLOW OF CONTENT	
	FLOW OF SPEECH	
	VOCAL PROJECTION	
	VOCAL VARIETY	
	USE OF BODY	
	AESTHETIC CONTROL	
	DICTION	
	Grade Total	

APPENDIX IV
MATERIALS FOR PROJECTS

The following anthologies are recommended as general sources for the oral class projects. They are compiled with the oral interpreter in mind.

Wallace A. Bacon and Robert S. Breen, *Literature for Interpretation*.
A good collection with stories, poems, letters, sections from diaries, and scenes from plays. (Holt, Rinehart and Winston, 1961)

Moiree Compere, *Living Literature for Oral Interpretation*.
This is still one of the best collections. It contains readable essays, stories, poems, and a complete lecture recital by the author. (Appleton-Century-Crofts, Inc., 1949)

Ruth Draper, *The Art of Ruth Draper, Her Dramas and Characters*.
Contains memorable monologues performed by Miss Draper in her lifetime, with a memoir by Morton Dauwen Zabel. (Doubleday and Co., Inc., 1960)

Helen Hayes, *A Gift of Joy*.
As Miss Hayes reflects on her life and philosophy she is reminded of what writers have had to say about these matters. She quotes favorite prose descriptions, poems, and scenes from plays. Her choices are generally well known, but usable. One might find an idea for a lecture recital here. (M. Evans and Company, Inc., and distributed in association with J. B. Lippincott Co., 1965)

Charles Laughton, *The Fabulous Country*.
Stories and descriptions that Charles Laughton "loved best and personally found the most evocative of American life and the American scene." This collection may suggest ideas for a lecture recital. (McGraw-Hill Book Co., Inc., 1962)

Oral Project III   Suggestions for the essay assignment

James Baldwin, *Nobody Knows My Name*.
In this book, and in others by James Baldwin, the essays are on themes that deeply concern the author. Some might be used for a particular audience. (The Dial Press, 1961)

Jacques Barzun, *The House of Intellect*.
Stimulating writing concerning American culture. Sections of the book are usable. (Torchbooks, 1961)

Peg Bracken, *I Hate to Housekeep Book* (1964) and *I Try to Behave Myself* (1963). "Peg Bracken is very funny." Some parts make good entertaining essay readings. (Harcourt, Brace & World, 1964 and 1963, resp.)

Art Buchwald, *Don't Forget to Write*.
There are some usable short pieces here. For instance, "Let's See Who Salutes" makes a serious point beneath its playfulness. (The World Publishing Co., 1958)

Clifton Fadiman, *Enter Conversing*.
Clifton Fadiman's essays may be used to make an audience laugh, reminisce, wonder, and think. Earlier collections also have good material. (The World Publishing Co., 1962)

William Faulkner, *Essays, Speeches and Public Letters,* ed. James B. Meriwether. A collection of Faulkner's nonfiction concerning the latter part of his career. Some are usable. (Random House, Inc., 1965)

John Gould, *You Should Start Sooner*.
Short humorous selections can be found here. Mr. Gould's humor is the "Down East" variety—dry and strong. The pieces are from his popular column "Dispatches from the Farm" in the *Christian Science Monitor*. (Little, Brown, 1964)

Joseph Wood Krutch, *If You Don't Mind My Saying So*.
"A thought provoking collection of fact and opinion about the modern world." In *The Measure of Man* (Grosset and Dunlap, 1954) there are also good selections to use.

Elinor Goulding Smith, *The Complete Book of Absolutely Perfect Housekeeping*. "An uproarious guide for disorganized housewives (with neat solutions to sloppy problems)." (Harcourt, Brace and Company, 1956)

James Thurber, *The Thurber Carnival*.
Humorous stories and essays assembled from various Thurber collections. Good. (Random House, 1945; Modern Library)

E. B. White, *Here Is New York* (Harper, 1949), *The Second Tree from the Corner* (Harper, 1954), *The Points of My Compass* (Harper & Row, 1961), *Credos and Curios* (Harper & Row, 1962).
Good sources of short, well-written material.

Hans Zinsser, *As I Remember Him*.
Humorous and philosophical biography (or autobiography). Descriptive sections make delightful readings. The chapter "R. S. and Women" is especially good. (Little, Brown, 1964)

Other essayists with sources for material

Irwin Edman	Adlai Stevenson	*The New Yorker:* "Talk of the Town"
D. H. Lawrence	Jonathan Swift	*The Atlantic Monthly*
G. B. Shaw	Mark Twain	*Harper's*

Oral Project IV   The narrative

Anthologies

Lynn Altenbernd and Leslie L. Lewis, *Stories.*
 Contains stories from early nineteenth century to recent times. Arranged for
 college literature course. A good collection. (The Macmillan Co., 1963)
Whit Burnett, *This Is My Best.*
 Each contributor, an outstanding author, selected his "best." (World, 1942)
Whit and Hallie Burnett, *Story Jubilee.*
 The thirty-three-year selection of contributors to the magazine *Story.* (Double-
 day and Company, Inc., 1965)
Charles Laughton, *Tell Me a Story.*
 Stories that Charles Laughton read aloud for the enjoyment of American
 audiences. His introductions add interest. (McGraw-Hill Book Co., Inc., 1957)
Winifred Lynskey, ed., *Reading Modern Fiction,* 3rd edition.
 Stories selected for enjoyment. Most of them read well aloud. (Charles Scribner's
 Sons, 1962)

Specific suggestions for the narrative

James Agee, *A Death in the Family.*
 Many selections in this novel make good readings. Especially recommended: the
 scene ("in the dark") where the father comforts the young son and the scene
 where the boy and uncle talk after the funeral.
James Baldwin, *Another Country.*
 Not many parts of this novel are usable, but the scene of the Negro funeral in
 Harlem is adaptable.
Stephen Vincent Benét, *The Devil and Daniel Webster.*
 This well-known story is adaptable for this assignment or for Chamber Theatre.
Roark Bradford, "Sin" and other ageless stories in Negro dialect on which Marc
 Connelly based his play *Green Pastures.* Found in the collection *O'Man Adam
 an' his Chillun* (Harper and Brothers, 1928). *How Come Christmas* (Harper,
 1948) is a Negro Sunday school lesson which makes a good humorous Christmas
 reading.
Hortense Calisher, "The Rehabilitation of Ginevra Leake."
 A delightfully ironic and timely situation. A protected southern maiden lady
 finds an answer to loneliness in the Communist Party, "but the party is to the
 lady a categorical man!" This and other good selections found in *Tale of the
 Mirror* require cutting.
Truman Capote, "A Christmas Memory."
 A beautiful story of an old lady, who never grew up, and her seven-year-old
 friend. Humorous and touching, but needs careful cutting.

Maureen Daly, "Sixteen."

At sixteen it's tragic to know that "He" won't call. The story makes a good monologue.

William Faulkner, "Dry September."

Restraint increases the tension of this story of violence in the South. There are many characters, but some can be cut. "A Rose for Emily" and "The Bear" are good choices but require careful cutting.

Ernest Hemingway, "A Clean Well Lighted Place."

The characters are male, the scene dramatic, the dialogue leaves a sense of things unspoken. Good length for a reading and a good possibility for Chamber Theatre. There are many other stories and sections of Hemingway's novels that might be recommended. His terse, vivid style reads well aloud.

Sarah Orne Jewett, *The Country of the Pointed Furs.*

A long short story in episodes depicting New England life. "Sentimental, but there is a strong sense of human dignity." Good possibility for Chamber Theatre.

James Joyce, "The Little Cloud."

The dream sequence in this story might suggest the use of modern dance in a Chamber Theatre adaptation.

D. H. Lawrence, "The Rocking-Horse Winner."

A famous suspense story. Must be carefully cut for reading.

Bernard Malamud, "The Magic Barrel."

Delightful story of a young Jewish Rabbi and a clever marriage broker. Can be found in collection by the same name; other selections are also good.

Katherine Mansfield, "Miss Brill."

An old lady's happy world of fantasy is shattered. Would need only slight cuts. "The Doll's House" and many others also are suitable.

Somerset Maugham, "The Luncheon."

Right length; humorous incident involving a poor writer and a food-conscious female guest.

Herman Melville, "Bartleby the Scrivener."

Dramatizes the irony of the truth that men are interdependent and, yet, alone-forlorn. A man's reading that would require careful cutting and subtle handling. Good possibility for Chamber Theatre.

George Orwell, *Animal Farm.*

Animal characters are suggestive of "stock" human characters. Could be used with cutting and summary remarks. This would make an interesting project for Chamber Theatre.

Dorothy Parker, "Here We Are."

A newly married couple furnishes a humorous situation. There are other clever stories usable for certain audiences. All of Miss Parker's prose is "bright, knowing, and sharp."

Alan Paton, *Tales from a Troubled Land.*

A collection of short stories that concern the relationships between the black man and the white man in South Africa. The story called "Wasteland" makes a short, deeply moving reading. There are also scenes in the novels *Cry the Beloved Country* and *Too Late the Phalarope* that are usable.

Katherine Anne Porter, "The Downward Path to Wisdom."

The effect of chaotic family relationships on a child is made vivid and disturbing. Requires cutting. "Noon Wine" and others are also good.

Leonard Ross, "Mr. Kaplan and Shakespeare."

Good for anyone who wants to try dialects. Humorous. The collection *The Education of Hyman Kaplan* has many such.

Saki (H. H. Munro), "The Open Window," "The Story Teller."

In the first, suspense and an imaginative young woman. In the second, the "why" of a child is an experience that rings true to life. Both would require only slight cuts.

J. D. Salinger, "A Perfect Day for Bananafish," "For Esme—With Love and Squalor."

These stories, or a section from *Catcher in the Rye,* read aloud well. Salinger's "ear picks up with stunning exactness the speech of many kinds of people."

Max Steele, "Ah Love, Ah Me!"

A boy recalls that awful first date! A good humorous monologue.

John Steinbeck, "Flight."

A stark, pathetic story that moves with excitement. Steinbeck's novels *Of Mice and Men, Grapes of Wrath,* and others have good climactic scenes.

Dylan Thomas, "A Child's Christmas in Wales."

Beautiful writing and lots of action. A good reading for a man. There are many usable stories in the book *Quite Early One Morning.*

James Thurber, "The Secret Life of Walter Mitty."

A familiar but delightful story concerning Mitty's daydreams. Good reading for a man if done well. Needs cutting. Good possibility for Chamber Theatre. "The Catbird Seat," "If Grant Had Been Drinking at Appomattox," and many others make good humorous readings.

Eudora Welty, "Why I Live at the P. O."

A delightful reading for a girl who has a good sense of timing. Requires much cutting. There are many others: "Worn Path" is a beautiful story of an old Negro woman's thoughts and experiences; "Lily Daw and the Three Ladies" satirizes the "do-gooders" in a small southern town.

Tennessee Williams, "The Yellow Bird."

The story of a minister's daughter who finds a rather violent way of escaping inherited Puritan guilt. This and others of interest found in the collection, *One Arm* (New Directions).

Other suggestions (novels or long stories)

My Little Boy by Carl Ewald
The Snow Goose by Paul Gallico
The Turn of the Screw by Henry James
To Kill a Mockingbird by Harper Lee
A Long and Happy Life by Reynolds Price
The Little Prince by Antoine de Saint-Exupéry
The Pearl by John Steinbeck

Oral Project V   Poetry

Collected works and anthologies

e. e. cummings, *Poems 1923–1954* (Harcourt, Brace and Company)
Collected Poems of Thomas Hardy (The Macmillan Company)
Collected Poems of Siegfried Sassoon (The Viking Press, Inc.)
Collected Poems of Robert Frost (Holt, Rinehart and Winston)
Collected Poems of Edwin Arlington Robinson (The Macmillan Company)
The Complete Poems of Emily Dickinson (Little, Brown and Company)
Edna St. Vincent Millay, Collected Works (Harper & Brothers)
The Portable Dorothy Parker (The Viking Press)
Modern American Poetry and Modern British Poetry.
   Midcentury Edition, edited by Louis Untermeyer. (Harcourt, Brace, and Company, 1950)
Shakespeare's Songs and Poems.
   Edited by Edward Hubler. (McGraw-Hill Book Co., 1959)
Story Poems.
   Edited by Louis Untermeyer. (Washington Square Press, Inc., W. 555)
Light Verse.
   Edited by Oscar Williams. (Mentor T 372)
15 Modern American Poets.
   Edited by George P. Elliott. (Holt, Rinehart and Winston, 1964)
The Modern Poets, An American-British Anthology.
   (McGraw-Hill Book Co., 1963)

Suggestions for the lyric

W. H. Auden, "O What Is That Sound?"
William Blake, "The Little Black Boy."
Louise Bogan, "Women."
Padraic Colum, "The Old Woman of the Roads."
e. e. cummings, "in just," "somewhere i have never traveled," "my father moved through dooms of love," "anyone lived in a pretty how town."
Emily Dickinson, "Because I Could Not Stop for Death" and others.
John Donne, "The Bait," "Sonnet X," "Song."
Richard Eberhart, "The Fury of Aerial Bombardment."
T. S. Eliot, "The Love Song of J. Alfred Prufrock," "Preludes," "Journey of the Magi," and sections from *Four Quartets.*
Robert Frost, "Acquainted with the Night," "Birches," "A Minor Bird," "The Sound of the Trees," and others.
Robert Graves, "In Procession."
Hermann Hagedorn, *The Bomb That Fell on America.*
Thomas Hardy, "The Darkling Thrush."
Gerard Manley Hopkins, "God's Grandeur."
Langston Hughes, "Jazz Fantasia" and others.

Randall Jarrell, "Eighth Air Force."
Amy Lowell, "Lilacs," "Free Fantasia on Japanese Themes."
Robert Lowell, "Christmas Eve Under Hooker's Statue."
Louis MacNeice, "Snow," "Bagpipe Music," "Prayer Before Birth."
Edgar Lee Masters, "Silence."
Edna St. Vincent Millay, "Renascence," "God's World," "Departure."
John Crowe Ransom, "Bells for John Whiteside's Daughter."
Henry Reed, "Naming of Parts."
Theodore Roethke, "The Abyss," "The Waking."
Muriel Rukeyser, "Effort at Speech Between Two People."
Carl Sandburg, "Wind Song," "Four Preludes on Playthings to the Wind," "The
    Hangman at Work," sections from *The People Yes.*
Lew Sarrett, "Four Little Foxes."
Siegfried Sassoon, "Falling Asleep," "Does it Matter?"
Winfield T. Scott, "Three American Women and a German Bayonet."
William Shakespeare, "Spring," the Sonnets.
Karl Shapiro, "Hollywood," "Nostalgia," "Drug Store."
Stephen Spender, "An Elementary School Classroom in a Slum," "The Express."
James Stephens, "What Tomas Said in a Pub."
Wallace Stevens, "Peter Quince at the Clavier."
Algernon C. Swinburne, "A Ballad of Dreamland."
Allen Tate, "Death of Little Boys."
Dylan Thomas, "Poem in October," "Fern Hill."
Walt Whitman, "There Was a Child Went Forth."
William Carlos Williams, "Tract."
Elinor Wylie, "Pretty Words," "Velvet Shoes."

Suggestions for the narrative

Old ballads: "Lord Randal," "Get Up and Bar the Door," "The Twa Corbies."
Stephen Vincent Benét, "Mountain Whippoorwill," sections from *John Brown's
    Body.*
Tristram Coffin, "The Race," "Departure," and others from *Maine Ballads.*
Robert Frost, "The Death of the Hired Man," "Out-Out," "Home Burial," "The
    Star-Splitter," "The Fear," "Wild Grapes," "Snow," and others.
Thomas Hardy, short poems: *Satires of Circumstance.*
Roy Helton, "Old Christmas Morning."
Dubose Heyward, "The Mountain Woman."
Edna St. Vincent Millay, "The Ballad of the Harp Weaver."
Ezra Pound, "The Ballad of Goodly Fere."
E. A. Robinson, "Richard Cory," "Mr. Flood's Party," "Anaranth."
William B. Yeats, "The Ballad of Moll Magee," "The Fiddler of Donney."

Suggestions for the dramatic

Robert Browning, "My Last Duchess," "Soliloquy of the Spanish Cloister."
e. e. cummings, "sweet let me go."

Robert Frost, "The Witch of Coos," "The Pauper Witch of Crafton," "Servant to Servants."

James W. Johnson, "The Creation" and other sermons from *God's Trombone*.

D. H. Lawrence, "Love on the Farm."

Amy Lowell, "Patterns," "Appuldercombe Park."

Edgar Lee Masters, epitaphs from *Spoon River Anthology*.

E. A. Robinson, "Ben Johnson Entertains a Man from Stratford."

Monologues or soliloquies from verse plays

Maxwell Anderson, from *Key Largo* (in Act II: D'Alcola's address to King Mc-Cloud); from *Anne of the Thousand Days* (Henry's speech at the beginning of Act II, sc. 4, or Anne's speech at the end of Act III, sc. 4).

Euripides, from *Medea* (translated by Gilbert Murray) (Medea's speech beginning "Women of Corinth I am come . . ."); from *The Trojan Women* (Hecuba's speech at the burial of Hector's son).

Christopher Fry, from *The Lady's Not for Burning* (one of Thomas' long speeches).

Christopher Marlowe, from *The Tragical History of Dr. Faustus* (Faustus' speech that concludes the play).

John Milton, from *Samson Agonistes* (combined speeches of Delila asking Samson's forgiveness).

Edmond Rostand, from *Cyrano de Bergerac* (nose speech or the no-thank-you speech by Cyrano).

William Shakespeare, from *Macbeth* (dagger speech Act II, sc. 1); from *The Merchant of Venice* (Gratiano's speech Act I, sc. 1); from *King Henry IV, Part I* (Hotspur's speech Act I, sc. 3); and many others.

Suggestions for humorous poetry

Cedric C. Adams, "Intelligence Test."

W. H. Auden, "The Unknown Citizen."

e. e. cummings, "My Sweet Old Etcetera."

Arthur Guiterman, "Pershing at the Front."

Thomas Hardy, "Ah, Are You Digging on My Grave?", "The Ruined Maid."

A. P. Hubert, "It May Be Life," "Song for Parents."

Langston Hughes, "Seven Moments of Love."

Rudyard Kipling, "The Ladies."

Phyllis McGinley, "Apology for Husbands" and others.

Edna St. Vincent Millay, "She Is Overheard Singing."

A. A. Milne, "Disobedience" and other children's poems.

Ogden Nash, "The Strange Case of Professor Primrose," "Very Like a Whale," "Is There an Oculist in the House?" and others.

Dorothy Parker, "Recital," "Folk Tune," and others.

John Crowe Ransom, "Survey of Literature."

Jonathan Swift, "Stella's Birthday."

Oral Project VI   Drama Reading

Clare Boothe (Luce), *The Women* (Many scenes are usable).

Marc Connelly, *The Green Pastures* (Opening scene might be used with a part of the Fish Fry scene).

Jean Giraudoux, *The Madwoman of Chaillot* (A cutting of the Tea Party scene with the three mad women makes an excellent reading).

Hugh Herbert, *The Moon Is Blue* (A cutting of the first act of this delightful comedy makes a good two-character reading).

Carson McCullers, *The Member of the Wedding* (Act II sc. 1, the climactic wedding scene makes a good reading).

William Saroyan, *Hello Out There* (This one act play reads aloud well. Dialogue is between a young man and a girl; characters entering at end of play can be cut).

G. B. Shaw, *Pygmalion* (A good selection is the scene where Colonel Pickering first introduces Liza Doolittle to society).

Thornton Wilder, *The Matchmaker* (A section of the dinner conversation between Mrs. Levi and Vandergelder in Act III might be combined with Mrs. Levi's long speech in Act IV and a portion of the proposal that follows. *Our Town* (The drug store scene and others are good).

Tennessee Williams, *A Streetcar Named Desire* (A short reading might be made from the first scene in the play where Blanche tells her sister Stella what has happened to their home, Belle Reve).

APPENDIX V
TO THE INSTRUCTOR

THE SPEECH LABORATORY

It is generally believed that the use of a speech laboratory adds to the interest and effectiveness of the work in an introductory oral interpretation course. It enables the teacher to set up a plan of work based on applied theory which will enable him to handle increasingly large classes while likewise dealing with individual needs through the laboratory. For whatever assistance it may be, a small but efficient laboratory set-up is described below.

An ideal (small) speech laboratory would provide approximately twelve small recording and listening rooms, completely soundproofed and well ventilated. The rooms should be large enough for two people to work in comfortably. Each room would be provided with a tape recorder and speaker (Ampex E 65 series is a good choice),[1] two neck microphones and ear phones, a speaker's stand, two chairs and a small table.

A console system in the connecting room (or hall) would provide a means by which master tapes could be played into the various listening and recording rooms. This, with the individual neck microphones and ear phones, would increase the diversity of material being worked on at any one time by individual students. Three different master tapes could be piped into the various rooms; ear phones and a two-way intercommunications system could be used from the control console, and students could signal the central control from each room by means of an intercom button.

[1] Ampex Corporation, Professional Audio Products, 401 Broadway, Redwood City, California 94063.

Two of the recording rooms (say A and B) might be separated from each other by glass paneling so that the *larger* one, A, could be utilized as a central recording room for large groups and for the making of tapes, while room B could be used as a master recording and control room.

To make a speech laboratory of benefit to the largest number of people and to assure the proper care and handling of equipment, some responsible person must be given authority and assistance. This may rightfully fall to the director of the audio-visual-aid program. The scheduling of various speech classes in the laboratory and the assigning of adequate supervision must be handled efficiently from a central office.

Additional equipment, especially useful for the oral interpretation class, would include:

A supply of tapes (to be sold or rented to the students).

A record player.

Master tapes of selected readings by professionals (recorded from records) and recorded readings by former students and groups.

Master tapes with mimeographed scripts of vowels, diphthongs, consonants, strong and weak forms, stress, etc. should be available for those students with specific diction problems.[2]

A piano in one of the rooms would be useful for finding pitch levels and range of voices.

The financing of laboratory equipment and supplies may be done through a special fee to be administered by the director of audio-visual aids. Other college departments may help to make some of the equipment available.

In addition to servicing all speech courses, the speech laboratory may also serve the dramatics program, discussion and debate groups, and various campus and outside groups.

SUGGESTED CLASS PLAN

The following is a plan suitable for a class of approximately twenty students meeting three hours a week for an eighteen-week semester. The plan applies specifically to this text, and it is based on the assumption that speech laboratory equipment is available and that practice and conference periods can be scheduled outside of class. The plan can be used without the laboratory procedures or otherwise modified to suit the needs of varying class levels, different-sized classes, or courses of different lengths.

[2] Such tapes might be prepared by teachers in the department, or they might be recorded from Standard Linguaphone Sets.

Class Meetings	Laboratory
1 Introduction to course. Assignment: Chapters 1, 2, 3, and 4.	
2 Lecture-discussion: literary analysis: Chapters 3, 4. Assignment: Oral Project I (Form 1, pp. 223–25).	
3 Oral Project I: Ex. 1, 2, 3, and 4 (pp. 52–55) as assigned. Assignment: Written analysis of Ex. 17 and 18 *or* 19.	Instructions in operating laboratory equipment. Individual tapes purchased or borrowed.
4 Oral Project I: Ex. 5, 6, 7 and 8 (pp. 55–60) as assigned.	*Recording* prose and poetry of own choice, sentences and impromptu reading (Form 2, pp. 225–26).
5 Oral Project I: Ex. 9, 10, 11, and 12 (pp. 60–63). Advanced assignment: Chapter 9, "Oral Interpretation of Prose" and Oral Project III: reading narrative fiction.	
6 Oral Project I: Ex. 13, 14, 15 (pp. 63–66). Written analysis due.	
7 Oral Project I: Ex. 16 (p.67). Discussion of written analysis. Evaluation of Oral Project I. Assignment: Chapter 6, Voice Production (pp. 83–91).	
8 Discussion: breathing, phonation, resonance. Demonstration of exercises. Assignment: Chapter 6, Vocal Variety (pp. 106–114) with specific exercises assigned.	*Listening* to recording with instructor's written evaluation of voice and speech in hand (Form 3, pp. 227–28).
9 Discussion of vocal variety and demonstration of exercises. Assignment: Chapter 6, Word Production (pp. 91–106).	

10	Discussion of vowel-consonant production, flow of speech and demonstration of exercises. Assignment: Chapter 5, "Reading Techniques" (pp. 71–79).	*Conference* to discuss voice and speech evaluation and to plan individual laboratory program (Form 4, pp. 229–30).
11	Discussion: reading techniques. Exercises: grouping and inflectional endings. Assignment: Chapter 5 (pp. 71–79).	*Oral Project II* Recording and Listening (as assigned on form 4) for voice and diction improvement.
12	Exercises: emphasis and subordination. Assignment: Chapter 5, Direct Techniques for Projecting Emotional Meaning (pp. 79–82); Chapter 8, "Techniques for Psychological Approach" (pp. 125–33).	*Oral Project II* Recording and Listening
13	Discussion and demonstration of exercises for projecting emotion. Assignment: Chapter 7, "Techniques for Body Control."	*Listening:* narrative prose tape (selected readings by former students and professional readers)
14	Discussion and demonstration of exercises for body control.	*Oral Project II* Recording and Listening
15	Lecture-discussion: Chapter 9, "Oral Interpretation of Prose." Assignment: Chapter 10, "Oral Interpretation of Poetry" and Oral Project IV: reading poetry.	*Oral Project II* Recording and Listening
16	Oral Project III (4 readings). (Evaluations Form 7, p. 232).	*Oral Project III* Recording and Listening: reading narrative fiction
17	Oral Project III (cont.)	*Oral Project II* Recording and Listening
18	Oral Project III (cont.)	*Listening:* poetry tape
19	Oral Project III (cont.)	*Re-recording* of narrative

20	Oral Project III (cont.)	*Oral Project IV* Recording and Listening: poetry
21	Oral Evaluation of Project III. Assignment: Oral Project V *or* VI and Chapters 11 and 12.	
22	Lecture-discussion: Chapter 10 "Oral Interpretation of Poetry."	*Listening:* drama tape
23	Oral Project IV: poetry read- ings (4). (Evaluation Form 8, pp. 233–34).	
24	Oral Project IV (cont.)	
25	Project IV (cont.)	
26	Project IV (cont.)	
27	Project IV (cont.)	*Re-recording* of poetry.
28	Evaluation of Project IV Discussion: Chapter 12, "Drama," Chapter 12, "Special Forms," lecture recital.	
29	Class discussion and demonstra- tion of Chamber Theatre. Assignment: Chamber Theatre arrangement (tentative).	*Recording-Listening:* Project V or VI.
30	Discussion: Reader's Theatre. Try-out readings for Reader's Theatre production.	
31	Continuation of try-outs.	
32	Oral Project V or VI.	
33	Oral Project V or VI (cont.)	*Recording-Listening:* Individual parts in Reader's Theatre
34	Oral Project V or VI (cont.)	
35	Oral Project V or VI (cont.)	
36	Oral Project V or VI (cont.)	Group meetings for Chamber The- atre (tentative)
37	Reader's Theatre Rehearsal	
38	Reader's Theatre Rehearsal	

39 Reader's Theatre Rehearsal   Group meetings for Reader's
                                        Theatre

40 Reader's Theatre Rehearsal

41 Reader's Theatre Rehearsal

42 Reader's Theatre Rehearsal   Outside rehearsals for Reader's
                                        Theatre

43 Reader's Theatre Rehearsal

44 Reader's Theatre Rehearsal

45 Reader's Theatre Rehearsal   *Re-recording* of drama or lecture
                                        recital

46 Reader's Theatre Rehearsal

47 READER'S THEATRE PRODUCTION

48 Evaluations

49 Chamber Theatre Rehearsals   First Recording repeated (tape
                                        turned in with: first recording—
                                        original and final; re-recording of
                                        narrative, poetry, drama or lecture
                                        recital)

50 Chamber Theatre Rehearsals

51 Chamber   Theatre   Perform-
    ances

52 Chamber   Theatre   Perform-
    ances

53-54 Final Examination

CLASS PROJECTS AND METHODS
(SUGGESTED IN CLASS PLAN)

The series of oral class projects (described in detail for the student in
Appendix II, are intended as suggestions only. Some of the projects described must, of necessity, be omitted; any one can readily be contracted,
expanded, or modified to meet the class needs and interests.

Oral Project I

In an introductory oral interpretation class, this project may seem to be a
sudden plunge into class performance. This is intended, however, to set a
good beginning class level. The activity puts each student on his mettle to

make a good showing in his first appearance before his teacher and class-mates. The project also encourages discussion which can make for interest and a good class atmosphere at the beginning. In addition, it offers the teacher an immediate opportunity to get acquainted with the group.

There are advantages in having each student in the class responsible for one oral analysis exercise, but in a large class this may involve too much time. If necessary, two or three students may be assigned the same exercise to present as a group discussion. Form 1 (p. 223) is provided for a quick clarification of the assignment.

Oral Project II   (Voice and Diction)

If a speech laboratory is available, work on voice and diction can be started immediately and can be continued throughout the semester as needed by the individual student.

While the oral analysis exercises are in progress in the classroom, the teacher may schedule two laboratory periods for the purposes of: (1) pro-viding instruction for operating the laboratory equipment, (2) determin-ing each student's voice and speech needs through individual recordings (Form 2, p. 225).

A good laboratory set-up provides adequate assistance so that the instruc-tor's presence is not required for these sessions. His job is to listen to the recordings and to evaluate (on Form 3, pp. 227–28) the voice and diction of each student in the class. This is time-consuming for the teacher, but it is the basis for an individual's improvement in this area. When the evalua-tion form is completed, the teacher meets with the student in conference and together they plan a program and schedule laboratory periods. This is shown on Form 4 (pp. 229–30). In the class plan offered here, it is suggested that work on voice and diction exercises be concentrated in a two- or three-week period. Each student is scheduled for five laboratory periods, during which assistance is available to guide his work on specific voice and diction problems. After this, he is expected to proceed on his own, according to his individual needs.

It is usually impossible for a teacher to work with each student privately on the voice and diction project or on the class projects throughout the semester. The provision of laboratory assistance is sometimes possible. Carefully selected students who are majors in the speech department may sit in on the course and serve as helpers to the students under the super-vision of the teacher. When this cannot be provided, a substitute method is to assign the students of the class in pairs to work with each other. Such a plan, however, requires general supervision. Usually this can be provided in a short concentrated period.

The student's laboratory work should continue throughout the semester in at least one fifty-minute scheduled period each week. This time is used according to needs. Some students may need to continue work on voice and diction exercises, others may use the time for class preparations alone. According to the class plan each student is expected to record, listen to, and evaluate his readings of prose, poetry, or drama, *before* he reads these in class. A re-recording of the same material after he has been given constructive criticism in class serves as a measure of progress for both him and the teacher. If the teacher wishes to place emphasis on this recorded evidence of progress, he can request that the individual tapes be turned in at the end of the course with certain recordings intact: first recording, re-recording of narrative, re-recording of poetry, re-recording of drama or lecture recital, re-recording of first recording.

Students should be encouraged to realize that the speech laboratory not only provides a needed place for oral practice, but offers the facilities for more rapid individual improvement.

Oral Projects III, IV, V, VI

These projects are described in detail in Appendix II.

One of the chief concerns of the teacher is finding the best procedure to use for the critical evaluation of each student's reading. Ideally, perhaps, an oral evaluation from the teacher and the students immediately follows each reading. In a small class this is possible, but in a large class some compromise has to be made. The class plan offered here suggests that the teacher ask for written criticisms from members of the class, confining the oral criticisms to the teacher's evaluation at the end of each project.

The written criticisms are made at the time of the reading. The teacher and several student evaluators fill out an evaluation form (including comments). This can be worked out so that each student in the class criticizes about four of his classmates during each oral project. If students work in pairs in the laboratory, each student includes his partner in his group. Since partners know the material in advance, this serves to make the criticism more significant. Some teachers feel it best to collect the student evaluations and to sift through them to see if there are any misleading or worthless criticisms. The instructor may make a few notes in regard to these, which he gives to the student reader with his own criticism. In this way, the teacher keeps some control on the evaluations. Sometimes, through his written comments, he can help the reader receive the criticism profitably. At the same time, this check gives the teacher an opportunity to spot the student who invariably turns in a worthless criticism.

The teacher's oral evaluations come at the end of each oral project. At least half a class period is used to bring the whole project, its successes and failures, into focus as a learning experience for the students. Here, too, the teacher may wish to call attention to the written evaluations.

Projects VII and VIII   Chamber Theatre and Reader's Theatre

These two projects are "extras" which may be included in the semester plan or not. There are, of course, various ways in which they may be used to lessen the teacher's load.

A Chamber Theatre adaptation and class production might be assigned as a third alternate with projects 6 and 7 (drama reading and lecture recital). The whole class would gain something from the class demonstration and the student-directed productions, but the work would fall to the more capable and interested students.

Reader's Theatre may be given as a fully staged production for the public, or a simple production may be given in the classroom for invited guests. In either case, it can serve as a challenging and memorable class finale.

Index

DATE DUE
